Consciousness as Representing One's Mind

PHILOSOPHY OF MIND SERIES

Series Editor
David J. Chalmers, *Australian National University*

The Conscious Brain
Jesse Prinz

Simulating Minds
The Philosophy, Psychology, and Neuroscience of Mindreading
Alvin I. Goldman

Supersizing the Mind
Embodiment, Action, and Cognitive Extension
Andy Clark

Perception, Hallucination, and Illusion
William Fish

Phenomenal Concepts and Phenomenal Knowledge
New Essays on Consciousness and Physicalism
Torin Alter and Sven Walter

Phenomenal Intentionality
George Graham, John Tienson and Terry Horgan

The Character of Consciousness
David J. Chalmers

The Senses
Classic and Contemporary Philosophical Perspectives
Fiona Macpherson

Attention is Cognitive Unison
An Essay in Philosophical Psychology
Christopher Mole

The Contents of Visual Experience
Susanna Siegel

Consciousness and the Prospects of Physicalism
Derk Pereboom

Consciousness and Fundamental Reality
Philip Goff

The Phenomenal Basis of Intentionality
Angela Mendelovici

Seeing and Saying
The Language of Perception and the Representational View of Experience
Berit Brogaard

Perceptual Learning
The Flexibility of the Senses
Kevin Connolly

Combining Minds
How to Think About Composite Subjectivity
Luke Roelofs

The Epistemic Role of Consciousness
Declan Smithies

The Epistemology of Non-Visual Perception
Berit Brogaard and Dimitria Electra Gatzia

What are Mental Representations?
Joulia Smortchkova, Krzysztof Dołęga, and Tobias Schlicht

The Border Between Seeing and Thinking
Ned Block

Consciousness as Representing One's Mind
Richard Brown

CONSCIOUSNESS AS REPRESENTING ONE'S MIND

THE HIGHER-ORDER APPROACH TO CONSCIOUSNESS EXPLAINED

RICHARD BROWN

OXFORD
UNIVERSITY PRESS

Oxford University Press is a department of the University of Oxford.
It furthers the University's objective of excellence in research, scholarship,
and education by publishing worldwide. Oxford is a registered trade mark of
Oxford University Press in the UK and certain other countries.

Published in the United States of America by Oxford University Press
198 Madison Avenue, New York, NY 10016, United States of America.

© Oxford University Press 2025

All rights reserved. No part of this publication may be reproduced, stored in a retrieval system, transmitted, used for text and data mining, or used for training artificial intelligence, in any form or by any means, without the prior permission in writing of Oxford University Press, or as expressly permitted by law, by license or under terms agreed with the appropriate reprographics rights organization. Inquiries concerning reproduction outside the scope of the above should be sent to the Rights Department, Oxford University Press, at the address above.

You must not circulate this work in any other form
and you must impose this same condition on any acquirer

CIP data is on file at the Library of Congress

ISBN 978-0-19-778400-6

DOI: 10.1093/oso/9780197784006.001.0001

Printed by Integrated Books International, United States of America

The manufacturer's authorised representative in the EU for product safety is Oxford University Press España S.A. of El Parque Empresarial San Fernando de Henares, Avenida de Castilla, 2 – 28830 Madrid (www.oup.es/en or product.safety@oup.com). OUP España S.A. alsoacts as importer into Spain of products made by the manufacturer.

*For Ryland and Caden,
whose consciousness makes life more interesting*

Contents

Introduction   1

1. Constructing a Scientific Theory of Phenomenal Consciousness   26
2. The Higher-Order Representation of a Representation (HOROR) Theory of Phenomenal Consciousness   57
3. The Contents of HORORs   83
4. HOROR in the Brain   115
5. The Traditional Higher-Order Approach to Consciousness   143
6. Non-Relational Versions of Traditional Higher-Order Theories   167
7. Relational Versions of Traditional Higher-Order Theories   194
8. Conclusion   224

Appendix: The 2D Argument against Non-Physicalism   225
Acknowledgments   229
Works Cited   231
Index   243

Introduction

My goal in this book is to introduce and explore one of the most wildly counter-intuitive ideas about the nature of consciousness that I have ever come across. No, I am not talking about the claim that consciousness is a fundamental aspect of reality—far from it! I am talking about the idea that consciousness might ultimately turn out just to be representing one's own mental life. And what's more, that the right kind of representation might itself be something more like a thought than it is like a picture or image. I still remember when I first encountered this idea as an undergraduate in my philosophy of mind class. When the professor asked what we thought about it, I spontaneously blurted out that it was possibly the second-most-absurd idea I had ever heard. How could the experience of listening to music, or being terrified in the dark, or anything for that matter, be a thought-like representation of something else happening in my mind? I left that day thinking that the higher-order thought theory, as it was called, had to be obviously false.

As it very often turns out, the ideas that challenge us the most are also the ones that influence us the most. I continued to think about and struggle with this counter-intuitive idea. As I soon discovered, it apparently had a long history in philosophy. It was a contemporary version of a family of theories known as higher-order theories of consciousness. These theories were explicitly introduced into the contemporary Western philosophical discussion by authors like David Armstrong (1968), who took themselves to be developing the claims made by philosophers from the seventeenth and eighteenth centuries. For example, John Locke (1690) famously wrote that "consciousness is the perception of what passes in one's own mind." Immanuel Kant (1724) appealed to a kind of inner sense and spoke of the "I think" that must accompany all our conscious experiences. It is an interesting philosophical question whether these historical thinkers meant to be discussing something we would recognize as consciousness. Whether historically accurate or not, these ideas suggested an account of the nature of consciousness to contemporary readers. We have an awareness of things in the world, but also, and possibly simultaneously, we have 'higher-order' awareness—an awareness of our awareness of the world; an inner awareness that puts us in touch with our own minds.

Higher-order theories, then, take explaining consciousness to importantly involve inner awareness. Some take that kind of inner awareness to be a thought-like representation. There are those who find this very intuitive, but I am not one of them. This still seems wildly implausible to me. Why should we take the theory seriously? And why am I writing a book on it? If it seems obviously false, then can't we dismiss it out of hand? This does seem to reflect the attitude of many, my former self included, but it is a mistake.

Everyone Should Care about Higher-Order Theories

I had to admit that the general idea of the higher-order approach to consciousness appealed to me at an intuitive level. Gradually it started to seem to me that the thought-like version of inner awareness I met as an undergraduate might not be so *obviously* false. There were no logical inconsistencies in the theory, nor were any philosophical objections to it unanswerable. There were many interesting issues one had to navigate before one could dismiss the theory. By the time one had succeeded in navigating all of them, one had the feeling of almost losing sight of one's initial worries. Besides, something wildly counter-intuitive is probably going to have to be the case when it comes to consciousness anyway (Schwitzgebel 2014). If that were all that there was to it, this approach to consciousness may be more of a niche topic, suitable for a few diehard enthusiasts, but of less interest to the general discussion about the nature of consciousness. However, I think there are at least two reasons that make this approach worth exploring no matter what one antecedently thinks about it.

First, if one thinks the view is obviously false, then it should not be difficult to decisively challenge it empirically. Given that there is no logical contradiction entailed by the view, 'obvious falseness' should imply that there is some conflict with already existing empirical data. But when one looks at the contemporary findings from psychology and neuroscience, one finds that higher-order theories can mostly be fit to the empirical data (Kriegel 2009; Lau and Rosenthal 2011; Brown 2012c; Gennaro 2012; Lau and Brown 2019; Lau 2022; Fleming 2020). This has led to many theorists developing different versions of the higher-order approach and arguing that their version is consistent with empirical data.

So, contrary to our assumption, it doesn't seem to be the case that already existing empirical data outright conflicts with the higher-order approach. There are, of course, empirically based arguments against specific versions of the theory. We will discuss many of them throughout this book. Even so, there are seemingly consistent interpretations of the empirical data that align with the higher-order approach. The empirical arguments against higher-order theories are far from decisive. Higher-order theories continue to be mainstream contenders for at least part of a scientific theory of consciousness. The various versions of higher-order theory offer us one possible consistent interpretation of a wide swath of psychological and neuroscientific data (Brown 2012a; Brown 2012c; Lau and Brown 2019: Brown et al. 2019). That doesn't make these theories true, obviously, but it is a noteworthy achievement all by itself.

While it is true that a good theory effectively organizes what we think we already know, the true test of a theory lies in the falsifying predictions that it entails. I do not mean to endorse the simplistic idea that we can falsify a theoretical approach with an experimental silver bullet. There is often a complex dance between empirical evidence and theoretical assessment. Still, *obviously false* theories should make some predictions that would leave them vulnerable to empirical disconfirmation. At the very least, it shouldn't be too hard to challenge the theory enough to convince the general scientific community of the problems. This hasn't been done. Even worse, what few attempts there have been to interpret existing data as tests of key predictions have been stymied by confusion over what would count as a true test of the theory in the first place.

Counter-intuitive theories with testable predictions are ripe for empirical investigation—even if only to be crossed off, or moved down, our list of viable candidates. It turns out that the different versions of the higher-order approach make differing predictions about key cases. So, to test them we must carefully work out what these differing predictions might be, and that requires developing the specific versions of the theory in enough detail to do so. Just to be able to dismiss higher-order theories as viable candidates requires understanding what would count as a challenge. It turns out that doing this is harder than it seems.

Consciousness is a psychological phenomenon. As such, the natural place to find the empirical tests we are looking for would be cognitive neuroscience. This is the interdisciplinary science that aims to understand the neural processes that implement the mind. Where do higher-order theories fit in there? What we find when we look at the current cognitive neuroscience of consciousness is that proposed theories have tended to center on five main ideas (Seth and Bayne 2022).

The first is the idea of the Global Workspace. Initially inspired by computer science, the basic idea is that consciousness involves the widespread sharing of information among specialized processing modules (Baars et al. 2013). In its current form Global Neuronal Workspace Theory (GNWT) proposes that the global workspace consists in a set of widely interconnected neurons in the frontal and parietal regions of the brain (Mashour et al. 2020; Sergent et al. 2021).

Second, we have more local views, like the local recurrency theory of Victor Lamme (Lamme 2018), which suggests that it is recurrent feedback to, for example, visual areas that is critical for consciousness. The key idea here is that information processed in an entirely feedforward manner is not conscious. Consciousness requires feedback. The kind of feedback that is required can occur 'locally' in a somewhat confined area of the brain, for example the sensory cortices. Local theories do not require the kind of 'global ignition,' which GNWT interprets as wide-spread sharing of information among other areas of the brain.

Third is information and integration, especially in the form of integrated information theory, or IIT (Tononi et al. 2016). Information and integration are key ideas in the neurosciences, but IIT proposes that consciousness is identical to integrated information. Integration here, roughly, means causal powers of the system that go beyond the causal power of the components of the system. Fourth, attention is often thought to be very important, either because attention is itself importantly involved in consciousness (Prinz 2012; Mole 2020) or, more recently, perhaps consciousness is our model of attention (Graziano et al. 2020).

Each of these four theoretical approaches has some claim to providing an interpretation of at least some of our current empirical data. As a result, each has its defenders and detractors. Where in this list do higher-order theories fit? Unlike these other theories, which mostly were developed by working scientists, higher-order theories were explicitly developed by philosophers. It is only recently that these kinds of theories have been explicitly connected to the empirical literature (Lau and Rosenthal 2011; Gennaro 2012). Since that time, there has been a sustained effort to extend the philosophical theorizing into empirically tractable questions (Brown, Lau, and LeDoux 2019). Some progress has been made, but there is still some confusion on how the overall landscape of scientific theories of consciousness should be mapped.

For example, sometimes we find people presenting things as though higher-order theories are just a fifth kind of theory to add to the list of currently viable contenders (Seth and Bayne 2022). Other times we find people trying to unify versions of the other ideas with higher-order awareness (for example Peter Carruthers 2000; Van Gulick 2022; Schurger and Graziano 2022). This is the second reason that anyone interested in the empirical nature of consciousness should care about higher-order theories. As these other theories are usually presented by the people who defend them, they happen to be first-order theories. This is because these theorists do not see a role for inner awareness in a theory of consciousness. But that is an accidental feature of these theorists, not their theories. We can see that each of the first four theories mentioned above could come in higher-order or first-order versions, even if no one currently defends that version of the theory now.

Take GNWT, which says, roughly, that a state is conscious when it is made available to a wide range of systems. This could require a kind of higher-order representation or not. For example, if one thinks of the global workspace as a kind of blackboard architecture, as Baars seemed to have when he introduced it (Baars 1988), then it would seem to entail re-representation of the original content on the 'blackboard.' Does this re-representation constitute a kind of higher-order awareness of the original content? If not, does it have to be made available to a self-system to count as conscious (Baars 1988; Caruthers 2000)?

Others have argued that we ought to think of the Global Workspace less like a blackboard and more like an information conduit connecting modules directly (Wu 2014). This way of thinking of the Global Workspace may not need to involve inner awareness. It may all just be representations of the world and other non-mental phenomena that are directly connected. Perhaps the wide-spread sharing of that kind of first-order, which is to say, non-higher-order, awareness is all one requires for consciousness. But, just when one thought it was safe, one might argue that these interconnections themselves constitute a kind of higher-order awareness (VanGulick 2022). So, what reasons do we have for preferring versions of GNWT that reject a role for inner awareness?

The same goes for IIT. The defenders of IIT start with some intuitive axioms they take to reflect the basic nature of consciousness. As they are stated now, they reflect a first-order approach to consciousness. One could modify IIT to include an axiom capturing the need for higher-order awareness. Or one might argue that one of the current axioms ought to be interpreted in a higher-order way. Deciding between these two options requires understanding why we should accept or deny a higher-order theory.

Similarly, attention may be a kind of inner sense (Sauret and Lycan 2014), and local recurrency may be the neural implementation of an inner awareness (as some higher-order theorists have suggested, e.g., Gennaro 2012). Indeed, even panpsychism could come in first-order and higher-order varieties. Some philosophers have argued that consciousness is fundamental, and that the particles of microphysics may be identical to consciousness (Strawson 1994; Chalmers 2013a). One could hold that these fundamental bits of consciousness require higher-order awareness. Or one could hold that they do not.

Evidently, higher-order theories are not just a fifth kind of theory to be added to the list. Every theory of consciousness is either a higher-order theory or not. So, at this point what we have found in the literature are several versions of first-order theory (GNWT, IIT, etc.), and one or two versions of higher-order theory (higher-order perception and higher-order thought). But there are many more possible versions of each of these specific kinds of theories. We now stand in need of a way to empirically arbitrate between them. We need to work out the theories in enough detail to determine whether the Attention Schema, for example, involves elements of higher-order theory (Graziano et al. 2020) or whether they are competing models of consciousness (Rosenthal 2020).

Those who support higher-order theories have reasons to develop these views so that they can be appropriately tested empirically. Those who do not support higher-order theories also have reasons to see the view developed, even if only to disconfirm it, or to empirically justify their preferred first-order theory. Doing either of these requires understanding far more than a caricature of the nuanced landscape surrounding higher-order theories.

Organization of the Book

I have split the book into two parts. In the first part, consisting of Chapters 2 through 4, I try to take a fresh perspective on the higher-order approach. Starting from the ground up, I try to set out a version of higher-order theory that I think is under-appreciated. In the second part of the book, which consists of Chapters 5 through 7, I step back and situate the theory developed in the first part in the existing higher-order literature. What emerges overall is an argument that this version is worth considering. At the conclusion of the book, I offer an appendix where some of the more technical material is discussed.

In a way this is backward from the order in which a typical philosophical manuscript would be presented. Ordinarily one might expect Chapters 5 through 7 to follow the first chapter. These chapters canvas the existing higher-order views, develop a new taxonomy to categorize them, and argue that a new approach is perhaps required. Chapters two through four then develop the view suggested by the shortcomings of the canvassed views.

There are a few reasons I have chosen to organize things this way, but the main reason is straightforward. As I discussed above, higher-order theories have only recently been introduced into the cognitive neuroscience literature. There is a desire to see where this set of ideas fits in with the other ideas already in play. Yet much of the debate within and between higher-order theorists took place in the philosophical literature in the late twentieth century. As a result, it is framed in a way that seems to me to be at odds with the best way to present the ideas to contemporary theorists who want to test it empirically. Making that argument is itself a tricky issue. Not everyone may be interested in the minutia of the various attempts to develop a higher-order theory over the past forty years. I find it very interesting, but I don't want to obscure the main message. There is a version of the higher-order theory that is interesting and overlooked/conflated with other versions.

Different people may want to take different paths through the book. Everyone should start with the first chapter. For those interested in general issues about higher-order theory and ways in which these theories can, and should, be empirically tested, start at Chapter 2. For those old hands who want an insider's perspective into the debate on higher-order theories from the last twenty years or so, start with Chapter 5. There are plenty of cross-references to help one jump around if one is not inclined to read it straight through.

I start, in Chapter 1, by defending what I thought was an obvious truism: the science of consciousness is in the business of understanding and explaining many phenomena, but chief among them is phenomenal consciousness. This involves what Thomas Nagel (1974) famously called there being something that it is like for one. Saying anything in this area is fraught with danger, as the terminology has been used and reused in so many ways by theorists with very different goals. The result is a confusing mess rather than an orderly set of distinctions. I start by trying to define how I will be using the terms in this book. Doing this requires some care. To help with this I introduce the phrase 'phenomenologically manifest' to talk about what occurs in one's stream of consciousness. When one is phenomenally conscious, there is something that it is like for one, from one's point of view. We can call this one's phenomenology. What it is like for one, specifically, is what is phenomenologically manifest. It is the overall character of one's experience. This will allow us to separate two questions that are very often run together. The first is a question about what exactly is phenomenologically manifest. Different theorists have postulated different answers to this question, as we will see. The second is a question of how those things that are phenomenologically manifest get explained by a theory of consciousness. It turns out, perhaps surprisingly, that these two questions may get different answers.

I distinguish phenomenal consciousness from several others that you find in the literature, some from first-order theorists and some from higher-order theorists. These other uses of the word 'consciousness' pick out real and important phenomena, all of which need to be explained. I argue that there is at least a *prima facie* case that each of these other notions can be disassociated from phenomenal consciousness. We need a theory of phenomenal consciousness that can make sense of these disassociations, and which is developed philosophically in enough detail to make empirically testable predictions. I then address two related issues concerning phenomenal consciousness. On the one hand, some think that it must be non-physical. On the other hand, partially because of the former consideration, some have adopted 'illusionism,' which is the view that phenomenal consciousness does not really exist but only seems to. I strongly disagree with both claims.

I argue that we can address both concerns with the same counterargument. Non-physicalism and illusionism stem from differing reactions to the a priori arguments against physicalism. However, these a priori arguments can themselves be countered by exactly parallel a priori arguments against non-physicalism. I provide the details of this argument in the Appendix but go over its application in Chapter 1. At the very least, the existence of the a priori counterarguments against dualism show that there is no pressing need to give up robust physicalism with a commitment to phenomenal consciousness.

Phenomenal consciousness is a real subjective component of physical reality. There is no reason, as of now, to think that we cannot explain this real subjective phenomenon in a way that is acceptable to the physicalist. The science of consciousness, at the point where we find ourselves now, should address what I call the 'central challenge' of consciousness science. This is the challenge of empirically deciding among the major theories of phenomenal consciousness currently being offered. We are beginning to have enough resources to start attempting to narrow down the pool of contenders. Meeting the central challenge would be to construct a 'standard model' of, at the very least, human consciousness. It might not be a complete account, and it may not garner universal support, but it would provide a basic framework for research in the cognitive neuroscience of consciousness.

In Chapter 2 I begin to develop a version of the higher-order approach I call the Higher-Order Representation of a Representation, or HOROR, theory of phenomenal consciousness. This is a representational theory of phenomenal consciousness from the higher-order perspective. I begin the chapter by arguing that higher-order theories are those that postulate a role for inner awareness in explaining phenomenal consciousness. A theory of consciousness is a higher-order theory just when it posits a crucial role for inner awareness in its explanation of what it is like to be the system in question. First-order theories are those which deny any role for inner awareness in the explanation of the nature of phenomenal consciousness.

First-order theories can also posit a special role for inner awareness in one of two ways. The first is to offer a deflationary notion of inner awareness, but I do not see any way to make that kind of view work. The second is to take what Nicolas Silins has called the Ascending Road. To take this path is to accept that one is always conscious of one's conscious states. One then needs to argue that the first-order state's being conscious is due to a factor other than the inner awareness with which it is necessarily associated. This helps us to clarify what it means to be a higher-order theory of consciousness.

We next need to discuss what it means to be mental. Some theorists appeal to folk-psychology to define what mentality is. My preference is for a pluralist, inclusive, notion of what makes something mental. My strategy is to appeal to the cognitive sciences. Whatever states and/or processes are postulated to play a role in the theories of mental processes developed by cognitive scientists should count as mental. If that means that there are low-level states of my brain that count as mental states, we should accept that. This allows us to include in our discussion theories that appeal to folk-psychology, like David Rosenthal's higher-order thought theory, as well as theories that appeal to computational neuroscience, like Steve Fleming's HOSS model, or

Hakwan Lau's Perceptual Reality Monitoring theory (both discussed in Chapter 7).

I then try to clarify my notion of representation as placing satisfaction conditions. The claim of representational theories of consciousness is that phenomenal consciousness consists in the appropriate representation. A higher-order representational view will hold that these representations, which are what consciousness consists in, have satisfaction conditions that involve mental states and processes. Put more informally, the HOROR theory says that phenomenal consciousness just is a representation of oneself as having a mental life. As I argue, representing oneself as having a mental life amounts to representing oneself as being is some targeted first-order mental state and in effect conceptually describing that mental state in some way.

Since the higher-order state is itself the phenomenally conscious state on the HOROR theory, and we are not typically aware of these higher-order states, it follows that there can be states of consciousness of which I am not aware. This makes the HOROR theory a nontraditional higher-order theory in a couple of ways. First, I reject what has come to be known as the Transitivity Principle, which says that a conscious state is one of which I am aware. The Transitivity Principle has been used both as the primary motivator for the higher-order approach and to delimit the data that a theory of consciousness must account for. I do not think that the higher-order approach to consciousness needs to rely on the Transitivity Principle for either of these tasks. Furthermore, it seems to me to be an empirical question whether it really is the case that phenomenally conscious states are ones of which we are aware. The only evidence I have seen given by traditional higher-order theorists is the intuitive pull of the Transitivity Principle. Not everyone finds this pull as intuitive, and these clashes of intuitions are best translated into empirical questions, in my view.

Second, and because I reject the Transitivity Principle, I argue that we need to separate phenomenal consciousness and state-consciousness. State-consciousness involves the state of which I am aware, while phenomenal consciousness involves what it is like for me. On the face of it these are conceptually distinct. There are some theorists who try to identify them, but that requires additional arguments. On the HOROR theory the higher-order state is phenomenally but not state conscious, and the lower-order state targeted by the higher-order state is state- but not phenomenally conscious. This allows us to formulate a modified principle that says that a phenomenally conscious state is one that appropriately makes me aware of my own mental life. In this way we can try to capture, in modern terms, what the slogan "consciousness is an awareness of what passes in our own minds," seems to suggest. That is what phenomenal consciousness is.

Third, HOROR theory might be considered non-traditional because of the emphasis on representations rather than perception or thought. Higher-order thought theories take the inner awareness posited for phenomenal consciousness to be akin to ordinary thoughts from folk-psychology, whereas higher-order perception views take them to be more like folk perceptions. I think the folk platitude that involves inner awareness is all we need. The rest is theorizing, and the workhorse of today's cognitive neuroscience is the representation, not perception or thought. I expect the relevant HORORs to perhaps be sub-personal states found in a specialized network or module, but these empirical and philosophical matters are a long way from being resolved.

I then try to say something about the kind of content I envision these higher-order states will have at the psychological level. I discuss these at a general level before going into more detail in Chapter 3. I start by introducing my distinction between what I call *phenomenally active* and *phenomenally silent* content in the relevant HORORs. The content of the HOROR is phenomenally active when it results in a phenomenologically manifest aspect of one's stream of consciousness. A content is phenomenally silent when it does not result in a phenomenologically manifest aspect of one's stream of consciousness. I connect these two kinds of content to descriptive and pointer contents. Descriptive contents of HORORs involve concepts being deployed to produce intentional content, which I take is what it is to think. I model pointer content as metaphorically akin to HTML code for hyperlinks, though this is just one way to think of them. The part of the hyperlink that points to the website one wants to link to is not part of what shows up on one's screen. What is on the screen is the blue-underlined text that indicates click-ability. We can think of what is on the screen as what is phenomenologically manifest—the part of the HTML code that determines that is phenomenally active. The other aspects of the line of code are phenomenally silent, though they play an important role in generating the link.

In Chapter 3, I develop the content I envision these states as having in more detail. The basic idea is that the HORORs represent the subject as being in a special relationship with perceptible properties in the world. As I set out in Chapter 1, phenomenally conscious states can be thought of as having two components, the subjective and phenomenal characters, as they have been called (Kriegel 2009). Part of my goal is to map the space of possibilities here, and the other part of my goal is to argue for my way of thinking of things. On the mapping side of things, there are various ways in which one might see phenomenal and subjective character as going together. Some theorists use them in such a way as to make subjective character a subspecies of phenomenal character (Kriegel 2009), in which case both are phenomenologically manifest. Others reject this (Gennaro 2012) and insist that phenomenal character does not include subjective character. For these theorists, subjective character is not phenomenologically manifest.

As for myself, I understand phenomenal and subjective character to be aspects of one's phenomenology, or what it is like to be you at any given moment. They are aspects of what is phenomenologically manifest. The phenomenal character captures the way in which my conscious experiences differ—some are like seeing red, some like hearing a sound, and so on. The subjective character is common to all these experiences and picks out that it is from my point of view that there is something that it is like to see red, and so on. The concepts that one applies to the targeted lower-order states describe it in mixed language as one's own self mentally encountering a non-mental worldly property, say redness, which is represented as being a basic property of the physical world, or one's environment. The satisfaction conditions for this state involve the first-order representation of red in the world as well as the self. The state will be accurate just when it is me, not you, who is seeing red. According to the HOROR theory both phenomenal character and subjective character are phenomenologically manifest. Importantly, this is not because I am aware of the higher-order state. It follows from the claim that this element of the relevant higher-order state's content is phenomenally active.

This departs from traditional higher-order views in another way. The concept postulated to occur in the HOROR is that of 'seeing red.' This is not controversial. However, I suggest that we should distinguish at least three concepts of RED. The first is what I call *physical red*. This is the physical property of objects that first-order sensory states represent. This is most likely surface reflectance profiles but could be a power, or disposition of physical bodies. Second is the concept of *mental red*, of a mental quality. This is the concept of something mental and is what is traditionally thought to occur in the relevant higher-order states. But on the HOROR theory that I defend, the concept is that of *perceptible red*. I take this to be the concept of a primitive color that physical objects possess. If this weren't a book on philosophy, I might dare to say that this is the ordinary commonsense concept of red. According to the HOROR theory, one, rather confusedly, describes one's first-order mental states/processes as a visual encounter with the perceptible property. 'I am visually encountering perceptible red, which is a property of the tomato I am seeing,' or some such, might approximate the kind of content that is postulated.

The reason that the version of higher-order theory I favor postulates the use of the concept of perceptible red, as opposed to mental red as traditional theorists do, is that I am skeptical that we have a concept of mental red that can do the work required (Byrne 2022). I do, however, think we have a concept of mental red that plays some other role in the HORORs. As just discussed, we have conceptual/intentional descriptive content, but there is likely some kind of indexical or 'pointer' content in the relevant higher-order states as well. This indexical/pointer content will 'pick out' the relevant lower-order states and thus will give us an answer to the question 'which state/process am I currently aware of myself as being in?' This indexical/pointer content can be thought of as a kind of concept of mental red. It allows us to become aware of the first-order state, but this content is phenomenally silent. The lower-order states so referred to are the ones that the subject is aware of being in and so will have some functional effects on the mental life of the creature. But *the way in which* the subject is aware of those first-order states is determined by the conceptual/descriptive content of the relevant HORORs, and that is what it is like for the subject.

Having laid out the philosophical aspects of HOROR theory, we can then look at some of the possible empirical predictions that the theory makes. I focus on the kinds of mismatches that may occur among these three kinds of representational contents (the first-order state, and the conceptual and 'pointer' contents, of the higher-order states). I view these cases as predictions made by specific versions of the HOROR theory and try to separate two major versions of the theory: rich and sparse HOROR. These versions of the theory disagree on whether the descriptive contents of the higher-order states represent all the detail that the first-order states themselves are representing. Rich versions of HOROR affirm that this is the case. The relevant higher-order states will target first-order representations and conceptually represent all, or most, of the content of those targeted first-order states. Sparse versions of HOROR will deny this. They hold that at least in some cases the relevant higher-order states target the very same kind of first-order states and represent them in either a partial, or generic and abstract way. When the first-order states are represented in a partial way, the higher-order state will leave out a lot of the detail, as in representing a small portion of a large image. When the higher-order state represents the first-order state in an abstract or generic way, it will be glossing over the detail, as in representing a specific sentence like 'the dog is hungry' simply as 'some words written in English forming a sentence.' My intuitive sympathies lie with the rich HOROR, but we are not yet able to adjudicate between rich and sparse HOROR.

This naturally leads to a discussion of introspective consciousness, and I close the chapter by sketching the account of the HOROR theory of introspective consciousness. According to the HOROR theory, one becomes introspectively conscious when one has an introspective HOROR, one that represents you as in effect experiencing yourself mentally encountering a perceptible property (as opposed to representing oneself as simply mentally encountering that perceptible property). This account of introspection is distinct from the traditional higher-order approach in that it does not postulate a third-order representation. Instead, it postulates a change in the contents of the second-order HOROR.

I do not think that philosophical arguments, all by themselves, will ever be able to advance these debates. Nor do I think that empirical results alone will decide these issues (if that were so I wouldn't need to write this book!). Even so, empirical results are ultimately going to decide many of these issues for us, or so I will argue. Because of this, Chapter 4 is dedicated to sorting through some of the empirical issues related to HOROR theory. I begin by arguing for my claim that the only reason to accept a theory of consciousness, higher-order theories included, is because of empirical results. A priori reasoning and folk-psychological platitudes can give us insight into which questions we should empirically ask and help us interpret the results. They cannot establish, or refute, a theory of consciousness in the absence of empirical evidence. To answer any of the empirical questions we need to map the psychological concepts we have been discussing onto the states of the brain/brain states (Brown 2006). It is often assumed that the first-order states we are interested in will be found in the sensory cortices and that the higher-order states that we are interested in will be found in the prefrontal cortex. This intuitive idea may not be correct, and that leads us to see that there are different neural implementations of the various versions of the HOROR theory discussed in Chapter 3. Some theorists champion a prefrontally implemented higher-order theory (Lau 2022), others a more parietally implemented version (Gennaro 2012). We can then distinguish versions of the theory that invoke a rich and detailed phenomenology due to the higher-order state and there being rich and detailed content in the first-order states. Once all these distinctions are in place, we can then start to look at the few empirical results that are relevant.

Perhaps the earliest use of empirical work to press the attack against higher-order theory was by Fred Dretske and his use of change blindness. Dretske's intuitive idea was that in the case where there is something changing right in front of one and yet one doesn't notice this change, we have some evidence for a conscious state of which you are unaware. Finding states that are phenomenally conscious, but of which we are unaware, has been thought to the best way to challenge higher-order theories empirically. This tradition has been carried on in the work of Ned Block, who also presses the attack against higher-order theories using descendants of the original change-blindness arguments. After close examination, these arguments based on change blindness turn out to be inconclusive. They fail to take into consideration the details of the higher-order account. The issues are complicated, but in short, the problem is that the objectors do not recognize the possibility that what it is like to be in a conscious state may diverge from what the content of the (first-order) conscious state actually is! This may sound obscure, but by the time one has read through Chapter 4, it should hopefully be a bit less obscure.

Change blindness still seems like a promising avenue to test specific versions of the HOROR theory, and together with Ned Block, David Chalmers, BiYu He, Jan Brascamp, and others, we have come up with a version of a change-blindness experiment that we think might address the rich prefrontally implemented version of HOROR theory (Koenig et al. 2023). This project is in progress as I am writing this, but I go over the basics of it in Chapter 4 and what we hope it might be able to show with respect to this debate. The basic idea is to try to see whether there are any traces of rich HORORs in the prefrontal cortex. This suggests a way to empirically decide among positions in this area and mitigates the worry that these issues are not empirically tractable.

Before closing this chapter, I examine some of the work done by Hakwan Lau (Lau 2022). Lau is one of a few scientists who explicitly attempts to test aspects of the higher-order theory. Lau defends the prefrontal implementation of his specific version of higher-order theory to be discussed in detail in Chapter 7. Still his work can be taken to bear on the HOROR theory in that he is testing for an element that the theories have in common (the pointer content). We will discuss this more recent work in Chapter 7. Lau's earlier work was aiming to test whether there may be some aspect of one's phenomenology that outstripped what was represented at the first-order level (Lau and Brown 2019). Lau's work is very interesting and important, but I think the results are inconclusive there as well. What does become very clear is that we have two competing models of the data, one where there is phenomenal consciousness at the first-order level and results in a judgment in the prefrontal areas and the other where the prefrontal areas play an important role in producing phenomenal consciousness. We thus stand on the verge of answering these questions, but, tantalizingly close as we might be, the central questions await further work.

That completes my introduction and defense of what I think of as an interesting version of the higher-order approach. It is at odds with the traditional higher-order approach in many ways, and seeing how it is at odds with the traditional higher-order approach lets us see that there is a way of carving up the theoretical landscape that has been mostly overlooked until recently.

In the fifth chapter we backtrack to take a closer look at what I call the traditional higher-order approach to consciousness. Higher-order theories count as 'traditional' on my reading if they accept the Transitivity Principle, which states that a phenomenally conscious state is one of which I am aware. The state that is conscious on the traditional approach is the target of higher-order awareness. What has largely gone unnoticed until recently is that there are at least two distinct readings of the traditional Transitivity Principle. I have called these the relational and non-relational readings (Brown 2012b). Relational versions of the traditional higher-order approach argue that a phenomenally conscious mental state involves that very state being related in the right way to a higher-order state that makes the subject aware of (being in) that first-order state. Further, they hold that the first-order state's content is phenomenologically manifest. Traditional non-relational versions of the theory hold that a phenomenally conscious mental state is one that the subject represents herself as being in, and so is the targeted first-order state, while still holding that it is the content of the higher-order state that entirely and exhaustively determines what it is like for the subject.

There are two kinds of traditional non-relational theories depending on how they respond to the possibility of an 'empty' higher-order state, or one where the targeted first-order state does not exist. Pure non-relational theories argue that in such cases the subject is nonetheless in a conscious state and that the state that is conscious is the non-existent first-order state. These theories are purely non-relational in that the higher-order state employs solely descriptive contents. The first-order state that is targeted is simply the one that best fits the description issued by the higher-order state, and it may be the case that there is no existing first-order state that is so best described.

Mixed non-relational theories attempt to rule out non-existent conscious states by arguing for a relational aspect of the higher-order awareness that secures reference to a first-order state, which is then the conscious state, but at the same time they hold that it is still the higher-order content that entirely determines what it is like for one. Mixed non-relational theories are non-relational in the sense that, even though the first-order state is the phenomenally conscious state, what it is like for the subject is determined by the way the higher-order state represents it. The first-order state does not contribute its content to the phenomenology of the subject except insofar as it influences the contents of that higher-order representation. The first-order state is phenomenally silent, and its content is not phenomenologically manifest. This way of carving up the conceptual space lets us see that some theories, like the traditional higher-order thought theory (Rosenthal 2005) and the self-representational theories (Kriegel 2009), are similar in an important respect. They are all traditional non-relational higher-order theories.

On the relational side we can similarly distinguish between joint-determination and spotlight views. Joint-determination views are mixed in that they hold that both higher-order and first-order elements are phenomenologically manifest, or that one's experience is jointly determined by the contents of the higher-order and lower-order states. Spotlight views are pure in that they hold that one's phenomenology is completely determined by the contents of the first-order states and the higher-order state merely serves to make one aware of their content.

HOROR theory as discussed in the previous chapters is a non-traditional higher-order theory in my sense. It is non-traditional because it denies that the phenomenally conscious state is the first-order state. That is to say that the HOROR theory rejects the Transitivity Principle as a way of fixing the data for a theory of consciousness and as a motivator for accepting the theory. HOROR theory has a lot in common with traditional non-relational views in that HOROR accepts that the subject's phenomenology is completely and exhaustively accounted for by the higher-order representation and its contents. HOROR theory also shares limited similarity to relational views in that the posited relational/pointer content, though phenomenally silent, is thought to have some functional effect on the first-order states. A first-order state's being 'pointed at' will likely serve to keep it active longer and route it to working memory, or to other areas for use in reasoning, control of action, and so on. In this way HOROR theory tries to capture the spirit of Block's slogan that "consciousness greases the wheels of access," which I interpret to mean that phenomenally conscious states have some functional role to play. The HOROR theory allows us to flesh out the claim that phenomenal consciousness must be involved "somehow in powering the wheels and pulleys of access" (Block 1995). The pointer content in the HOROR may not be the only such greasing mechanism, but phenomenally conscious states do enhance the availability of first-order states on the HOROR theory.

The discussion reveals that there are, in general, six overarching types of higher-order theory. Two types of non-traditional non-relational views like HOROR (pure and mixed) and at least four versions of traditional approaches: pure and mixed versions of non-relationalism and pure and mixed versions of relationalism, which I called spotlight and joint-determination. Spotlight versions of relationalism can be considered pure in that they assign all of the work to the relation that makes the first-order content phenomenologically manifest. Joint-determination views are a form of mixed relationalism in that they posit that both elements are phenomenally active. There is a nice symmetry there. On pure non-relational views, what it is like for one is completely determined by the content of the higher-order state. On pure relationalism, what it is like for one is completely determined by the first-order state. Mixed non-relationalism adds in a relation but denies that it plays a role in what it is like for one. Mixed relationalism insists that the higher-order state and the relation it has to the first-order state must both play a role in what it is like for the subject.

The fact that this taxonomy has been obscured for so long is my primary reason for thinking that we should present things in a different way, but there are some other reasons as well. These all revolve around the Transitivity Principle. So, at the end of Chapter 5 I give my reasons for thinking that we should move beyond this traditional way of thinking about the higher-order theory. Is the claim that all conscious states are states we are aware of really a conceptual truth? Are all higher-order theories committed to the existence of unconscious qualitative aspects of the mind? And is state consciousness really the explanatory goal of a theory of consciousness? Spoiler alert: the answer to each of these questions is 'no.' Rather than being diagnostic of the higher-order approach in general, answering these questions helps to determine various versions of the overall approach.

In the sixth chapter we take a close look at non-relational versions of the traditional approach. We first start by examining the traditional pure non-relationalism of David Rosenthal's higher-order thought theory. Non-relational versions of the theory invoke conceptual/intentional contents of higher-order representations as the explanation of phenomenal consciousness. As it is typically presented, the intentional content of the THOT (I use this as a name for the traditional higher-order thought as it occurs in the mind of an individual) is purely descriptive. One major drawback to this kind of traditional pure non-relationalism is that there can be conscious mental states that are merely notional—that is, conscious mental states that do not exist. As we will discuss in Chapter 6, this paradoxical-sounding statement can be made sense of with some fancy footwork, but there are other problems with traditional pure non-relationalism. Without any kind of relational content being posited in the relevant higher-order states, pure non-relational higher-order theories have no way to say what the actual conscious mental states of the subject are. One is left grasping at third-person measures and gets the feeling that which states of the subject count as conscious are merely an honorific without any real consequences. This may be acceptable to some theorists, but others may take it as a reason to look elsewhere.

It was precisely these consequences that led other traditional non-relational theorists to attempt to find some way to secure the first-order content. These kinds of theories are exemplified by Uriah Kriegel and Rocco Gennaro. This may be surprising to think of these authors as endorsing non-relational versions of higher-order theory. Their motivation is precisely to find some relation that ties the first-order and higher-order elements into a single unified state. However, these theorists deny that this relation has any role to play in determining what it is like for the subject. The theories they offer are mixed non-relational theories in that they hold that there is some mental relation that makes it the case that there is always a first-order state/content when we have a conscious mental state, but they also hold that it is the higher-order content that determines what it is like for one. This allows us to see that the difference between self-representational views (like Uriah Kriegel's) and higher-order thought views (like Gennaro's wide-intentionality account) differ over whether the kind of inner awareness posited in their explanation of phenomenal consciousness is itself conscious. Because they accept the traditional Transitivity Principle, this amounts to the claim that inner awareness is itself something of which we are aware. This is a real and important difference between the views on the issue of subjective character being phenomenologically manifest. They do not differ on whether one's phenomenology is entirely dependent on the content of the higher-order representation.

Traditional non-relational accounts also have issues with specifying the nature of the self. To see this, we discuss an argument based on somataparaphrenia, which shows, I think, that there is a problem for traditional non-relationalism. Traditional non-relational theories all have the same issues. They are traditional, and so want there to be some existing first-order state which is conscious. This can be done, as in pure non-relationalism, by offering a philosophical analysis of the term 'conscious state' as just being the occurrence of the THOT. Or it can be done, as in mixed-non-relationalism, by finding some relation that might exist among the relevant states/contents. The problem is that once one works through the details, one finds that the very motivation for the Transitivity Principle is undermined. This provides us with some philosophical reasons to prefer a non-traditional higher-order theory.

We conclude Chapter 6 with a discussion of the ways in which the HOROR theory differs from these traditional versions of non-relationalism. There are many interesting philosophical issues that come up when thinking about these various kinds of higher-order theory, but I tend to want to sidestep those issues. I prefer to reframe these philosophical differences as empirical predictions each version of the theory makes. The main difference in predictions is over the neural correlates of consciousness, whether prefrontal cortex or something more distributed. But there are also the predictions about mis-representation cases. Each of these views makes claims about what we should expect to find at the neural level in particular cases. For example, consider someone who looks at a hammer but says they don't know what it is. This is called visual form agnosia and is a case of not being able to identify something based on visually perceiving it. The different versions of higher-order theory seem to make different predictions about these kinds of cases. Whatever one's philosophical predilections, I think it is these kinds of empirical cases that will help us to decide among the various views we have been discussing.

In the seventh chapter, I turn to an examination of several attempts to develop versions of relational higher-order theories. Most relational versions of the higher-order approach are motivated by the desire to allow the first-order state of which we are aware to become phenomenally active. They long to find some more intimate connection between our first-order representations/qualities aimed at the world and our awareness of them, which allows those first-order states to become phenomenologically manifest (Coleman 2015). There is a widespread conviction that we need something like acquaintance to capture the relation between our awareness and the qualities of which we are aware. So, to set the stage we discuss the higher-order acquaintance view of Benj Hellie and (separately) David Chalmers. These are not, strictly speaking, higher-order theories in my sense. They do not aim to explain consciousness, but they do offer a nice illustration of what many theorists would like to have. Chalmers endorses the idea that phenomenal awareness is by its nature also an awareness of that awareness. This is introduced as a primitive, non-reducible aspect of reality and so is not compatible with physicalism. But is there any way that we might be able to capture something like this picture without the heavy burden of conflicting with physicalism? As argued in Chapter 2, we don't know that physicalism is true, but we can see that it hasn't been obviously ruled out either. So, what are the prospects for this kind of project?

This idea has been developed in several ways, but all relational versions of the traditional higher-order approach can be classified as either 'spotlight' (pure) or 'joint-determination' (mixed) views. The difference between these views lies in whether what is phenomenologically manifest to the subject can be captured solely by the first-order content of the states. Spotlight views affirm that this is the case. On the other side are those who argue that what is phenomenologically manifest will be jointly determined by both first-order and higher-order contents. On the joint-determination views, one's phenomenal properties are jointly determined by both higher-order and first-order components. When what it is like for one is jointly determined in this way, it will be the case that both the higher-order pointer and the first-order states are phenomenally active, thus each will result in a phenomenologically manifest aspect of one's stream of consciousness.

Spotlight views have been the most popular, but there are some joint-determination views as well. Contemporary spotlight views include Mental Quotation views (Picciuto 2014; Coleman 2015), (what I call) Attentional Sifting views (Lycan and Sauret 2014), and more recently Perceptual Reality Monitoring (Lau 2022) and (what I call) acquaintance + first-order representation views (Guistina forthcoming). On the joint-determination side there are fewer, but there are some. From the classic literature I think we can see that the traditional higher-order perception view defended by William Lycan is a form of joint-determinism as I defined it. More recently, we have the Higher-Order State Space, or HOSS, model (Fleming 2020), and even the Attention Schema theory can be seen as an implementation of this kind of theory (though with an illusionist flavor). Each of these accounts is interesting, and ultimately a lot of the issues among the various theories will be empirically settled, but there is a general reason that I am uneasy with relational theories.

The desire for intimacy leads these theorists to postulate such a thin notion of awareness that the way in which the content of the first-order state gets into the stream of consciousness becomes entirely mysterious. How does it become phenomenologically manifest? One can intone the words 'because that is what I am aware of', but how does it really work? I argue that one is led to the view that the mental qualities, the redness of mental red and so on, must exist in an 'inner-awareness independent' manner. This either comes with a certain metaphysical cost, collapses the view into a first-order theory, or else renders the whole process a matter of stipulation. One must either simply stipulate that consciousness results from the relevant relation or admit that the first-order qualities already had the property we were trying to explain, in which case the higher-order awareness does nothing to explain those properties.

The relevant lesson that I draw from the exploration of the various versions of the traditional higher-order approach over the last few chapters is that we want a hybrid non-traditional view that postulates both descriptive and relational content in the higher-order state. But, as our exploration also reveals, these two kinds of contents are suited for different roles related to consciousness. The relational content is needed to rule out non-existent conscious states. It supplies an answer to the question 'which state is it that the subject is aware of at this moment?' and so it secures the reference to the first-order states. This relation arguably has functional consequences for the lower-order states. It likely serves to route them for further processing, keep them online for further causal efficacy, and so on. However, the relational content of the higher-order states likely does not play any role in determining what it is like for the subject. This is completely and exhaustively determined by the conceptual/descriptive content of the higher-order state. The descriptive content describes the subject as having the relevant kind of mental life. So, the overall conclusion is that a theory like HOROR theory is missing and desirable. Good thing we provided it in the first part of the book!

Hopefully the two parts of the book together constitute both an argument that the HOROR theory should be taken seriously as a distinctive non-traditional version of the non-relational higher-order approach to phenomenal consciousness and a clarification of the subtleties of the theoretical landscape surrounding higher-order theories.

1
Constructing a Scientific Theory of Phenomenal Consciousness

Understanding consciousness has presented a long-standing challenge to the science of the mind (see Michel 2020 for a recent review). There are many interesting phenomena, unanswered questions, and challenging methodological puzzles in the scientific study of consciousness. As a result, there are many avenues for research in consciousness science. At the core of them all is phenomenal consciousness. I will argue that phenomenal consciousness is the primary explanatory target for a theory of consciousness. The central challenge for the emerging cognitive neuroscience of consciousness is to arbitrate, in so far as it can, among currently existing theories of human phenomenal consciousness.

To get clarity on these issues we first must separate out the various things that we might mean when we talk about 'consciousness.' In section 1.1, I introduce several distinctions among concepts of consciousness and argue that in each case phenomenal consciousness is what a theory of consciousness is called on to explain. In section 1.2, I argue that we should be optimistic about the prospects for an account of phenomenal consciousness in physicalist terms. Finally in section 1.3, we will turn to the goal of a science of consciousness. In section 1.3.1, I introduce what I call the central challenge of consciousness science. After millennia of theorizing about the nature of consciousness, it is time to start testing our big ideas. We need a standard model of the human mind, which will include many phenomena. Part of that standard model will have to include phenomenal consciousness.

1.1 Kinds of Consciousness

There are many concepts of consciousness, and many ways that people use the word 'consciousness'. Here I will set out how I use these various terms and will try my best to follow what I take to be a standard way of using the relevant terms. Unfortunately, there are different 'standard' uses in different subgroups (Mehta 2022), so we may not avoid stepping on some toes. Where this happens, I will try to be as clear as I can about the way I will use the terms in this book.

1.1.1 Phenomenal Consciousness and our Cast of Characters

The most fundamental sense of 'consciousness' is phenomenal consciousness. This is a technical term for a commonsense notion. A creature is phenomenally conscious when there is something that it is like for the creature from its subjective point of view (Nagel 1974). To have phenomenally conscious states is to be in states that, when one is in those states, there is something that it is like for you to be in them. This 'stream of consciousness' that constitutes one's phenomenology is the overall character of one's experience. We can call this the *phenomenal character* of an experience, which is the overall specific way that it is like for one at any given moment in one's stream of consciousness, or from time to time.[1]

Another way of speaking of phenomenal character is by introducing phenomenal properties. These are the properties of either subjects, or phenomenal states, which distinguish one phenomenally conscious state (or subjective experience) from another phenomenally conscious state. We can say that phenomenal states are individuated by what it is like for one to be in them. So, for example, the phenomenal redness of a visual experience is what distinguishes it from a visual experience of green. Both visual experiences would be distinguished from the

---

[1] I use 'phenomenal character' to talk about the overall character of one's experience as well as some specific individual aspect of one's overall experience. Context makes it clear which is meant.

phenomenal character of the sound of a trumpet, thinking about the moon landing, and so on.[2]

Because the terminology in this area is so cursed, it is hard to say anything beyond this that isn't controversial. Indeed, what we have said so far is controversial in its own right! To help discuss the various technical bits of jargon and the ensuing options for how to use them, I will often speak of something being *phenomenologically manifest*. Something is phenomenologically manifest when it is conveyed to the subject by one's phenomenology. To be phenomenologically manifest is to be occurrent in one's stream of consciousness. To put it in the terms above, phenomenal character is what is overall phenomenologically manifest, and the specific things that are manifest in this way are the phenomenal properties of one's phenomenally conscious states.

One very influential way to think of phenomenal character is to take it to be comprised of subjective character and qualitative character (Kriegel 2009). On this reading, 'qualitative character' denotes the specific phenomenal properties that vary between phenomenally conscious states. When I have a phenomenally conscious experience of red, when what it is like for me is like seeing red, the phenomenal redness of that experience is often called its qualitative character. And this qualitative character will differ from the qualitative character of an experience of hearing a sound, and so on. However, all these experiences, which vary in qualitative character, have in common that they are for me, from my point of view, and are subjective in that sense. Thus, they all have the same subjective character, which is thought to be common to all phenomenally conscious states of an individual.

I am in general sympathetic to this division, but we must be careful. As these terms are often used, subjective and qualitative character are postulated to be phenomenologically manifest. However, this is controversial for both proposed aspects of phenomenal character.

---

[2] I will largely set aside so-called phenomenal externalism on which the phenomenal character of red is a property of the external world (identical duplicates could have distinct phenomenal character depending on their environment according to phenomenal externalism). This is related to naïve realism, set aside in footnote 3. My goal here is simply to make clear how I will use the terms in this book. Any non-terminological philosophical issues will be dealt with when we discuss transparency and the content of the higher-order states involving perceptible red in Chapters 2 and 3.

Starting with subjective character first, many treat it not only as a subspecies of phenomenal character, but as the most pressing part for a theory of consciousness to account for (Zahavi 2005; Kriegel 2009; Zahavi and Kriegel 2015). It would therefore be phenomenologically manifest as I use the term. Other theorists hold that there is indeed something that distinguishes phenomenally conscious states from states that are not phenomenally conscious, and that this is something that is common to all conscious states. They thus agree that there is subjective character, yet they deny that subjective character is phenomenologically manifest (Rosenthal 2005; Gennaro 2012). We will leave discussion of the details until later chapters (Chapter 3, section 3.1, for my own views on how subjective character fits into phenomenal consciousness, and Chapter 6, section 6.1.3, for discussion of Rosenthal's view of the self, and section 6.2.2 for discussion of Gennaro's view, if one would like to skip ahead). As I use these terms, phenomenal character is always phenomenologically manifest, but subjective character will only be so for certain theoretical approaches and not others. I will do my best to flag any areas where there may be cause for ambiguity.

Moving to qualitative character, we see a similar debate playing out. This time things are even more complicated because often there are really two debates about qualitative character that are conflated. One of these debates is largely orthogonal to the debate about phenomenal consciousness. The other is central to this debate, so conflating these two issues is very dangerous for our project.

The first debate involves first-order sensory and perceptual states. Suppose that some creature is perceiving a red object. Is the state in this animal's mind that allows it to respond to this worldly property 'qualitative' in the sense of being non-intentional/non-conceptual? Here the question of qualitative character is one of what kind of properties sensory states have. Some hold a purely conceptual/intentional account of the mind. These theorists want to deny that there are any mental qualities in this sense. Representations and/or concepts of qualities are fine. Others hold that the defining characteristic of sensory mental states is their non-intentional/non-conceptual qualitative character. Higher-order theorists are split on this question as well, suggesting that it is independent of one's specific version of the higher-order approach. Some higher-order theorists endorse mental qualities (Rosenthal 2005).

Some higher-order theorists endorse representationalism about qualities (Kriegel 2009; Gennaro 2012). Others argue that mental qualities are a special kind of non-intentional/non-conceptual representation (Berger and Brown 2022).

The second debate concerns whether the sensory first-order states can occur unconsciously and still be qualitative in the above sense. Are sensory and perceptual states necessarily phenomenologically manifest when they occur? Can one have a pain, or a visual experience of red, that is well and truly qualitative, but that there is nothing it is like for one to have? A pain that is painful in some sense, but that is not phenomenologically manifest? Some theorists use 'qualitative' just to mean 'the phenomenologically manifest aspect of the state' (Kriegel 2009). In that case it is obvious that these kinds of states cannot occur without being phenomenally conscious. Other theorists have tended to use 'qualitative character' as a way of talking about the mental qualities of *first-order* sensory states *that may or may not be phenomenologically manifest* (Rosenthal 2005). In this case, qualitative character and phenomenal character are distinct. Used in this way, qualitative states can occur without there being anything it is like for you to have them occur. They can occur without being phenomenologically manifest. We will discuss this extensively in Chapter 7.

As in the case of subjective character discussed above, I will continue to use 'phenomenal consciousness,' 'phenomenal properties,' and 'phenomenal character' to discuss what it is like for one and what is phenomenologically manifest in one's stream of consciousness. As I use these terms, there can be no doubt that these states and properties must be phenomenally conscious in the sense of there being something that it is like for one to be in these states or to insatiate these properties. Nor can there be any doubt that they are phenomenologically manifest in the sense of being a distinct part or aspect of what it is like to be you overall when they occur. When it comes to 'qualitative character,' whether the properties in question are first-order, or phenomenologically manifest, depends on the theory in which this term is employed. I am happy with either usage, but unlike talk about phenomenal character, talking about qualitative character needs further clarification to make clear in which of the above senses it is being used. I will take extra care to ensure that any use of 'qualitative' is used in such a way as to make it clear how it relates to my primary notion of phenomenal consciousness and phenomenal character.

We don't use these technical terms in our ordinary folk-psychological discourse. We do use related terms like 'experience,' 'conscious experience,' and 'subjective experience,' which I take to be the commonsense equivalent of the technical term. It is familiar from commonsense that we can distinguish our mental life in terms of what it is like for us. What it is like to see the red tomato, particularly its phenomenal redness, the way in which I experience the redness of the tomato, is very different from what it is like for me to see a rotten and withered tomato, or an unripe green one. There are many ways in which these experiences differ, but one is that the phenomenal redness is distinct from the phenomenal greenness. Both visual phenomenal properties are distinct from the phenomenal sounds and emotions that populate my subjective experience. We often use aspects of phenomenal consciousness to convey experiences to others. We might say 'you know that feeling you get when you are about to go over the rollercoaster? It's a bit like that' or 'it tastes a little like an orange but more bitter.' And so on.

For the most part, we typically think of these properties as being in the world, but the familiar experience of dreams, illusions, and hallucinations suggest that they are at least also properties of experience. And it is these properties that we arguably attend to when we introspect.[3]

People typically introduce phenomenal consciousness, and especially phenomenal character, via sensory experience like seeing red or experiencing pain, but it is generally meant to pick out what it is like for us overall. The phenomenal character of an experience may include qualitative sensory components as well as emotional and cognitive states like thoughts. Phenomenal properties, the properties of phenomenal states—individuate things more fine-grained in terms of what is phenomenologically manifest. This can include the

---

[3] I will largely set aside the debate about naïve and/or direct realism and representationalism in the philosophy of perception, though it is currently very interesting and lively (see, e.g., Beck 2019; Raineri 2021; Pautz forthcoming). As we will see, there is a kind of analog to this debate that occurs between defenders of higher-order theories of consciousness.

phenomenal aspects of emotions, and cognition in general (LeDoux and Brown 2017, Brown and Mandik 2012). We will tend, as almost everyone does, to focus on visual experience, but it is helpful to keep in mind that phenomenal consciousness includes the entirety of our experience. Phenomenal consciousness is what it is like to be you, and that is a vastly more complex thing than what it is like to simply see red.

To fully understand consciousness, we need to develop and explore our phenomenology as well as our science of the brain. There are many controversies surrounding phenomenology (Brown 2013). We will largely focus on issues on the brain side of things, but I think it is important to realize that work needs to be done on the phenomenological side of things as well. The phenomenological part of our standard model of the mind is not yet complete.

Phenomenal consciousness is contrasted with a creature's lack of experience altogether. A creature that lacked phenomenal consciousness would be a philosophical zombie (Chalmers 1996). There would be nothing that it was like for this creature. States that are not phenomenally conscious are not like anything for the creature in which they occur. From the creature's point of view, it would be as if they weren't there at all. They would be absent from the stream of consciousness. A philosophical zombie is a more extreme version of this. These hypothetical creatures have internal states, and allegedly may even be a physical duplicate of you, but *ex hypothesi*, there is nothing that it is like for this creature to be in any of these states. A philosophical zombie is alleged to have no subjective point of view at all. These creatures have been used to argue against physicalism, and we are not doing that here (we will discuss physicalism in the next section). Here we are simply using zombies as a way of pointing to the thing we want to understand. We do not mean to merely explain how certain behaviors are produced, though that is a fine and interesting task for science. We want to explain the subjective, seemingly private, and ineffable inner world that zombies are alleged to lack.

As another illustration, we can think about the super-scientist Mary in her black and white room (Ludlow, Nagasawa, and Stoljar 2004). Mary, as the familiar story goes, has never seen red even though she knows everything there is to know about the physical processes involved in producing color experiences. When Mary looks at a ripe strawberry for the first time, seeing its color with her own eyes, she learns what it is like for her to see red. It is this learned property that a theory of consciousness aims to explain. Alternatively, and perhaps more realistically, we could contrast a recording of my voice on a smartphone with your hearing me speak. In both cases there is sensitivity to the environment, complex processing—Siri can recognize its name!, and so on. Yet in my case I have an experience of the sound of the voice. There is something that it is like for me to have all that complex processing occur. In the phone's case, much like a philosophical zombie, one presumes 'all is dark inside.'

What is this thing that Mary learns when seeing red for the first time, that philosophical zombies are alleged to lack, that the iPhone does lack (currently at least), and that is usually present in my ordinary waking hours—seeing, hearing, feeling, thinking, willing, doubting, and so on? It is this that we aim to understand.

This is what a theory of consciousness needs to account for. To do so we must distinguish phenomenal consciousness from several other concepts of consciousness for which it is often confused.

1.1.2 Creature Consciousness

In another sense of the word 'consciousness,' we have what has been called Creature Consciousness (Rosenthal 2005). This picks out the property of a creature's being awake and responsive to stimuli. Usually these go together. When one is awake, one is usually alert and responsive to the world, at least to some degree. When one is alert and responsive to the world, one is usually phenomenally conscious. There is something that it is like for me to be drowsy, or hyper-vigilant. There is something that it is like for me to feel sluggish and slow to respond as opposed to mentally 'light on my feet.' In this sense creature consciousness is just phenomenal consciousness.

On more careful reflection, however, these various aspects come apart. To start with we can consider dreams. When one sleeps there are periods of times when one is not creature conscious, but where one is phenomenally conscious. One is not awake and is not responding to stimuli, but one is dreaming and so arguably enjoying phenomenal consciousness. There is something that it is like for one to dream, or at least it seems that way for many people. Philosophers like Norman Malcolm and Daniel Dennett have questioned whether we are right about that (Malcolm 1956; Dennett 1976). They insist that much, if not all, of what we report about dreams is embellished. What we report as the content of our dream reflects what I think it would be like to have the experiences we report, or a false preprepared memory. If I dream that I am chased by a monster, and this happens without there being anything that it is like for me to do so, then when I wake up it may be the case that my remembering this content creates the feeling that I would have been scared, and seen various colors and shapes, heard sounds, and so on. How do I know I had phenomenal consciousness in my sleep instead of this second more skeptical scenario? Even if you wake someone from sleep and immediately ask them to report any dream content, they may spontaneously start filling in 'what it is like' details that were not actually present while they slept.

This skeptical position is widely rejected (Windt 2019), but we do not need to resolve this issue here. I use it to illustrate one side of a possible dissociation. The question of whether a creature is phenomenally conscious is distinct from whether it is creature conscious in the sense above. We want to know whether there can be phenomenal consciousness in the absence of creature consciousness defined as being awake and responsive to stimuli. The answer appears to be 'yes,' but how can we scientifically settle this question?

Even in periods of dreamless sleep, the question of phenomenal consciousness arises. Is there nothing that it is like for me in a dreamless sleep? Many contemporary researchers take 'no' to be the obvious answer. On the other hand, some people have argued there is something that it is like for one to be in a dreamless sleep (Windt et al. 2016). Indeed, how can I wake up in the morning and announce that I slept well (or poorly), if not by having some kind of experience of my sleeping? Answering this question is very tricky, and it turns out that there has been a very long discussion in Eastern traditions about whether this kind of report is based on experience during dreamless sleep, or on an inference I make when I wake up (see Thompson 2014 for helpful discussion of this issue). In this respect the issue is somewhat like that of dreams. Is there something that it is like for me to be dreamlessly asleep? To have dreams? Or are these things that I mistakenly infer that I experienced when I wake up?

We can also see the possibility of the disassociation in the other direction. We can have a creature being awake and responsive to stimuli without being phenomenally conscious. To begin, we can consider the case of Roomba, the robotic vacuum cleaner. Once one purchases a Roomba and brings it home, it will learn the layout of your home. If Roomba gets stuck in a corner, it will attempt to free itself. If the Roomba bumps into a toy on the ground, it will back up and go around it. If the Roomba comes near a staircase, it will stop and reverse course. The fancier models even have the Roomba unit return to its charging base when it is low on power or needs maintenance. Roomba seems in some sense to be creature conscious. These units are responsive to the environment in a way like a robotic insect that collects dirt. When it returns to its base it eliminates waste by emptying its receptacle. While it is charging, it is non-responsive to the environment in a way that suggests that it is no longer creature conscious.

If you think that it is strange to call Roomba creature conscious, it is probably because you are associating phenomenal consciousness with creature consciousness. As I see things, it is quite likely that Roomba is to some degree creature conscious, but entirely phenomenally unconscious. There is almost certainly nothing that it is like to be Roomba as it navigates the room, detects that its battery is low, and returns to the charging station, and so on. If we separate phenomenal consciousness from creature consciousness, then there is no issue with thinking that Roomba, or even a philosophical zombie, has creature consciousness. I am also happy with those that insist that Roomba is not creature conscious. All I ask is that we agree that the important question is whether there is anything that it is like for Roombas as they operate.

Moving from the realm of the non-biological to the biological, we can consider the case of plant life. There is a very interesting debate about the status of so-called plant cognition (J. Lee 2023) currently taking place. It may seem strange to think of plants as creature conscious. Do they count as creatures? Regardless of one's feelings about that, we are learning that plants are surprisingly complex. They display circadian rhythms, respond to predators, and seemingly can learn by association. Plants therefore offer one possible case of a kind of creature consciousness in the absence of phenomenal consciousness. One reason for thinking so is that even though their abilities are interesting and complex, they all involve the sort of thing that many take to be unconscious in the case of animals. Others take the hypothesis that plants are indeed phenomenally conscious seriously (Segundo-Ortin and Calvo 2022). Do plants engage in cognition? Is there anything that it is like to be a plant engaged in plant cognition?

We can even see potential dissociations in the human case as well. In the so-called vegetative state (now called 'non-responsive wakefulness'), the brainstem activates but the cortex does not. As a result, patients display wakefulness without responsiveness and merely reflexive movements. In the minimally conscious state, patients exhibit sleep-wake cycles and have some limited responsiveness to stimuli (Giancino et al. 2002). It appears that creature consciousness can come in degrees. One can be awake without being alert or responsive to stimuli, and one can have those latter two properties to varying degrees. On the other hand, it is a matter of dispute whether phenomenal consciousness can come in degrees in this way (A. Lee 2023). Is there anything that it is like, from the vegetative subjects' point of view, when they are awake but non-responsive? Or is the sleep-waking cycle something that is just an automatic process that is not experienced by the person? Is this something that could admit of degrees? Does it really make sense to say that there is some degree or other of there being something that it is like for these patients?

The questions raised by the preceding paragraphs are difficult, and we are not in the position to attempt to answer them at this point. My only goal is to offer a characterization of the phenomenon that we are attempting to explain. In the case of creature consciousness, it seems that the central questions and issues surround phenomenal consciousness. We can in principle give an account of the sleep-waking cycle of mammals in terms of brain functioning without encountering too many difficult philosophical problems (Brown 2006, 2012c; Hobson 2021). The issues surrounding phenomenal consciousness remain though.

1.1.3 Awareness

Creature consciousness involves an organism being awake and responsive to the environment. We saw that these various aspects may come apart. One may have wakefulness seemingly without any kind of awareness of the environment. To be aware of something, at an intuitive level, is to be able to sense, perceive, or think about that thing. What exactly these folk-psychological categories turn out to be is a matter of a lot of contention, but we can put that aside. Awareness, as we are using it here, puts one in touch with the environment (where our own body counts as being a part of the environment in this sense). To be aware of the environment is to be in states that will be useful for engaging with that environment.[4]

As before we see possible dissociations among phenomenal consciousness, creature consciousness, and awareness. Consider the case of somnambulism, or sleepwalking as it is often called. In this case someone is asleep but is responding to the environment in a certain way. Someone who sleepwalks to the kitchen must in some sense be aware of the room they are in even though they are asleep. How else could they have made it all the way from their bed to the kitchen without trashing the house? In extreme cases somnambulists have driven cars![5] Is this a case of limited awareness without being awake and alert? It is tempting to interpret it that way. In whatever way one interprets this case, we would like to know what it is like for the sleepwalking subject. Is someone who is making a sandwich out of cigarettes and mayonnaise while engaged in a bout of sleepwalking phenomenally conscious while doing so?

There is another case that suggests a dissociation between awareness and phenomenal consciousness. The case of locked-in syndrome suggests that some who appear to be unconscious in the creature sense

---

[4] Some philosophers have used the term 'transitive consciousness' for this (Rosenthal 2005), but I find that terminology cumbersome, and so will continue to use 'awareness.' It is sometimes claimed that we should use 'transitive consciousness' because the word takes a complement, conscious *of* something. However, we do see complement free uses of 'aware,' in fact I used it as such in the main text!

[5] Some have argued that these extreme cases should be thought of as distinct from somnambulism due to the involvement of sleep medication (Pressman 2011).

may be aware. One classic demonstration of this was to ask subjects to imagine playing tennis as opposed to walking through a familiar place, such as their home (Owen et al. 2006). In healthy subjects this elicits typical neurological activity in different areas of the brain. As we would expect, these are the areas associated with motor commands (moving arms, legs, etc.), and ones associated with memories of familiar places (Perihippocampal Place Area [PPA], for example), respectively. Some subjects in coma, and thought to be non-responsive, showed brain activity similar to healthy controls when instructed to imagine playing tennis versus walking through a familiar place. This strongly suggests that these subjects heard, understood, and followed the instructions of the researcher. It is hard not to take this as evidence that these subjects were aware of these instructions despite lack of creature consciousness.

One cannot assume that demonstrating awareness in this way means that these subjects are 'awake' in the sense of being phenomenally conscious. It could be the case that this brain activity is completely non-conscious in the phenomenal sense. Perhaps there is nothing that it is like for the subject to have these processes carried out. Perhaps they are aware of the instructions, and can follow them, even without the lights being on. Could there be an awareness of the environment without phenomenal consciousness?

I think Roomba may be creature conscious, but with very little in the way of awareness of the environment. There is a more complex example that provides a more compelling case of awareness without phenomenal consciousness. What I have in mind is the case of the self-driving car. The self-driving car can recognize a stop sign, as shown by the fact that it stops there. The self-driving car puts on its blinker and turns right. Isn't this a case where we would say that the self-driving car is aware of the stop sign? That it is aware of the traffic as it accelerates while turning? It seems to me that this is the right way to think about it. The car has a sensitivity to the environment, and so counts as aware of the environment. The car can be activated and deactivated, during which time it is not responsive to stimuli (it will not stop at the stop sign if it is off and rolling down a hill). But the question of whether the self-driving car is phenomenally conscious seems easy to answer. It has an awareness of the stop sign, but it does not have a phenomenally conscious experience of the stop sign. There is nothing that it is like, from the car's point of view, to process the information about the stop sign.

Could the locked-in patients be in a similar situation? Could their responses be produced by a kind of awareness that is not phenomenally conscious? I am not suggesting that the answer is obvious. I am only using these examples as various ways to isolate phenomenal consciousness. It is at least conceptually distinct from these other notions of consciousness. Even if you disagree with this assessment of the self-driving car, or Roomba, or locked-in patients, the point here is that the philosophically and scientifically important issues revolve around phenomenal consciousness. Knowing that something is creature conscious or has awareness is one thing, a creature having phenomenal consciousness is another matter. I am hoping that the reader finds themself thinking at this point that it would be nice if we had a decent theory of phenomenal consciousness that would allow us to address these questions.

1.1.4 State Consciousness

There is another notion of consciousness that is often introduced, and that is the notion of 'state consciousness.'[6] State consciousness is meant to pick out the notion that some mental states can occur consciously at some time and unconsciously at another time. Once again, we must be cautious here, because there is a sense of 'state consciousness' where it just means phenomenal consciousness. In fact, in Nagel's original 1974 paper introducing the 'what it is like' terminology, he explicitly says that a conscious mental state is one which there is something that it is like for one to be in. A state is unconscious in this sense just when there is nothing that it is like for one to be in the state. If state consciousness is used this way, then there is no question about whether state consciousness and phenomenal consciousness can come apart.

---

[6] Sometimes this is called 'intransitive consciousness,' to contrast with 'transitive consciousness.' As before I will skip this terminology and stick with 'state.'

There is, though, another sense of 'state consciousness' where it is meant to pick out an awareness of a mental state of my own. So, maybe I have an unconscious belief, like say the belief that I was born in Los Angeles. It is natural to think that my belief is conscious now because I am aware of believing it, and that it was unconscious before because I was not aware of believing it. This belief of mine was not what we would call an occurring state of my mind. It is a dispositional state of mine. Many theorists think that, in additional to these kinds of unconscious states, there are currently occurring mental states of which we are not aware. The question of the relation of this kind of awareness to phenomenal consciousness has been hotly debated.

Take, for example, inattentional blindness. In this case subjects are presented with a scene and given a task. Originally it was to count the number of times a basketball is passed by the team in a certain color jersey. Meanwhile, something unusual happens—a gorilla-suited person strolls through the scene, complete with mid-stroll pause, and waves to the camera before strolling off the other side of the screen. The surprising thing is that subjects often don't notice (Chabris and Simons 2011). Given that the subjects are tracking the basketball as the players pass it back and forth while they all move about, one assumes that at some point the subject's eyes hit upon the gorilla-suited person. Since their attention was elsewhere, they were not aware of the mental state corresponding to the visual representation of the gorilla. Thus, we seem to have a state that the subject is not aware of being in.

As we will see in Chapter 4, a great deal of debate exists about the right way to interpret these kinds of results. For now, let us just assume that there is a visual state of which you are not aware, and so therefore, that state does not have the property of being state conscious. Is that state phenomenally conscious? Is there something that it is like for the subject to see the gorilla-suited person even when they don't know what it is like? Or is it that there is nothing that it is like for one to see the gorilla-suited person? The subjects say that they don't see it, after all. Once again, the crucial questions center on the notion of phenomenal consciousness. Even if one could establish that there were mental states of which one was not aware, we would still need to address the question of whether these states were, or could be, phenomenally conscious.

The paradigmatic case for unconscious mental processing comes from the study of a phenomenon known as Blindsight. This seemingly paradoxical phenomenon was discovered by Larry Weiskrantz (1997) in the 1980s and studied extensively since then. The seeming paradox is that we have someone with damage to their primary visual cortex, and who correspondingly says that they cannot see things in the relevant area of their visual field. At the same time, this person is also able to perform above chance on various discrimination tasks when forced to guess. For example, a famous case involving the human subject GY had him correctly saying whether something was an X or an O when forced to guess. This was even though he also said that he did not see anything when those stimuli were presented. This has been offered as a case of mental processing that is unconscious. This is convincingly a case of awareness of the environment without state consciousness. Is it also a case of visual states without phenomenal consciousness? Many typically assume that it is, but this has been questioned (Philips 2021b).

More generally, it is widely believed, and routinely asserted in introductory textbooks, that a great deal of mental processing occurs unconsciously. However, though this belief is wide-spread and has some support (Berger and Mylopoulos 2019), it is also controversial (Peters and Lau 2015; Peters et al. 2017; Philips 2021a). I will largely ignore this issue, though it will come up again in Chapter 5 when I explain my reasons for rejecting the traditional Transitivity Principle. I bring it up here to illustrate once again how the central questions revolve around phenomenal consciousness.

There is a theme that is developing here. There are some questions that cannot be answered scientifically without first having a theory of phenomenal consciousness. We need a well-confirmed theory of consciousness that will allow us to interpret these findings and disassociations.

1.1.5 Self and Introspective Consciousness

Self-consciousness itself has a long and distinguished history of discussion (see Smith 2020 for a recent overview). Self-consciousness involves a kind of awareness of oneself as being oneself. The role that self-consciousness plays in phenomenal consciousness is much debated. Here the proposed dissociation often goes the other direction. Aren't there phenomenally consciousness states without any form of self-consciousness? Does every kind of phenomenally conscious state involve some form of self-consciousness? We will come back to this issue in detail in Chapters 3 and 5. Some theories of consciousness deny that phenomenal and self-consciousness are related in any significant way. Other theories rely on there being a crucial connection between the two. We need a way to arbitrate between them.

Just as self-consciousness is a kind of awareness, it is natural to think of introspective consciousness as being a kind of awareness as well. Introspection, generally, involves the ability one has of coming to know about one's own mind. *Introspective consciousness*, as I use the term, is a kind of phenomenal consciousness. It is what it is like for you to be consciously aware of your own mind. When we are introspectively conscious, we can examine or probe our experience, and make judgments about what it is that we are experiencing (Renero and Brown 2022). Experiencing red, by gazing at a ripe strawberry for example, is one thing. Introspecting my experience of the strawberry, thereby becoming aware of my experiencing red and, on that basis, forming the conscious judgment that I am experiencing red, seems distinct from that.

It is natural to think that when I engage in introspection, I have a special kind of awareness of my own experience. In so having that kind of awareness I come to know in a direct way what the experience is like for me. I do not thereby introduce any new properties of my experience. When I am experiencing the redness of the ripe strawberry, which appears to be a property of the strawberry itself, not my experience of the strawberry, I represent the environment as being a certain way. When I then focus my attention on the experience of the strawberry, as opposed to focusing on the strawberry, I can become aware of what it is like for me to represent the environment as being a certain way. I do not thereby introduce any new phenomenal property of 'introspective redness.' I just get a good clear grip on what is already there.

Putting things in this way is a bit tendentious due to claims about the transparency of experience (Harman 1990). I will argue later that we do at least sometimes come to be aware of our own experiences in this way (Chapter 3). Even if we don't, one could have a 'displaced perception' account of introspection. On these kinds of accounts, one does not become aware of one's experience when one introspects. One instead is aware of the world, and then infers what one's experience is from that. On this kind of view, I look at the strawberry, and then when I try to introspect my experience, I end up focusing on the strawberry itself. I attend more carefully to the redness of *the strawberry*, and then I infer that I must be in a state that represents this property of the strawberry, and so on. By this indirect method I arrive at the introspective judgment 'I am seeing red.' There is no reason why this account of introspection can't be joined with a higher-order theory of phenomenal consciousness, though this is not my preferred way to think about it.

These issues are complicated, and we will return to them later in the book (in Chapter 3 section 3.7). There are those in the higher-order camp that do in fact appeal to this kind of indirect introspective method. Amusingly, the issue here is the same as we have encountered all along. Is there a kind of phenomenal consciousness involved in introspection? Some say yes, one has the phenomenal character of deliberate and attentive focus on one's current experience. Others say no, we infer from the world that we must in certain mental states, but they cannot become introspectively conscious in the way just discussed.

We have thus reduced our central concepts of consciousness to three: creature consciousness, awareness (of the world, of our mental states, of ourselves), and phenomenal consciousness. In each case what we saw was that we need to understand how phenomenal consciousness is related to the other two.

1.1.6 Access Consciousness

Access consciousness is typically defined as a state's being "poised for control of action or rational deliberation" (Block 1995). This notion as introduced by Ned Block was originally meant to explicitly contrast with phenomenal consciousness. Block's original idea was that it was at least conceptually possible that one could have access consciousness without phenomenal consciousness, a hypothetical condition he dubbed 'super blindsight,' and phenomenal consciousness without any kind of access consciousness, an extreme version of what has come to be called 'phenomenological overflow.'

We can see that the various kinds of consciousness discussed above, besides that of phenomenal consciousness, can all be thought of as a kind of access consciousness. To be creature conscious is to be awake and responsive to stimuli, and that requires having states that are poised for the control of action or deliberation. To be aware of the environment requires that one have these poised states as well. State consciousness also counts as a form of access consciousness. The states we count as being aware of typically are typically those states which are poised for control of action and so on. To introspect or have self-consciousness involves another kind of access to one's mental life. The question that has kept coming up in our discussion is this: what is the relationship among the various kinds of access consciousness—creature consciousness, state consciousness, awareness, introspection, and phenomenal consciousness?

Is it really possible, as Block suggested, that there is a double dissociation between access and phenomenal consciousness? Some of the cases we have gone through in the discussion might seem to suggest so. However, we cannot answer these questions without having a well-tested and confirmed theory of each of these concepts of consciousness. Primary among them, though, is phenomenal consciousness. That is the center around which all the other problems revolve.

To summarize our discussion, these are some of the questions that a theory of consciousness needs to address and that the science of consciousness needs to arbitrate.

1. Can there be creature consciousness in the absence of phenomenal consciousness?
    - Can there be phenomenal consciousness without creature consciousness?
2. Can there be awareness without phenomenal consciousness?
    - Can there be phenomenal consciousness without awareness?
3. Can there be state consciousness without phenomenal consciousness?

- Can there be phenomenal consciousness without state consciousness?
4. Can there be phenomenal consciousness without self-consciousness?
5. Can there be phenomenal consciousness without introspective consciousness?
   - Can there be introspection without phenomenal consciousness?

Many people have thought that this presents science with an almost insurmountable hurdle. Can there even be an empirical science of phenomenal consciousness?

1.2 99 Problems, but Is Consciousness One?

Perhaps the most well-known problem in the study of consciousness, the Hard Problem, is that of explaining why the neural activity correlated with any phenomenally conscious state is the neural correlate of that state, as opposed to some other state, or no phenomenally conscious state at all (Chalmers 1996). Neurons tend to fire action potentials that are nearly identical in electrical and chemical properties. What distinguishes the neural firing related to experiencing seeing red as opposed to that regulating my breathing rate? One is part of what it is like to be me. The other is invisible and does not show up in my stream of consciousness at all. Neuroscience reveals that they are mainly distinguished by neurotransmitters that control the electrical activity of the neurons, and their timing and relation to other neural firing. How could that account for phenomenal consciousness? It can start to seem a bit arbitrary in that there seems to be no good reason why any given experience should feel like it does because of its neural realization. Why isn't the activity regulating my breathing experienced? What is the difference that makes all the difference?

The Hard Problem is contrasted with the so-called easy problems, which involve analyzing some function and finding a mechanism that performs that function. So, if memory is just the encoding, storage, and retrieval of information (to take semantic memory as an example), then we need to find the neural mechanisms that preform those functions. This problem is 'easy' in the sense that we generally understand how it is that we are supposed to answer the challenge, and what tools we will need to do it. Memory so defined is a functional notion. So, if we find that long-term potentiation in the brain, which involves changes at the synaptic level, is the mechanism via which information is stored in the brain, then we have offered an account of memory, at least the storage part. We then will have to give an account of encoding, retrieval, and so on, but we see how that could be done, at least in principle.

The Hard Problem is different, so the story goes, because consciousness itself is not obviously associated with any physical structure or psychological/biological function. It seems at least conceptually possible that any experience be associated with any neural state, or with none. It seems to many that one could have a physical duplicate—the philosophical zombie discussed previously—that had all the same physical states that you did but lacked consciousness altogether. According to the philpapers survey (Bourget and Chalmers 2021), 60 percent of surveyed philosophers say zombies are conceivable and/or possible (only 24% say they are possible *and* conceivable). If so, then phenomenal consciousness is itself arguably not a physical state, since the zombie had all of those.

This has led some theorists to be quite squeamish about phenomenal consciousness. There are those who argue that phenomenal consciousness must be non-physical (Graziano et al. 2020). Others argue that phenomenal consciousness is somehow mysterious and should be avoided (Mandik 2016). Still others have argued that phenomenal consciousness is merely an illusion (Frankish 2016). The surprising thing here is that those cited in this paragraph think they are defending physicalism!

The HOROR theory, as I see it, is in principle neutral on the metaphysics of consciousness. There are both dualist and illusionist readings of the theory I will develop. My reading of the theory is largely as a mind-brain identity theory or functionalist account of phenomenal consciousness. In a way this is a side issue from my main project. The important point for my purposes is that these metaphysical positions are not forced on one by being friendly to phenomenal consciousness. As I see the theory, it is an account of the nature of phenomenal consciousness—whatever its ultimate metaphysical nature is. The reason for this is that I do not find any of the pessimistic takes from the previous paragraph even remotely convincing (Brown and LeDoux 2020). I am in general friendly to physicalism, but if physicalism is true, then it had better be able to give an account of real genuine phenomenal consciousness. It seems to me that many physicalists give up the game too early and admit defeat prematurely.

1.2.1 Consciousness Might have been Physical All Along

One way to emphasize this is by pointing out that the arguments against physicalism depend mostly on a priori theorizing and conceptual analysis (Kripke 1980; Chalmers 2009; Renero forthcoming). This usually involves fanciful thought experiments populated with strange creatures like philosophical zombies, and Mary the super scientist raised in a black-and-white room we discussed above. And more to boot! All these arguments have something in common. They start with some intuitive judgment about consciousness, and the way in which we are epistemically related to it and infer a metaphysical conclusion (Chalmers 2009). Less appreciated is that the physicalist can (and has) done this as well. For every a priori argument against physicalism, there is one against dualism just like it (Brown 2010). In what follows I will focus just on the case of philosophical zombies, but I think that the argument generalizes to all a priori arguments against physicalism.

I have called creatures that are purely physical and phenomenally conscious 'shombies' as a playful take on the zombies offered by the dualist. It seems only an accident of history that made it the case that the conceivability arguments against physicalism were explored before those against non-physicalism. For those interested in the gory details I have gone through them in detail in the Appendix. Consciousness being physical is no more absurd than idealism, panpsychism, quantum dualism, or any of the other philosophical accounts of the metaphysical nature of phenomenal consciousness. We have some sense of what it would mean for consciousness to be physical. There is nothing absurd or contradictory in that idea unless one mistakes one's epistemic access to phenomenal consciousness with the thing itself.

At the very least, we can see that it is a mistake to give up on phenomenal consciousness if one is a physicalist. Acknowledging the reality of phenomenal consciousness does not imply that we accept something inherently spooky or non-physical. It is simply the acknowledgment that there is something that it is like to be me, something that it is like for me. Phenomenal consciousness is conceivably physical, and that is enough for us to look for an empirically adequate account of what its nature might be.

1.2.2 Illusionism

We do not quite know how phenomenal consciousness could be physical. Some might think it is quite a bit worse than that! Yet, if consciousness is physical, this is because it is fundamentally related to, or identical with, either some functional property, or some physical structural property. To put my cards fully on the table I split my credence between these kinds of views. On some days I find myself thinking that phenomenal consciousness must be identical to some biological property of the brain (Block 2023). Other days I find myself thinking it might be identical to some functional property that the brain happens to instantiate. It is hard to see what else would count as a physical property, but only time will tell.

Some will be unhappy with this and see it as a kind of cheating. From one side there will be accusations of not really talking about consciousness. How could it be identical to some physical structural or functional property of the brain? You haven't, they might continue, even provided a response to the arguments against physicalism. Once we consider the physicalist parody-arguments the originals are called into question (Brown 2010). The shombie argument shows that it is possible that consciousness is physical. So, it might be a biologically instantiated higher-order representation. Of course, it might not, but once the shombie argument is on the table we need independent reasons to reject physicalism.

There will also be complaints from the other side. There has been a vocal minority in philosophy who have endorsed Illusionism about phenomenal consciousness (Frankish 2016; Kammerer 2022). Making sense of what exactly the illusionist is trying to persuade us of is somewhat difficult, but they seem to deny that phenomenal consciousness exists at all. Whatever their claim ultimately is, I think this is a mistake. The illusionist appears to be someone who says something like the following, "Whatever you're talking about, this 'what it's like' business, these 'phenomenal properties' we already know that those things can't be physical. But we want to be physicalists! We love science! So we must be under the misapprehension that those things are real or exist when they don't." If I hadn't met these philosophers and talked with them, I would have thought that they are being disingenuous. How can one deny one of the most obvious and basic facts about reality? Even if this is not an accurate portrayal of their views, the appearance of this view is bad! I think instead they are making a rhetorical mistake.

What the illusionist really wants to deny is that phenomenal consciousness must be non-physical. If you use the words 'phenomenal consciousness' to mean 'the non-physical aspect of our experience,' then I could see why you would want to deny that there is any such thing. I am highly skeptical that there is any non-physical component to reality! However, this is to tilt at windmills. This is not how the term is used by most philosophers writing about consciousness. Phenomenal consciousness is simply what it is like to be. The nature of that kind of property is not given just by how it appears to us. It is the job of science to tell us what its physical nature is—not to convince us that it isn't there!

What this shows is that the shombie argument works against illusionism just as well as it does against non-physicalism. Once one sees that phenomenal consciousness is possibly physical, one has no reason to deny that it exists in the physical reality we live in.

If you're a physicalist, you shouldn't start by admitting that the challenge is too hard! I think that phenomenal properties can be physical. When I say that, I mean that genuine actual honest-to-goodness Real Deal phenomenal consciousness could have been physical all along! This whole time, even Plato and Aristotle were phenomenally conscious in this way. It was probably just a physical property then as well. Complete with honest-to-goodness subjectivity and the whole nine yards at no extra cost. I think that this is possible for the same reasons that the dualists think phenomenal consciousness can't be physical. It just seems unintelligible (and so inconceivable) to me how one could have the same physical creature, with exactly the same physical states, and exactly the same physical laws, and yet fail to have a phenomenally conscious being. It sounds like saying there is a world where there is H_2O and our physical laws but no water. It seems like you can conceive of that, as when you imagine a certain view to be false. However, if that view is actually true, then you must have been mistaken in some sense.

It turns out that before endorsing illusionism about phenomenal consciousness Keith Frankish (Frankish 2007) also made an argument like the shombie argument. Whereas I have called these creatures 'shombies' Frankish has called them 'anti-zombies,' saying, "we can define anti-zombies as beings which are bare physical duplicates of us, inhabiting a universe which is a bare physical duplicate of ours, but nonetheless having exactly the same conscious experiences as we do." To me there's a bit of problem with the way Frankish introduces anti-zombies. The phrase "having exactly the same conscious experiences as we do" is ambiguous. When I read it, I think that the anti-zombie will have phenomenal consciousness in the way that we have been discussing it. They will have phenomenal properties and subjective character, and so on. There will be a point of view from which certain things are phenomenologically manifest. Indeed this seems to be the way that Frankish intended the argument to be understood in his original paper. If this is the way you interpret that phrase, then what I have called shombies just are anti-zombies. But if that's the case, then why have two names for the same thing? Shouldn't I be using 'anti-zombie' as well?

The problem is, as mentioned already, Frankish is known to defend illusionism (Frankish 2016). In doing so he denies that phenomenal consciousness is real. It merely *seems* to be real, argues Frankish, because we suffer from an 'introspective illusion' according to his view. Therefore, when he says that anti-zombies have 'exactly the same conscious experience as we do,' I worry that he thinks they have this illusionist experience. At the very least, an opponent will think that. Conceiving of creatures for which illusionism about phenomenal consciousness is true is most decidedly not to conceive of creatures with "exactly the same conscious experience" as ours according to me! Let us call a possible world where illusionism about phenomenal consciousness is true 'Deluded Earth.' The creatures who inhabit Deluded

Earth are physically and functionally just like us, but do not have phenomenal consciousness. They merely mistakenly believe that they have phenomenal consciousness. They mistakenly believe that there is something that it is like to be them. Deluded Earth is a zombie world. Our world is decidedly not a zombie world. So, a world where illusionism is true is not a world like ours.

As I see things Frankish's anti-zombies are just re-described zombies plus some rhetoric trying to get us to be ok with being zombies. I am not ok with being a zombie! This is why I keep the term 'shombie.' Shombies have actual phenomenal consciousness, the thing that some people think is so very hard to see how it could be physical. My shombie twin is phenomenally conscious in the way that the panpsychist thinks they are conscious, just while being wholly and exhaustively physical.

Either way, and whichever term you prefer, the point is that unless you can show that there is some kind of contradiction in the conceivability of phenomenal consciousness being physical (i.e., in the conceivability of shombies as having genuine phenomenal consciousness), I think we shouldn't be illusionists. That's what it would take for me to be an illusionist. You'd have to show that there's literally a contradiction in the claim that phenomenal consciousness is physical. As far as I can tell here is no such contradiction.

It is important to note that one cannot appeal to zombies, or related thought experiments, to rule out shombies. The (ideal negative) conceivability of zombies is exactly what is at issue, and what shombies are meant to challenge. It would be question begging to simply re-assert the conceivability arguments against physicalism. Both non-physicalists and illusionists takes these *prima facie* epistemological considerations about consciousness too seriously. So, I reject illusionism.[7]

---

[7] To be wholly honest I would probably try out being a non-physicalist before endorsing illusionism and am most partial to a form of quantum dualism (Okan and Sebastián 2020; Chalmers and McQueen 2022). As I said in the Introduction something very strange may have to be true about consciousness. In fact, I think that one could be a non-physicalist and still endorse much of what is argued for in this book as being about the neural and psychological correlates of phenomenal consciousness. It should also be noted that one could be an illusionist and take much of what is argued for in the book as being an account of the origin of the illusion.

Until such time as some non-zombie related contradiction in physicalism is derived, I will take physicalism to be the default position. I will also take the various theories of consciousness on offer as empirical conjectures about the scientific nature of phenomenal consciousness. The Hard Problem looms in the background, but it should be deprioritized so that we can focus on short-term achievable goals (Brown 2010).

1.3 Hard, Harder, Hard Enough: Problems Proliferate

We do not need to solve the Hard Problem to take the science of phenomenal consciousness seriously. What then do we need to do? Here authors have proposed several alternatives.

For example, Ned Block (2002) proposed the 'harder problem' of consciousness. This is a long and intricate problem with a lot of twists and turns. The basic idea is that we have reason to think that all conscious creatures must share a scientific nature. That is, they will likely share some physical—possibly neural—property. On the other hand, when we consider creatures that are very different from us in terms of their inner make-up, we have no reason to withhold consciousness from them. For example, Commander Data, from *Star Trek*, is a mere functional isomorph of humans. There are no neurons in Commander Data's head, and instead there is some non-biological machinery that does roughly the same job. Even so, we have no reason to deny phenomenal consciousness to commander Data. So, we seem to be in a position where we have reason to believe something (physicalism) but also reason to reject it (Commander Data–type cases of multiple constitution of the mental). Block does mention that a version of this problem arises for other biological creatures that are very different from us, like an octopus, but he does not draw out the implications for the science of consciousness in his original 2002 paper.

Scott Aaronson does offer a problem of this sort for us which he calls the 'Pretty Hard' problem (Aaronson 2014; see also Long 2021). Aaronson takes Block's Harder problem and explicitly draws out the implication for the science of consciousness. For Aaronson the Pretty

Hard problem involves giving a theory of consciousness that allows us to see which systems in nature are conscious. When thinking about the range of possible systems that may potentially have a mental life—from sea slugs, to bees, to cephalopods, to A.I. systems—we want a theory that tells us which of these systems are phenomenally conscious. Aaronson suggests that the Pretty Hard problem can be used to judge competing theories of consciousness.

In a related vein Hakwan Lau has proposed the 'Hard Enough' problem. This involves taking any given theory of consciousness and building a simple mechanism that implements that theory. We can then ask if the system is plausibly conscious (Lau 2022, 168). Lau suggests that this problem is 'hard enough,' not because it is 'pretty hard,' but rather because he thinks it is a hard enough problem to let us judge competing theories of consciousness.

Both the pretty hard and hard enough problems are on the right track in their focus on arbitrating between currently competing theories of consciousness. However, our intuitive judgments may mislead us or bias us in various ways. For example, Aaronson has suggested that integrated information theory can be ruled out by noting that it predicts that inactive logic gates will be more conscious than you or I. This is because the theory predicts they will have a great deal of integrated information. Lau agrees and finds this very implausible, or at least less plausible than its competitors, and therefore rejects IIT as a plausible account of consciousness. While I don't want to defend IIT, I think that empirical predictions in living systems are a better arbitrator than these kinds of intuitive arguments. I think that every theory of consciousness currently on offer makes some startling predictions about which systems will (or won't) be phenomenally conscious. In most of these cases the best strategy is to test theories of consciousness on humans, and then once there is a clear contender for an account of human consciousness, we can ask how widely it applies.

David Chalmers has made another contribution to our list of problems with his recent (2018) meta-problem of consciousness. This is, roughly, the problem of why it is that we find consciousness problematic. There is an empirical question about the mechanisms that allow us to form introspective judgments and make reports like 'it is hard to see how consciousness could be physical.' This empirical question will be among the so-called easy questions, which everyone agrees admit of a straightforward physical/functional explanation.

Chalmers argues that we can use the meta-problem to judge theories of consciousness by providing, "what we might call the meta-problem challenge for theories of consciousness. If a theory says that mechanism M is the basis of consciousness, then it needs to explain how mechanism M plays a central role in bringing about judgments about consciousness" (op. cit. 36). The meta-problem challenge, like the previous Pretty Hard and Hard Enough problems, focuses on theories of consciousness. Unlike those previous problems, the meta-problem challenge is a call for an explanation. I think this is an important issue and one we will come back to and discuss later in the book (in Chapter 3). For now, it is enough to say that this challenge gives us a *prima facie* reason for wondering if a theory may be on the right track, but by itself cannot refute a theory of consciousness.

According to the 'Real Problem' of Anil Seth, "the primary goals of consciousness science are to explain, predict, and control the phenomenological properties of conscious experience" (Seth 2021, 25–26). This is the approach that I agree with the most. In the first place, Seth does not back down from the phenomenological aspects of consciousness, as indicated in the definition of the Real Problem. Second, it focuses on the scientific issues of prediction, explanation, and control. If one could give a theory of consciousness that predicted what kind of phenomenally conscious states one would be in, allowed one to control those phenomenal states by holding them constant or shifting between various states by manipulating the brain, and allowed an explanation in terms of the brain's functioning of how those states were implemented, then that would go a long way towards establishing that theory as a Standard Model of Human Consciousness.

Each one of these problems, aside from the classic Hard Problem, offers a goal for the science of consciousness. We do need a theory of consciousness that tells us which systems are conscious, theories that have wildly implausible implications about which systems are conscious should recognize that this is a strike against them. Understanding how to predict, control, and ultimately explain phenomenal consciousness is important. Perhaps the meta-problem can be used to shed light on which theories of consciousness we can take seriously.

What all these problems have in common is the desire to find a plausible theory of consciousness and its implementation in the human brain. Each one of the various problems we canvassed was aimed at testing or providing benchmarks for theories of consciousness. I agree that this is what is needed. However, none of the various problems suggested what I take to be the standard way to test theories, which is empirical prediction and possible falsification. We have already met the five Big Ideas of the contemporary moment in time. These are Global Neuronal Workspace, local recurrency, Integrated Information, attention and/or models of attention, and versions of higher-order theory. None of these approaches to understanding consciousness may be right, or each of them may be onto a small part of the picture. Either way, we need to be able to say what the predictions of each theory are and test them against one another in specific cases. It is only then that we will make any progress on any of these other problems.

1.3.1 The Central Challenge of Consciousness Science

Thus, the central challenge of a science of consciousness, as I understand it, is to give an account of phenomenal consciousness, and its relation to the brain, that would allow us to see which, if any, of the *currently available* theories of human consciousness are on the right track. Being on the right track here means several things. First, it means being able to answer the kinds of questions that we listed at the end of the first section of this chapter (1.1.6). Second, we want to meet the Real Problem in humans, which is to say allowing us to explain, predict, and control the phenomenological properties of human beings. If some version, or combination of various ideas from different versions, of our Big Ideas allowed us to do that, then it would naturally explain why we make the judgments about consciousness we do (the metaproblem). It would also allow us to see which other systems in nature had conscious experience like humans (the Pretty Hard problem), as well as which artificial/non-biological systems implementing our Big Ideas might be conscious (the hard enough problem).

We have some major theories, and we have some understanding of what the philosophical issues are. What we need now are detailed accounts of the major theories that allow us to form empirically testable predictions. We then need to look at the competing accounts of consciousness and test them against one another in differentiating situations. To be clear, I am not suggesting that any experiment will decisively decide among theories of consciousness. The hope is that certain views will be forced to make so many emendations, patches, and ad hoc extensions, that overall, the view will seem unworkable. Other theories will handle the data more elegantly, will allow us to ask better questions, and will naturally occupy more of our attention.

Higher-order theories, having originated in philosophy rather than cognitive neuroscience, have yet to be fully developed in this way. My hope is to contribute to this goal by clarifying the conceptual landscape around higher-order theories of phenomenal consciousness.

2
The Higher-Order Representation of a Representation (HOROR) Theory of Phenomenal Consciousness

In the next three chapters I will develop the Higher-Order Representation of a Representation, or HOROR, theory of phenomenal consciousness (Brown 2015). In this chapter, I discuss issues about higher-order representationalism and HOROR at a very general level. In Chapter 3, I focus on the content that I take the HORORs to have in more detail. In Chapter 4, I evaluate the HOROR theory from an empirical standpoint. My primary goal is not to defend the theory from rivals or argue for its superiority. My interests lie in clarifying what the theory holds, as well as the ways in which it might be challenged empirically.

In section 2.1, I argue that the difference between first-order and higher-order theories is in the explanatory role of inner awareness. In section 2.1.1, I distinguish higher-order theories from first-order theories that also invoke inner awareness. In section 2.1.2, I discuss what it means to be mental. In section 2.2, I discuss what it means for a theory of consciousness to be a higher-order form of representationalism. In section 2.2.1, I connect inner awareness to higher-order representationalism and its relation to access consciousness. In section 2.3, I finally begin to lay out the basics of the HOROR theory. In section 2.3.1, I argue that we should separate state-consciousness from phenomenal consciousness. In section 2.3.2, I give my HORORibly simple argument for the HOROR theory. In section 2.4, I introduce the kinds of content I view the HORORs having at a general level. I begin by introducing my distinction between phenomenally silent and active content in section 2.4.1, and then briefly discuss intentionality in section 2.4.2, before finally, in section 2.4.3, discussing mental pointers.

Consciousness as Representing One's Mind. Richard Brown, Oxford University Press.
© Oxford University Press 2025. DOI: 10.1093/oso/9780197784006.003.0003

2.1 Higher-Order Theories of Phenomenal Consciousness

Higher-order theories of consciousness are usually associated with the idea that a conscious state is one of which I am conscious. This pithy statement has come to be known as the Transitivity Principle and encapsulates what many think of as the core commitment of higher-order theories. We will discuss these matters in detail in Chapters 5, 6, and 7. For now, I will note that commitment to the Transitivity Principle is entirely optional. At best, it helps us to delineate a particular class of higher-order theories. It cannot give us a general criterion for when a theory is a higher-order theory.

The key idea behind the higher-order approach is that, as Locke put it, "consciousness is the perception of what passes in [one's own] mind." The folk-psychological platitude here suggests that phenomenal consciousness may be a kind of *inner awareness*. There is no suggestion that a conscious state is one of which you are aware. There is certainly nothing like that explicitly in David Armstrong's (1968) work. The Transitivity Principle is a theoretical interpretation of what it means to have inner awareness that doesn't show up until the work of David Rosenthal (1980). If you're a higher-order theorist, then what that means is that you think that a form of inner awareness plays a crucial, fundamental role in accounting for phenomenal consciousness. First-order theories are simply theories that deny this. To be a higher-order theory is to appeal to an awareness of one's own mental life as a crucial part of the explanation of phenomenal consciousness. What it is like for the subject to have ordinary conscious experience is explained, at least in part, by inner awareness.

Inner awareness, in the sense that I am using it, is one kind of access that we have to our own mind. Access consciousness, as defined in Chapter 1, involved a state's being widely available for use in reasoning and control of behavior. This notion closely corresponds to the notion of the global workspace, where states can be made available to a wide variety of consumer systems. Global broadcast all by itself most likely doesn't suffice for inner awareness. If so, then inner awareness, as I see it, will not count as the traditional kind of access consciousness. However, as discussed in section 1.1.6, a state's being globally broadcast is just one way of accessing our mental lives. We will discuss this in more detail in the next chapter, where I will argue that inner awareness may help to route first-order states into the global workspace.

2.1.1. First-Order Theories and Inner Awareness

We must exercise caution here. First-order theorists may also invoke inner awareness as importantly connected to phenomenal consciousness. To do so they must also deny that this inner awareness plays any role in explaining the nature of consciousness. There are two ways of doing this. One is to deny that inner awareness is psychologically substantial. The other is to argue that inner awareness, whatever it is, has no role to play in explaining phenomenal consciousness. An example of the first strategy is exemplified by Ned Block (2011a), and the second by Nicolas Silins (Silins forthcoming). Let us look at each.

In response to Rosenthal (2011a) and Weisberg (2011) in their exchange in *Analysis*, Block says,

> Weisberg ascribes to me the view that "pains matter even if the subject is in no way aware of them." I strongly deny this view 2007a:484–85, noting that "to say that one is necessarily aware of one's phenomenally conscious states should not be taken to imply that every phenomenally conscious state is one that the subject notices or attends to or perceives or thinks about." I deny the Rosenthal–Weisberg theory of awareness, not awareness itself. (2011, 446)

This exchange occurred in 2011, and Block is citing himself from five years earlier saying that he accepts a kind of inner awareness as a crucial part of phenomenal consciousness. There is a lot to analyze in this passage, and we will return to these issues in Chapter 5. For our purposes here, we can take Block to be challenging the idea that inner awareness must be interpreted as a substantial psychological phenomenon. If so, then he can grant that every state is one we are conscious of without giving up on the first-order theory.

Block (2007) has suggested two possible ways this might be done. The first is self-representationalism. We will discuss self-representationalism in Chapters 6 and 7, so I will leave much of the discussion for there. For now, I will just note that it is unclear how self-representationalism can be formulated in a way that doesn't involve some form of "noticing, attending, perceiving, or thinking" about the state in question.

Block's second possibility is a deflationary account. This deflationary approach is inspired by Sosa's (2003) quip that "just as I smile my own smiles so too, I experience my own experiences." The thought is that perhaps just having a first-order phenomenally conscious state, all by itself, gives you a kind of inner awareness for free. That would be nice. This is akin to a kind of deflationary acquaintance view. So, just as whenever one is smiling one is also smiling one's smile by default, so too one may, just in having a phenomenally red experience, come to be aware of that phenomenal quality by default. The phenomenal red is itself an awareness of something in the environment. Just by having that awareness, so the hope goes, one also automatically comes to be aware of one's awareness. Just in a deflationary, non-substantial way.

It is not at all clear how this notion of deflationary awareness can distinguish the phenomenally conscious states from the rest of my psychological states. Take any old psychological state of mine. Isn't it the case that I will be aware of it in this deflationary way (Brown 2012a)? If so, then all my states will have this kind of deflationary self-awareness and so a "meishness." I am after all walking my own walks no matter whether marching, dancing, running, crawling, sleepwalking, and so on. Shouldn't the same hold in the mental case? But it is highly counterintuitive that every psychological state is phenomenally conscious!

As of now Block has offered us more of a wish list than an alternative account of inner awareness. At the very least, I think that this argument motivates exploring the prospects for a non-deflated notion of inner awareness. It would be nice if there were some kind of inner awareness that was understandably physical, and that wasn't a higher-order intentional/conceptual representation. We will examine the prospects for these kinds of views in Chapter 7. For those that are impatient, I hope you don't mind if I tell you now that I don't think that they work.

Nicolas Silins has recently argued that an inflated version of inner awareness is compatible with first-order theories. He has called this the Ascending Road (Silins forthcoming). The idea is that the nature of phenomenal consciousness will explain our inner awareness of it, not the other way around. As he puts it, "(**The Ascending Road**): For any conscious mental state M and subject S, if S is in M, then S is aware of M because M is conscious" (5). This makes clear that it is not just the invocation of inner awareness that makes a theory a higher-order theory. It is the role that inner awareness is posited to play that makes the crucial difference.

Silins argues that the ascending road makes better sense out of the alleged correlation between conscious states and inner awareness. Silins has a response to the kind of argument I presented against Block's deflationary account above. Not every state of my mind will meet the criteria set by the ascending road. As he says, "The key defining feature of a conscious mental state here is not quite the feature of our being aware of the state. The key feature of a conscious mental state here is instead the feature of being such that, if you are in the mental state, then you are aware of it because you are in it" (Silins forthcoming, 17). The idea is that you are aware of the conscious state *because* you are in the conscious state. The conscious states, on this view, are the ones that you are aware of because of their being phenomenally conscious (which they have for some other reason unrelated to inner awareness). This is compatible with the inner awareness occurring because of some other factor.

What kind of inner awareness can fulfil this task? Silins is open to a variety of options, but until such time as those options are filled in, we have a placeholder for a view. A lot depends on the details of any worked-out version of the ascending road. We will discuss a possible example of the ascending road in Chapter 7 when we discuss David Chalmers' view.

For now, we have a clearer grasp on what it means for a theory to be a higher-order theory of consciousness. In addition, we have a clearer grasp on how we can differentiate higher-order theories from first-order theories, even ones that invoke the necessity of a kind of inner awareness. Silins' account of what distinguishes phenomenally conscious states from ones that are not phenomenally conscious entails that inner awareness can occur without it accounting for the first-order state being phenomenally conscious. This opens the view to being empirically distinguished from higher-order views. We would first need a worked-out account of the kind of inner awareness in question. Especially important would be an account of what would happen if the inner awareness showed up without the first-order state. We don't have that yet. The ascending road is still under construction.

Higher-order theories of phenomenal consciousness are not merely claiming that inner awareness is correlated with phenomenal consciousness. Their claim is that phenomenal consciousness is at least partly explained by inner awareness of one's mental life. What, then, is it that passes through one's own mind?

2.1.2 Marking the Mental

A first pass at identifying the mental is noting that mental states/processes are the states of which we become aware through inner awareness. This reveals two kinds of properties that typically populate our stream of consciousness. These are intentional/conceptual and phenomenal properties (Rosenthal 2005, 25).

An intentional mental state is about something. Examples of intentional properties populating my mind include the standard thinking, willing, and doubting that we often hear about, but there are many more things than that. These include *wondering about the weather, realizing I am late for a zoom meeting, inferring the conclusion of a line of reasoning, intending to complete a task, remembering an epic summer trip, being anxious about a social event*, and many, many more. I follow the typical way of modeling these kinds of mental states as consisting of a mental attitude held toward some propositional content. I will discuss this in section 2.4, but I view these propositions toward which we hold attitudes to be mental representations. When I wonder about the weather, I am in a mental state of *wanting to know* information about the conditions outside. 'Wanting to know' is the mental attitude, and 'what are the current conditions like outside' is the content toward which I hold that attitude. I can hold various mental attitudes toward the same content and have various contents toward which I have the same mental attitude.

We have previously discussed phenomenal properties. These involve the phenomenologically manifest properties of our sensory and perceptual contact with the world. Here we find the phenomenal and qualitative character that we have discussed in Chapter 1.[1] This includes the redness of our ubiquitous red tomato, but also the painfulness of pain, the fearfulness of fear, and perhaps even the wonderingness of wondering, and the realizingness of realizing (Brown 2007; Brown and Mandik 2012).[2]

One could use these properties to define folk-psychologically what it is for something to be mental. One could argue that the above-mentioned states are always conscious, and so consciousness is the mark of the mental (Descartes 1650). Or one could argue that these kinds of states must be importantly connected to consciousness in the right way (Searle 2002). Or one could argue that these states can be characterized independently of consciousness (Rosenthal 2005). Or one could argue that these kinds of states are all connected to intentionality in the right sort of way, and so intentionality is the mark of the mental (Crane 1998). Finally, one might argue that being mental is a disjunctive property of either intentionality or qualitative character (Rosenthal 2005).

Another strategy is to leave the realm of folk-psychology and instead rely on the cognitive sciences. So, take for example memory. Memory is a folk-psychological category. Once we start to try to understand it scientifically, we quickly find ourselves theorizing and populating our theories with postulated entities. For example, in the case of memory we can start with a division between long-term and short-term memory. To make things simpler I will ignore other distinctions we could make for now. This distinction marks things that can be recalled only for a short time and then are forgotten, versus things that you will be able to recall for longer periods of time. Short-term memory has evolved into 'working memory', which is postulated

---

[1] Recall that 'qualitative character' is ambiguous between properties of first-order sensory states/events that may occur consciously or unconsciously versus properties that characterize some aspect of one's phenomenal character. Here I intentionally mean for it to cover both senses. 'Phenomenal character' or properties, as I use the term, is not ambiguous in this sense and must be phenomenologically manifest (i.e., there is necessarily something that it is like for the subject to be in these states).

[2] I have argued that there is a phenomenal aspect to conscious thinking and that there may also be a qualitative character associated with mental attitudes (Brown 2007; but see footnote 1 on qualitative character).

to have components and processes that, should they be implemented, would result in the kind of performance on memory tasks that we find in humans and animals.

Working memory was originally postulated to have three components. The first was a "phonological loop" where we could keep certain internal speech active (say, repeating a six-digit number or password). The second was a memory store (they called it an "episodic buffer"). The third was a "visio-spatial" scratch pad (Baddelay and Hitch 1974). This original idea has been very influential and gone through many updates and iterations. It is also currently prominently featured in introductory psychology and neuroscience textbooks (Myers and DeWall 2020; Kolb et al. 2023). Many cognitive scientists believe that there is a system like this in the human mind, though there are detractors (Gomez-Lavin 2021). If there is such a system, this suggests that the phonological loop, visual-spatial scratch pad, and memory store should count as mental. They are postulated to carry out what we folk-psychologically recognize as mental processes.

Perhaps that is unsurprising. The elements of working memory have a "mental-ish" feel to them. To continue with our example of memory, let's move to long-term memory. Memories are hypothesized to undergo a process called consolidation. This is the process whereby the temporarily held information in short-term/working memory is transferred to a more stable storage format. It is widely believed that this may depend on neurons in the hippocampus firing in rhythmic patterns that change the synaptic weights of targeted neurons in the neocortex. If so, then those processes in the hippocampus, and those processes in the targeted neurons in the neocortex, will both count as mental. It may be counter-intuitive to think of synaptic weights, action potentials in the hippocampus, or large-scale brain wave patterns as being mental (Brown 2006; Brown 2012c), but one can, and arguably should, get used to it.

This strategy takes inspiration from the debate about the metaphysics of the mind. What does it mean to be physical? One answer is that "the physical" is whatever it is that physicists appeal to in their theories (Braddon-Mitchel and Jackson 1996). Or, if this doesn't work out, perhaps the physical is whatever structure is preserved in the march of theorizing. Similarly, what counts as mental, on my view, depends on what the cognitive neuroscientists appeal to in their theories of the mind. A consequence of this is that we will count as mental states even low-level information-processing states, say in the lateral geniculate nucleus of the thalamus (cf. Shea 2018). It will then become an empirical matter which of these mental states are the ones with which our inner awareness puts us in touch.

Different versions of higher-order theory may want to take different versions of the above approaches to defining 'mental.' My preferred strategy is to endorse a kind of pluralism about the mental here. There is room for many marks of the mental. I will generally consider all the above as viable candidates for the higher-order theorist. One thing to note is that these states of which we are aware will be fully representational. They are fully constructed first-order states of the external environment (the non-mental world). We are not talking about a bare sensory quality getting targeted by inner awareness.

We can now turn our attention to inner awareness.

2.2 Higher-Order Representationalism

Representational theories of consciousness are well known in the literature, but they are all first-order theories. Higher-order theories are often classified as versions of representationalism, but then are immediately treated like a different class of theory afterward. In the philosophy of perception literature, for example, higher-order theories are hardly ever mentioned. Some perception may be unconscious, but for the ones that are conscious, higher-order representationalism should be discussed. My hope is to connect these discussions more directly by rooting higher-order theories in contemporary representationalism (Berger and Brown 2022).

2.2.1 Inner Awareness as Higher-Order Representation

The traditional approach, more fully discussed in Chapters 5 and 6, proceeds by arguing that there are just two ways in which we are aware of things. The first is by perceiving them, and the second is having thoughts about them as being present (Rosenthal 2005). In this way the traditional views largely use the postulates of folk-psychology in their account of inner awareness. As discussed in the previous section, this is one possible strategy, but it is not the only one. Nor is it the one I prefer to take.

This is one of the times at which we should leave folk-psychology and instead rely on the cognitive sciences. One popular strategy in the cognitive sciences is to explain perceiving and thinking in terms of representations. So, we can say more generally that we are aware of something when we represent it in a way that allows us to be informationally sensitive to that thing. If so, then the awareness there in that term 'inner awareness' should be thought of as a kind of representation. Ordinary thoughts are a kind of representation, but not every representational state is an ordinary thought. One of the motivations for the HOROR theory is the idea that the requisite representational states may be representational in a generally thought-like way, that is, by having intentional/conceptual contents. However, I do not think that these higher-order representations will be ordinary folk-psychological thoughts or employ just folk-psychological concepts. I suspect they are more like sub-personal representational states, perhaps in a specialized module or system in the brain, or perhaps more widely distributed throughout the brain. These would not be very much at all like ordinary thoughts (except in so far as they have a kind of intentional content).

'Inner' here means that what one is aware of is itself something mental in the sense discussed above. Following standard usage something is 'higher-order' in this sense when it represents something mental (as opposed to something non-mental). Inner awareness thus turns out to be a representation of something mental—a kind of higher-order representation.

Representationalism can be characterized in many ways. As I am using the term here a representation consists in a state that places satisfaction conditions on the thing being represented. A state's satisfaction conditions specify the way the represented objects would have to be for the representation to be accurate. For a propositional representation, the satisfaction conditions will be the truth conditions. For perceptual representations I prefer accuracy conditions as opposed to truth. These are both kinds of satisfaction conditions. I call that part of a representation that places the satisfaction conditions the state's *content*. The things on which these conditions are placed I call the state's *target*, though I am aware that these words are used in many ways.

To take a non-mental example, consider a painting of my desk, as seen from the point of view of someone sitting in the desk chair looking forward. The painting is a representation of my desk. The content of the painting, as I use it, is the image depicted on the canvas. The target of the painting is my actual desk. For the painting to be accurate, the objects must be depicted in the right way. Let's ignore everything else on my desk and just focus on the coffee cup to my left. Suppose the color of my coffee cup is depicted on the canvas as vertically split between equal amounts of black and white (black on top, white on bottom). Further, suppose the painting depicts the mug as in front of a notebook, and to the left (from the represented point of view) of an iPhone. Given this, you know what to expect walking into my office. At least with respect to some of the things on my desk. If the cup on the desk was other than it is depicted, then the painting does not accurately capture what the desk looks like.

It is in this sense of accuracy conditions that I use the term "satisfaction" conditions for conscious experience. There is a long history in philosophy of using imagistic representation to model what is phenomenologically manifest. I am not suggesting that. I am merely using this as a commonsense way to illustrate what it means for something to have these kinds of satisfaction conditions. The idea is that there are mental states that will have satisfaction conditions somewhat like these because, in order for them to be accurate, or true, the world will have to be a certain way.

Of course, one need not paint a picture of the mug on my desk to represent it. If I describe the mug on my desk in language, as I did above, then you likewise know under what conditions that sentence would be true, so its truth conditions are its satisfaction conditions. I will generally speak of satisfaction conditions and mean to include both accuracy and/or truth conditions as the case may dictate.

A first-order representation has satisfaction conditions that involve non-mental reality. First-order states target the world around us and place satisfaction conditions on it. A representation of a red circle may target some sensory stimulus, a ball, or an image on a screen, for example, and place satisfaction conditions on it, thereby representing it as being a certain way—in this case, hopefully as being red and spherical. For the representation to be satisfied, the target must be as the content dictates. Since the satisfaction conditions pertain to the animal's environment, and not its own mind, they are first-order representations.[3]

Higher-order representations have satisfaction conditions that involve mental reality, which is to say their targets are mental phenomena. So, for example, suppose I were to represent myself as seeing a red ball. By doing so, I am placing satisfaction conditions that require that I have a mental state, that of seeing, on the world. To be accurate, the world must have mental states like seeing. In addition, the mental state of seeing needs to also be one of *seeing a red ball*, as well as *being done by me*.

Higher-order representationalism about phenomenal consciousness is the claim that the kind of inner awareness required by higher-order theories amounts to higher-order representation in this sense.[4]

I will now begin to lay out the general version of the HOROR theory.

2.3 The Higher-Order Representation of a Representation (HOROR) Theory

For a creature to be phenomenally conscious, on the HOROR view, is for it to have the right kind of higher-order representation with the right kind of representational content. This HOROR is itself a kind of inner awareness of one's own mental life. What is the right kind of higher-order representational content here? Traditionally the idea has been that it's a representation of the subject as being in some mental

---

[3] How the brain might implement these representations is itself a matter of some dispute, as we will see in Chapter 4, but for my version of the story see Brown 2006 and Brown 2012c

[4] As promised, this way of formulating representationalism allows that the required representations might be physical states, but it also allows that these states may be non-physical as well. If the notion of phenomenal consciousness cannot be captured in physicalistic terms, one may none the less think that it depends on higher-order representations in the way here defined. The satisfaction conditions of these kinds of states would then involve non-physical properties.

state or having some mental process occurring. In the remainder of this chapter, I will discuss these states in an abstract way and will explore them in more detail in the next chapter.

As with any kind of representation, mental representations can represent their targets in different ways. One and the same first-order mental state may be represented as being one way at one time, and another way at another time. Because of this the content of the higher-order representations that we are interested in must have at least two components. One will specify what the target mental representation is, and the other will characterize that target in some way. We will discuss my proposed content of these higher-order states in the next chapter, but traditionally they have been loosely characterized as, for example, 'I am seeing red.'

As previously discussed in Chapter 1, we can distinguish between a phenomenally conscious state's phenomenal and subjective character. Subjective character, as I understand it, is an aspect of what is phenomenologically manifest. Phenomenally conscious states are typed by their phenomenal character such that two phenomenally conscious states with the same phenomenal character will be indistinguishable from the subjective point of view.[5] The subjective character of an experience is that part which is the same among all conscious experiences. It is the "for-me"-ness or subjectivity aspect of the experience. When I experience blueness and redness, as in a flashing siren light on a police car driving by me, I have phenomenally conscious states where phenomenal blueness and redness are manifest, but which are phenomenally conscious experiences at all because of their subjective character.[6]

We can now apply this to the HOROR with something like 'I am seeing red,' as its content. According to HOROR theory this kind of higher-order representation is what phenomenal consciousness is. It will then follow that the phenomenal character of this experience is

---

[5] I am not sure if the conditional goes in the other direction. I think, maybe, we could have two states that were subjectively indistinguishable, but have different phenomenal character due to a difference in what is phenomenologically manifest. We will discuss cases like this in Chapter 3.

[6] I tend to talk in terms of phenomenally conscious mental states, but if one is not happy with this way of speaking, one can talk in terms of subjects and their properties. A subject is phenomenally conscious when they undergo some phenomenal and subjective character. Whether these are properties of states or subjects is a matter of one's preferences.

determined by the '... seeing red' part of the higher-order state.[7] The subjective character is determined by the 'I am ...' part of the higher-order state. This is because if one varies 'I am seeing red' to 'I am seeing blue,' then one will undergo a change in experience from red to blue. Furthermore, if one changes 'I am seeing red' to 'Am I seeing red?' or 'I doubt I am seeing red,' then there can be no phenomenal consciousness according to the HOROR theory. It is only states that assert that something is *here* now that count as making one aware of the things those states represent. The HORORs postulated by the theory are not these sorts of ordinary folk-psychological states.

I am not saying that one cannot have a conscious experience of wondering. Only that if one did come to have a conscious experience of wondering it would be because the relevant HOROR represented one as wondering something. 'Am I seeing red?' does not make one aware of seeing red. Arguably it doesn't make you aware of anything at all (though, again, you can be aware of it). Higher-order theorists agree that the relevant higher-order state must show up in a seemingly spontaneous (non-inferential) way and represent one's mental life as *occurring now* in one's stream of consciousness. Questions and commands do not meet this latter requirement.

With all the preceding discussion in mind, the general form of a HOROR theory can be summed up in the following way:

> HOROR Theory: for subject S to be in a phenomenally conscious state C with phenomenal character P, is just for S to token an appropriate higher-order representation(=C) with the satisfaction conditions that *S is themselves in target mental representation R, which in turn has P as its satisfaction conditions.*

To have a higher-order representation of this kind is to represent oneself as representing the world. Given what we have said so far, this comes to representing the satisfaction conditions of the relevant first-order representations.

---

[7] If one insisted on calling that 'qualitative character,' I am ok with that. Just so long as we all agree that this is an aspect of the higher-order state and a part of what is phenomenologically manifest.

To take our toy example, when one is having a phenomenally conscious experience of seeing red, one will have a higher-order representation with content like 'I am seeing red.' In this case the target mental representation R would be the first-order visual representation of red (we can leave aside for now the nature of the targeting relation). The subject is representing themselves as being in that targeted state in a particular way captured by P. Let us suppose that the subject is enjoying a nice shade of crimson in the sunset. In this case R will be the seeing of the color at the first-order level. The relevant HOROR may represent R accurately, in which case P will be that the first-order state is a representation of crimson, and that will be what is phenomenologically manifest. The relevant HOROR may also represent R inaccurately, say as a generic red. In this case P will be that the first-order state R is a representation of generic red (even though in this case it is not). What will be phenomenologically manifest to the subject in that case will be generic red.

The theory says that any phenomenally conscious state consists in a higher-order representation with some precisification of this general kind of content. That's what phenomenal consciousness is, and when that shows up in the right way that's all there is to you having experience.

2.3.1 Separating State-Consciousness from Phenomenal Consciousness

In the first chapter we noted the different concepts of consciousness and noted that state-consciousness and phenomenal consciousness are at the very least conceptually distinct. We will explore the prospects for identifying state-consciousness and phenomenal consciousness in Chapter 5. As I see things the higher-order approach should separate state-consciousness from phenomenal consciousness in the following way:

State-consciousness=the state of which I am aware (i.e., the target of the HOROR)[8]

---

[8] I use "state-consciousness" with the hyphen to mark it as distinct from phenomenal consciousness.

> Phenomenal consciousness=the state which, when I am in it, there is something that it is like for me to be in it (i.e., the HOROR itself)

Accordingly, there can be phenomenally conscious states that are not state-conscious. That just means that there is an appropriate HOROR that one is not aware of oneself as being in (in other words one has an ordinary phenomenally conscious state).

On the HOROR theory, the relevant higher-order state targets a (set of) first-order representation(s) and puts satisfaction conditions on it(/them) thereby representing it(/them) as being a certain way. This is what it is to experientially represent the external world on HOROR theory.

We can put the core idea of HOROR theory in terms of what I call HTTP (HOROR Theory Transitivity Principle), which I put as follows:

> HTTP: a mental state is phenomenally conscious if and only if it appropriately makes one aware of one's mind.

Many states may make one aware of one's own mind, but HTTP builds into it that this must be done in an "appropriate" way. This just means that the relevant HOROR must occur in a seemingly spontaneous way and represent one's mental life as currently occurring. But while I think that HTTP captures phenomenal consciousness, I do not think that it captures the notion of state-consciousness as it is typically defined. State-consciousness, by definition, applies to the state that one is aware of, not the state of awareness itself. We will come back to this question when we go through the various views and situate the HOROR theory among them more technically. Since my goal here is to set out the theory, I will leave it at this for now.

The state that we are aware of is the target of the HOROR. As discussed previously, I see these HORORs as one kind of cognitive access to our mental life. One of the ways in which we have access to our own mental life is by being aware of it. The things we count as being aware of are the states that are referred to, or picked out by, the proposed targeting relation. However, the state that we are aware of in this way (which state is picked out or referred to) is not what is phenomenologically manifest. This is not what is conveyed to the subject. What is phenomenologically manifest is the *way in which* we are aware of our own mental life. The HOROR targets the first-order state via a theoretical targeting relation, and the way in which it represents the targeted state just is the phenomenal and subjective character we are seeking to explain. Of course, what it is like for you to be in that state is just like the way the higher-order state represents your mental life as being, which is you being visually presented with some property in the environment, red or whatever.

In a sense this is very similar to first-order theories of consciousness. First-order theorists hold that phenomenal consciousness consists in the right kind of representation. These theorists search for the appropriate kind of content that will distinguish phenomenal consciousness from other representational states. HOROR agrees but adds that it is a higher-order representation that is required. Both kinds of theories agree that it is the kind of content that matters for whether a state is phenomenally conscious or not. They diverge over whether the right kind of content is higher-order in the sense of involving inner awareness. Hence, what it is like for you to be in the relevant HOROR state is just the way the first-order theorist typically thinks about the world. One experiences just the visual presentation of a red thing out there (from a point of view); the transparency comes for free. However, the way in which that experience gets explained, or accounted for, by the HOROR theory is in terms of a higher-order representation making you aware of being in a first-order state by targeting that state and then also describing it in the way we have said. Thus, even though there are similarities to first-order theory, the HOROR theory is a higher-order representational theory of phenomenal consciousness.

2.3.2 A HORORibly Simple Argument

On the HOROR theory the phenomenally conscious state is the HOROR itself. This sets it apart from most other theories of consciousness that I am aware of. I think there is a principled reason that higher-order theories should take this route.

I will make the argument for HTTP in two stages. To start with we can look at Lycan's (2001) classic "simple argument" for higher-order representationalism. It will come up again in Chapter 7, so it is good to refresh our memory. It goes as follows.

(1) A conscious state is a mental state whose subject is aware of being in it. [Definition]
(2) The 'of' in (1) is the 'of' of intentionality; what one is aware of is an intentional object of the awareness.
(3) Intentionality is representation; a state has a thing as its intentional object only if it represents that thing.

Therefore,

(4) Awareness of a mental state is a representation of that state. [2,3]

And therefore,

(5) A conscious state is a state that is itself represented by another of the subject's mental states. [1,4] qed (Lycan 2001)

In the twenty-two years since Lycan first gave this simple argument, there have been higher-order theories that challenge each of Lycan's three premises.

Premises (2) and (3) have been questioned the most. Those who challenge premise (2) deny that intentionality is the right way to think of the way in which we are related to our first-order states. These theorists seek a non-intentional form of representation. Those who challenge premise (3) want to find some way to have non-representational intentionality. These debates need not concern us here. We will comb through those details in Chapter 7. What I want to point out here is that until very recently there haven't been any higher-order theorists who challenge premise (1).

We can see the HOROR theory as filling that gap. The HOROR theory allows that one's phenomenally conscious states can be conscious without one being aware of being in them. A phenomenally conscious state is not one I am aware of being in according to the

HOROR theory. At least not necessarily. HOROR theory allows there may be cases where the relevant higher-order state occurs without my being aware of it.

Lycan's simple argument does more than let us categorize certain recent higher-order theories. We can adapt Lycan's simple argument into what I call my HORORibly simple argument (I couldn't resist!). It goes as follows.

1. A phenomenally conscious state is one which, when one is in that state, there is something that it is like for one to be in it.
2. The state that, when one is in that state, there is something that there is like for one to be in it, is the state of inner awareness.
3. Thus, the phenomenally conscious state is the state of inner awareness.
4. Inner awareness is a representation of one's own mind.
5. Thus, a phenomenally conscious state is a representation of one's own mind.

This HORORibly simple argument makes it clear where an opponent can disagree.

Premise 1 follows from the definition of phenomenal consciousness I gave in Chapter 1 and seems to me like a commonsense truism. Alas, one quickly learns that there are no obvious truisms about consciousness! We will come back to premise 1 in Chapter 5 when we discuss the traditional higher-order approach in more detail. We will see that there are those who reject it, but let us save that discussion for the later chapter.

Traditional higher-order theorists will disagree with premise 2 and need to contend with my argument for it given above, and in Chapter 6. Line 3 follows from those two premises and is HTTP from the previous section. I will argue that premise 4 is supported by a careful examination of non-representational versions of higher-order theories in Chapter 7 as well as the arguments from this chapter (especially section 2.2.1). Those who reject premise 4 need to give an account of their proposed non-representational form of inner awareness. They will have to also deal with my arguments in Chapter 7. Line 5 follows from that and is the foundational claim of the HOROR theory.

The HOROR theory is in a sense itself a category of theories. What unites them is the allegiance to the conclusion of the HORORibly simple argument and HTTP. A phenomenally conscious state is one that makes one aware of one's mental life by representing it. Within this general category there will be many different ways to model to the content of the relevant higher-order representation. We will now turn to discussing this in more detail.

2.4 The Structural Elements of HORORs

HORORs are higher-order *representations* and so have content. They are also *higher-order* representations, and so their contents have targets that are mental. So much for what we can all agree on. In order to offer an account of how it is that these HORORs might be able to do the postulated work, we need to assess the mental elements at the higher-order system's disposal. This will amount to giving a model for the content and structure of the relevant higher-order representations. I will explore this in detail in Chapter 3. Before doing so I need to say something generally about the kinds of contents these higher-order states are thought to have. We have already, at an abstract level, laid out some of the constraints a HOROR theory must conform to, but how does it meet them?

I have always thought of the relevant higher-order states as having something like a complex demonstrative structure. If I say, "that dog is friendly," then the expression 'that dog' refers to some specific object in my environment (presumably but not necessarily an existing dog) and describes it as a dog. The satisfaction conditions for this kind of sentence intuitively involve both the object referred to and the descriptive concepts applied to it.

There is a vast literature on complex demonstratives in the philosophy of language, and I am hoping we can mostly avoid it. All that I want is the relatively naïve idea that a state's satisfaction conditions may depend on which thing is targeted as well as how that thing is described. In the case of HORORs, we can start by saying that the 'complex demonstrative' nature of the HOROR will account for the two kinds of consciousness we distinguished in the previous chapters.

'Pointer' contents will account for the targeting relation and, therefore, determine which state or mental process it is that I am aware of myself as being in. Thus, the pointer content of the HOROR will account for state-consciousness. However, it is the descriptive/intentional content of the HOROR that accounts for phenomenal consciousness and what it is like for one.

These two kinds of contents will have different satisfaction conditions as well as different roles to play. Some of the contents of the HOROR will have as their satisfaction conditions the occurrence of some mental state or process. This is the component that makes the view a higher-order view in that this instantiates a kind of inner awareness of my own mental life. However, according to HOROR theory, some of the contents of the relevant HOROR have as satisfaction conditions non-mental properties and objects. The claim, then, is that the higher-order states will have a mixed kind of content that is partially higher-order but also partially first-order. In addition, each of these contents will play a distinctive role in the psychology of the subject. To make sense of this we must first make a distinction that, as far as I know, hasn't been made before.

2.4.1 Phenomenally Silent and Active Contents

Phenomenal consciousness is the occurrence of the relevant HOROR, and what it is like for one is completely determined by the content of this HOROR. However, this does not mean that every element of the content of the relevant HOROR will play an active role in determining what it is like for the subject. I will argue that there is a *phenomenally silent* content in the higher-order representation. This will be in addition to the *phenomenally active* content that determines what it is like for one.

As we discussed in the first chapter, to be phenomenologically manifest is to be part of what it is like for one. It is to show up in my stream of consciousness as part of one's overall phenomenal character. Phenomenally silent content is a part of the phenomenally conscious state but does not result in anything being phenomenologically manifest. What it is like for one does not have anything related to the phenomenally silent content as I am using that term. There will be nothing in one's stream of consciousness produced by this phenomenally silent content. It will have some other job to do, as we will discuss below.

Phenomenally active content determines what is phenomenologically manifest to the subject. Since I view a representation's content to be a matter of how that state places satisfaction conditions on its target, I am happy to endorse a pluralism about content. I allow that there may be many varieties of satisfaction conditions, and that a state can have multiple contents in that it can place multiple satisfaction conditions on its target.

Having a part of the content of a phenomenally conscious state that is phenomenally silent may sound odd. However, I think a good case can be made for it on the HOROR theory (which I will make in the next chapter).[9]

2.4.2 Concepts/Intentionality

As discussed in section 2.1.2, I view concepts as mental representations that are the building blocks of thoughts and thought-like representations. I will treat concepts as akin to words in a language of thought (Fodor 1975). Representations with the right conceptual content will then come to have intentional content. These representations will be about something and will characterize that thing in various ways. They will have targets and content as I have been using those terms.

How do these mental representations come to acquire content? I am partial to two-factor views. At the base level I am attracted to causal/historical and teleological accounts (Kripke 1980; Millikan 1984; Neander 2017). From there one can build up inferential relations that secure the rest of the content (Chalmers 2021). If we can't get all

---

[9] Phenomenally silent content should be distinguished from Andrew Lee's microstructure thesis about phenomenal consciousness (Lee 2019). Lee argues that there can be microphenomenal structure that is phenomenally active but not phenomenologically manifest in my sense.

intentional content that way, we can opt for pure inferential role semantics for any stragglers (Block 1986).

Deciding among competitors in this area would require a separate book. I bring out the above just to note where my background proclivities lie. As much as possible, I would like it to be the case that one could pick one's favorite theory of concepts and intentionality and insert it here. I think for the most part that is true, but there are some constraints that emerge when one works through the details.

2.4.3. Mental Pointers

I have suggested that a natural starting point in thinking about the content of HORORs is that they will have something like a complex demonstrative structure. As discussed in the previous section, I hope that any theory of concepts or intentionality will fit with my picture, but what about the pointer contents? Use of demonstratives in language typically involves pointing and/or communicative intentions. What does it mean to point to something in one's mind? Many philosophers are skeptical that there are demonstrative concepts because there seems to be difficulty making sense of these notion in the mind (Pereplyotchik 2012).

I don't think there is a mental analogue of a natural language demonstrative in the content of HORORs. I don't view them as ordinary folk-psychological thoughts as some higher-order theorists do. When I say that there is a mental pointer in the content of the HOROR, what I mean is that there is some aspect of that state that determines which first-order states are being targeted. The mental pointers are postulated to secure the targeting relation on my view. As such there are different ways that one might model these mental pointers (remember that I will argue that we need some kind of targeting relation in Chapter 6).

One possibility is to appeal to the causal/historical and teleological accounts of intentionality mentioned above. Perhaps what it is for a HOROR to point to its target is for it to deploy concepts that have the function of picking out those lower-order representations. Another possibility is the use of attention to understand mental pointing (Prinz 2007). A more speculative option might be a higher-order version of

Pylyshyn's visual indexes or Fingers of INSTantiation, aka FINSTs (Pylyshyn 2001). I think all of these are interesting routes to explore. Out of these three options I think the first is the most promising, but this is not the way I prefer to think of the mental pointers I am proposing.

The way I prefer to think of mental pointers is as akin to an address as used in computer science. A simple example involves html links. If I wanted to have a link to a webpage, then I point to it using an html attribute as follows:

```
<a href= "http://example.com/index.html">this is a link</a>
```

In this example, "http://example.com/index.html" is the URL, or Universal Resource Locater, of the website one wishes to link to. The URL provides the location of the website and file one wants ("example.com/index.html") and instructions for how to access it ("http://," which indicates the Hyper Text Transfer Protocol). The 'href= "..."' part points to the URL. When implemented, this results in the text 'this is a link' being displayed in the familiar blue underlining of hyperlinks.

While I obviously do not think that the mind uses html, it does provide a simple example of the two types of content I have been discussing. The displayed text on the screen is akin to what is phenomenologically manifest. The 'this is a link' bit in the above code is akin to phenomenally active content. The pointer content, which is the 'href= "..."' part, is not displayed on the screen. This is the phenomenally silent content. It is required to generate the link, but it is not part of what one experiences on the screen.

There may also be phenomenally active content that doesn't match what is phenomenologically manifest. To stick with our example from html, we know that links are usually rendered in blue color with an underline. You can change this in html (let's ignore CSS for now to make my point). Sticking with our example from above we might do this as follows,

```
<a href= "http://example.com/index.html" style="color: #ae3668";>
this is a link</a>
```

This line of code has all the same content as before. In addition, though, it includes the "style" attribute and specifies a color (in hex color format) for the link text and underlining to be displayed in. This has the effect of changing the color of the text displayed. Keeping in mind that this analogy only goes so far, we have an example of content that is phenomenally active in the sense that I mean. To be phenomenally active is just to determine something that is phenomenologically manifest in one's stream of consciousness. In this metaphorical example what is phenomenologically manifest is the color. Being phenomenally active does not mean that the content must directly match what is phenomenologically manifest. Sometimes it may, other times it may not.

We can thus map our distinction between intentional and pointer contents onto the distinction between phenomenally active and phenomenally silent contents. The intentional/conceptual part of the HORORs content is phenomenally active in my sense. The pointer content, then, is a part of the HOROR and has some role to play, but it is the phenomenally silent component. It does not contribute to what it is like for the subject. The postulated pointer content will play a functional role. Perhaps it will serve to keep various mental activities 'online,' or to route them to working memory for further processing, and so on. This will show up in the system's behavior but does not determine what it is like for the subject. According to HOROR theory, that is completely exhausted by the descriptive/intentional representational content of the relevant HOROR. Both of these are thought of as aspects of the phenomenally conscious state. The HOROR, which is the phenomenally conscious state, will have both these contents, or aspects.

We will discuss this in more detail in Chapter 7 when we examine Hakwan Lau's Perceptual Reality Monitoring theory. He offers the most worked-out account of the above idea about pointers. In my view the discussion in Chapters 6 and 7 reveal that there are compelling theoretical reasons to think that we need some kind of pointer content in the mind. Also revealed by that discussion are two other things about pointer content. First, according to the HOROR theory, pointer contents must be phenomenally silent. In cases of a 'descriptively' empty HOROR that still has the targeting content, my feeling is that one would have a zombie or super-blindsight type case (see section 1.1.6). A creature with this kind of descriptively empty pure pointer HOROR would be fully capable of interacting with the environment, but for which there was nothing that it was like to do so.[10] Second is that pointer contents are not well understood. It remains unclear how we should think about them philosophically, how they should be modeled psychologically, and how they could be implemented in the brain.

Even granting all of this it is still useful to appeal to them as elements in our theorizing. Higher-order theories that postulate mental pointer contents make different empirical predictions than ones that don't. Further, different versions of higher-order theories make different use of pointer contents and so also have differing empirical predictions as well.

Now that we have developed the general structure of the HOROR theory and the kinds of content those higher-order states may have, we can turn to a closer examination of the specific kind of content I am proposing that these HORORs have.

---

[10] Indeed, perhaps this is how it started. We could have creatures with super-blindsight-like abilities due to having pure pointer content in the perceptual monitoring module, and gradually this comes to have intentional content as well. Purely speculative but interesting thought!

3
The Contents of HORORs

Non-traditional higher-order theories like HOROR are relatively new, and their final form is yet to be set. In this chapter, I will argue for what I take to be one promising way to think of these higher-order representations. Along the way we will take into consideration input from some recently emerging fellow travelers. There appears to be a growing recognition that theories like HOROR are worth taking seriously. Three recent theorists exploring this strategy are worth highlighting. Miguel Ángel Sebastián (Sebastián 2022a, 2022b) argues that these higher-order representations must have a certain (non-conceptual) *perspectival de se* content. Joseph Gottlieb (Gottlieb 2022) offers what he calls the Map View, where the relevant higher-order states are map-like in being partially iconic and partially intentional. Joseph LeDoux (LeDoux 2024) has articulated what he calls a multi-state hierarchical view and takes these higher-order representations to be purely intentional/conceptual states, perhaps in a kind of *mentalese*. These theories each present a non-traditional higher-order theory that can be interpreted as endorsing the conclusion of the HORORibly simple argument from Chapter 2. We all slightly disagree on how to model the higher-order representation involved.[1] Since the reasons that are given in favor of the non-conceptual content and mentalease in HORORs are often based on neuroscience and considerations of the richness of experience, we will wait until the next chapter (4) to discuss them.

Let's take as our example the phenomenal red property again so we can talk about the various components of the content according to HOROR. Higher-order theorists have typically glossed this as

---

[1] I do not think Gottlieb accepts his version of higher-order view. Rather, he puts it forward as what he thinks the higher-order theorist should say. LeDoux and Sebastián do endorse their views.

something like 'I am seeing red,' or 'I am visually aware of red.' I agree that, at the most general level, something like this could characterize the content of the HORORs, but I think we can say a little bit more about what the content of these higher-order states is supposed to be. First, there is the 'I am' part that contains the mental analogue of 'I' and the assertive force. This is the part of the representation that attributes the lower-order mental state or process to oneself and asserts that it is currently occurring. The second component is the 'seeing red' part that contains the 'visually aware' and '(perceptible) red' parts. Each of these will involve pointer (phenomenally silent) and descriptive/intentional (phenomenally active) contents as discussed in the previous chapter (see section 2.4).

In section 3.1, I discuss the portion of the content of the HOROR related to the self and subjective character. In section 3.1.1, I discuss Miguel Ángel Sebastián's argument for *perspectival de se* content and argue that HOROR theory can meet this constraint. In section 3.2, I discuss the portion of the content of the HOROR that is related to the specific phenomenal character that is phenomenologically manifest. In section 3.3, I examine some predictions of the HOROR theory by careful examination of mis-match cases (3.3.1). In section 3.3.2, I discuss the question of whether phenomenology is rich or sparse and the way in which this will result in different versions of the HOROR theory (in section 3.3.3). Finally, in section 3.4, I discuss introspection from the point of view of the HOROR theory.

3.1 Subjective Character: The Higher-Order Mental Analogue of 'I'

There is a long tradition in philosophy that posits a special kind of direct acquaintance with oneself. The idea is that we know about our own selves in a primitive way. This primitive way of knowing allows us to think thoughts about ourselves that seem importantly different from 'ordinary' thoughts. One of the ways in which this kind of self-thought is supposed to be different is that I can refer to myself in a way that philosophers have called the 'essential indexical.' To take a classic example from John Perry (1979), suppose I notice my own reflection in a dirty window and think, 'that person has a stain on their shirt,' without noticing that it is myself that has that stain. In this case I am thinking about myself, since it is my reflection, but I am not thinking about myself as such. To do that I would need to realize that *I, myself*, am that person with a stain. There is a difference between thinking about something that happens to be myself and thinking about myself as such.

This ambiguity shows up again when discussing higher-order theories (Sebastián 2022a). According to the HOROR theory, phenomenal consciousness just is inner awareness of one's mind. But is this inner awareness an awareness of something that just happens to be one's mind? Or is it an awareness of one's mind as such? In the former case there need not be any content related to the self in the HOROR. Perhaps there could be a Selfless-HOROR, a HOROR that included everything in a typical HOROR minus the awareness of a self and attribution of the mental state to the self. The content of the relevant Selfless-HOROR might be,

> *there's visual awareness of (perceptible) red*

This might result in a phenomenally conscious state that 'floats free' of any self. The resulting phenomenally conscious experience may just be as of a selfless seeing of red. One might want to claim that this kind of phenomenally conscious state could be found in relatively unsophisticated creatures that lacked any kind of self concept. It might even be a model for selfless experiences during meditation.

Given the usefulness of a selfless-HOROR, it is a little surprising no one has developed it in more detail. This may be at least in part due to a well-known argument from David Rosenthal against selfless higher-order views. One would not, argues Rosenthal, be aware of a token mental state in such a case. One would only be aware of an abstract mental state type (Rosenthal 2005, 2011b). We will deal with Rosenthal's account of self-reference in Chapter 6 when we discuss the traditional higher-order thought theory in detail. Here it is enough to point out that the proposed targeting relation, accounted for by the proposed pointer content, would handle this objection. It might be true that in our case we represent our experiences as being had from a point of view that is, as it were, my own. This doesn't give us any reason to think it is a universal feature of phenomenal consciousness. The above approximation of the content of a selfless-HOROR had 'there is' standing in for the pointer content. I have already pointed out that I don't really think it has that lexical item as part of its content. The point is that there is an aspect of the content that acts as a pointer and secures reference to a token mental state. The organism in question would succeed in being aware of some token mental state without explicitly representing that it is a mental state of its own mind. As a result, all that would be phenomenologically manifest would be the free-floating seeing of red.

So, Rosenthal's objection fails. It is possible for there to be phenomenally conscious states that may not be experienced as belonging to any subject. This is not the way that our typical day-to-day experience is, though. When we speak of phenomenal consciousness, we are talking about there being something that it is like for the creature in question. There is a point of view, a subjective origin point, from which one experiences the world. So, as I see things there is compelling first-person reason to think that there is an aspect of the HOROR that accounts for this phenomenologically manifest aspect of subjective character.

My way of thinking of the HOROR theory, then, posits that there will be some phenomenally active content related to subjective character in the content of the relevant HOROR. It is an open possibility that there could be phenomenologically silent content related to subjective character as well. This is why I defined subjective character independently from phenomenal character in Chapter 1. If one thinks that subjective character is phenomenally silent, akin to the 'href= " . . . "' part of the HOROR, then subjective character is not a part of phenomenal character. It is not phenomenologically manifest. If one thought that the subjective character of the HOROR was phenomenally active, then the self will be phenomenologically manifest as part of one's phenomenal character.

One could go either way here depending on what one thought the phenomenology was like. As mentioned above, I do find the self to be phenomenologically manifest in some way. According to the HOROR theory this is because I am aware of myself in the same way in which I am aware of my first-order mental states, which is just by representing it. We can take the 'I am visually aware of red' generic content and unpack the satisfaction conditions of the 'I am' part as something like the following,

The entity in which that/those very state(s) are occurring is visually aware of (perceptible) red

In this case, the higher-order state represents as 'themselves' the very entity in which the targeted first-order state occurs. On this way of construing things, the mental analogue of 'I' in the HOROR refers to the self as the very organism in which the mental life one is aware of is occurring. I use the term 'entity' here because it is very general and means something like 'existing object.' In English it is synonymous with 'being,' 'body,' and 'individual.' Any of these would do the trick in my book.[2]

If this is on the right track then the mental analogue of 'I' that occurs in the HOROR refers to the subject by, in effect, pointing to a certain set of mental states/processes, and then describing those states/processes as the ones a certain existing object is currently in. There will, in addition, be the further descriptive/intentional content characterizing how the referred-to existing object experiences those states. We could try to capture the satisfaction conditions formally as follows,

[the x: x is in the states at ADDRESS 123](x is visually aware of (perceptible) red)

Here I am adopting some notation from Stephan Neale (1990), though I don't mean to commit to his theory of descriptions. The phrase in brackets is a limited quantifier, and the phrase in parentheses is what the quantifier ranges over. We can read this in English as saying, "the

---

[2] Gennaro seems to agree with this minimal notion of self-as-merely-distinct-entity/body saying that "all that is needed for most [Higher-Order Thoughts] is the kind of minimal 'bodily self-consciousness' self-concept, that is, being able to distinguish one's own body from other things" (2012, 242).

unique x, such that x is in the sates at address 123, is visually aware of (perceptible) red."

The HOROR theory as I think of it assigns different roles to these aspects. The 'visually aware of (perceptible) red' part we will discuss in the next section, so let us set that aside for now. The mental analogue of 'I' that occurs in the HORORs has satisfaction conditions along the lines we have been indicating. As promised, there are two aspects to these conditions. One is the pointer aspect, which lists the address at which the first-order states can be found. This aspect is postulated to be phenomenally silent. It does not account for any phenomenologically manifest part of one's stream of consciousness. If one thought that was all there was to one's phenomenology, then one could stop here.[3] However, to account for the phenomenologically manifest aspect of subjective character that I personally find in my own experience, HOROR theory postulates that the mental analogue of 'I' will have phenomenally active content as well. This will be in addition to the phenomenally silent content we have already been discussing.

Before discussing the phenomenally active content in more detail, I should note that this is part of the reason why the phenomenally silent targeting content is postulated as part of the content of phenomenally conscious states. As we have seen the reasons are twofold. One reason is that we need something that allows us to say which first-order states the subject is aware of (as argued for in Chapter 6). The second reason is that we need a way to secure reference to the self. Who is it that is doing the seeing? The answer, according to the HOROR theory, is whatever it is that is in the states located at the listed address, that's who.[4]

Returning to the phenomenally active content in the mental analogue of 'I,' it is these contents that account for any phenomenologically

---

[3] It could be, perhaps, that instead of explicitly representing that it is some entity in which the states are occurring in a phenomenally active way, it might be the case that the organism represents this implicitly and thus in a phenomenally silent way. If this organism was disposed to answer the question 'who is seeing red' (if it ever came up) with 'the one those states are occurring in,' or 'the entity in which those states are occurring,' then that would not need to be part of the explicit content of the HOROR. I do not endorse this dispositional account, but someone could. In fact, I take it to be a version of Rosenthal's view (Rosenthal 2005; 2012).

[4] If one were pressed on this and made to answer the question, I take it that the correct answer would be that 'it's me, the one in front of you, who is writing this book...' etc.

manifest content involving the self. The HOROR, in virtue of having the mental analogue of 'I' as part of its content, makes it phenomenologically seem that there is a point of view on the world. It is this aspect of the higher-order content, captured by the descriptive content of the restricted quantifier in the above, that is responsible for attributing the state to the subject who is experiencing it. Since, according to HOROR theory, what it is like for one is exhausted by the representational content of the HOROR, and the HOROR represents (in a phenomenally active way) that there is a unique existing entity that has a mental life unfolding, what it is like for this creature will be like an existing entity having a mental life from an unspecified point of view—or maybe from some bodily point of view, depending on how one thinks the phenomenology turns out. In this way the HOROR theory can account for subjective character being phenomenologically manifest. I experience *myself* as having a mental life, and that is my subjective character. Importantly I do not do this, according to HOROR, by becoming aware of some part of the higher-order representation.

3.1.1 Perspectival *De Se* Content?

As we can see, there are many ways one can construe this content on a HOROR theory. Miguel Ángel Sebastián (2022a) argues that there is a further constraint here. The content must be, in his words, *perspectival* content. What does this mean? Sebastián aims to connect discussion in higher-order theories of consciousness to discussion about *de se* representation in the philosophy of mind more generally. 'De se' in Latin literally means 'about oneself', and this term came to be widely popularized because of the work of David Lewis (1979). Sebastián lays out two constraints that have emerged in the discussion of *de se* thoughts.

The two constraints are what he calls global and portable.

> Global: Thoughts have global truth values—as opposed to having truth values only relative to subjects or times. Given a complete description of the world, we can assign them a truth value

Portable: Thoughts are portable. Different individuals can entertain the same thought

He then argues that the kind of content that is required in the relevant higher-order states needs to be portable and not global. To be portable means that two different individuals can have states with the same phenomenal content. There must be some sense in which it is possible that what it is like for me to see red is the same as what it is like for you to see red. To be not global, in his sense, is for it to be the case that we can have two individuals who have the same phenomenology but one is accurate, and the other is not.

For example, suppose that we have two individuals, Alvin and Simon. Suppose that both Alvin and Simon are having an experience of the red apple in front of them. Suppose, though, that Alvin has an appropriate HOROR as well as the relevant first-order state while Simon merely has the appropriate HOROR without the occurrence of the first-order state (something extensively discussed in Chapters 5 and 6). Let us assume that all of the relevant contents are in every case the same, except for the difference between Alvin and Simon that I just stipulated. In that case Alvin and Simon each have the very same thing phenomenologically manifest. Each will have a phenomenally conscious state of seeing red (among other states). Each will be in a state with satisfaction conditions involving (among other things) being in a first-order state of seeing the apple. This is a portable content. However, Alvin will be in states that meet those satisfaction conditions, whereas Simon will not. The relevant HORORs will only have truth-values relative to a given individual and thus would not be global. This is required to make the content truly perspectival in Sebastián's view. There is an aspect of the content of the state that is true only relative to an individual's point of view only when it is not global.

This kind of content, the kind that is portable and not global, is contrasted with the non-portable and global kind of content. If Alvin and Simon had different things that were phenomenologically manifest such that for Alvin what is manifest is 'Alvin is seeing an apple,' while for Simon it is 'Simon is seeing an apple,' then this could be settled by knowing all of the objective facts about the world and the two contents could not be shared.

Sebastián argues that we need an account of how our minds could have these kinds of portable and non-global contents. I think that the version of HOROR theory I have been sketching meets these two constraints. To apply what we have discussed, let's allow that there can be these different kinds of contents. Then, when one is seeing a red apple consciously, one will have a HOROR with phenomenally active and silent content. This HOROR is the phenomenally conscious state, but it will have a phenomenally silent aspect. These two components, in turn, largely map onto the pointer versus the descriptive content of the HOROR. One could endorse the denial of global by pointing out that the targeting relation is going to be unique to each individual. As argued for in Chapter 7, the most plausible interpretation of these pointers is cast in terms of the topologically organized maps we find in early sensory cortices. When I represent myself as seeing red, I am targeting states in my mind using addresses rooted in my specific neurobiology. These states will have mental addresses that are presumably unique to me. If so, the satisfaction conditions crucially depend on me. The phenomenally conscious state I am in is not entirely portable, since there is an aspect of its content that crucially depends on it being me who has the state. Still, the phenomenology itself will nonetheless be portable because when you and I have a phenomenally conscious experience of a red apple (with differing pointer contents), we, in some sense, could be having states with the same phenomenally active content. We attribute to ourselves being in the same first-order state, that of seeing red. Because of this what is phenomenologically manifest in our two cases is the same even though these states are perspectival in Sebastián's sense.[5]

I want to turn to discussing the other component of the phenomenal state.

---

[5] Sebastián argues that those who endorse global give up portable and vice vera. As we have just seen, I think the HOROR theory can accept his preferred route of being portable and not global. However, it seems to me that there is a sense in which both can be true. On the one hand, we can respect portable by noting that in both cases what is phenomenologically manifest will be the same, or at least could be, as discussed above. On the other hand, one could endorse global by relying on the dispositionalist reading of these contents mentioned above. As emphasized by Rosenthal (2022), these dispositions are objectively a part of the non-mental world. This is not a strategy that I recommend, but it is one that is available for those that are interested.

3.2 Phenomenal Character: The Concept of Seeing Red

As we have seen, on the HOROR theory the mental analogue of 'I' in the HOROR turns out to rely on a mix of descriptive and pointer contents. The targeting relation picks out a certain set of mental states/processes and the HOROR describes the self as the entity in which those very states are occurring. Whether or not the self is phenomenologically manifest, on the HOROR theory, depends on whether there is descriptive/intentional content or whether one thinks the 'I' in the higher-order state is a mere pointer.

We need to say more about the second component of the HOROR, which is,

visually aware of (perceptible) red

What are the satisfaction conditions of this component of the higher-order state? Just as with the mental analogue of 'I,' the HOROR theory postulates mixed contents here.

There are at least two concepts that that make up the intentional/descriptive content here. One is the concept of *seeing*, which is the visual awareness. The other is the concept of *redness*, which I think of as perceptible red, the property that objects in the environment (appear to) have. We will discuss the traditional higher-order thought characterization of this concept as mental red in Chapter 7, but a word on it now may be appropriate.

3.2.1 The Concept of Perceptible Red

Traditionally higher-order theorists have argued that the concept that figures in the higher-order state is that of mental red (Rosenthal 2005). They will often start with the traditional 'I am seeing red' content attributed to the relevant higher-order state but will soon refine that statement. When they get more specific, they gloss the content of the relevant higher-order states as something like 'I am in a red* state,' where red* is *mental red* and is thought of as the first-order qualitative component of seeing red.[6] It would be the first-order red mental quality. For reasons to be discussed in Chapter 7, I am somewhat skeptical that we have traditional concepts of mental red (Byrne 2022).

So, on the HOROR theory the concept of red that is applied in the relevant higher-order representation has satisfaction conditions that involve the world. This concept will be satisfied when there is in the organism's environment something primitively red. It is the concept of a property in the environment.

As we have seen, I think that the way in which we pick out the first-order mental states in question is by pure pointer content. We simply list the address of the state (as discussed in section 3.2. and argued for in Chapter 7). If one allows that pointers can be concepts, then our concept of mental red may be this pure pointer with no content (or whose content is an address). That is the only concept of mental red that we have, on my view. If so, then the HOROR theory postulates both concepts of red occurring in the relevant HOROR. There will be the descriptive/intentional concept of perceptible red as well as the pure pointer/address concept of mental red. The former is phenomenally active, and the latter is phenomenally silent, but they both have a role to play in the phenomenally conscious state.

3.2.2 The Concept of Visual Awareness

But that is only part of the content. The other part is the *seeing* part, and this will have satisfaction conditions that are mental. Seeing is a mental state/process, and so a state that represents me as seeing is representing me as engaged in a mental activity, or as being in a mental state of some kind. This higher-order content will be satisfied if the creature is in fact in the relevant mental state, and the state is the way that the HOROR describes it. We are trying to capture the way things appear to us at the commonsense level. The HOROR use concepts to describe oneself as being presented with something that isn't itself conceptual (an object with such-and-such properties). We do this by

---

[6] As Rosenthal uses the term 'qualitative character,' it is a neutral term that does not bring any commitment to phenomenal consciousness with it.

targeting our mental life, but then describing it in a confused mixed sort of way.

I take it as a common starting point among theorists that conscious experience presents a world as of objects 'out there' having properties like color, shape, texture, and so on. They make sounds, they have tastes, and so on. The world as we experience it seems to be populated with all these so-called secondary properties, but they do not seem like secondary properties. That is, they do not seem like they are properties of my experience. The redness of red seems to characterize the book's cover, not my experience of the book's cover. In this way I very much take the correct phenomenology of consciously perceiving to be that of Eden, as pictured by David Chalmers (2006). This is a playful name for a possible world where subjects are directly acquainted with a primitive redness, which is in fact part of the external object's surface. In Eden, things are just as they appear.

Unfortunately, we have reason to think that our world is not Edenic, but that reason is not phenomenological! We can come to be convinced that (some of) these properties do not accurately characterize the external world, but that does not seem to me to change the way I experience it. No matter how much philosophy or science one learns, it still seems like the redness of the tomato is a property of that object.

To accommodate this, the HOROR represents one as, in effect, being in Eden. The HOROR targets one's first-order representation of red and describes it as one being directly presented—in a distinctly visual way—with a certain primitive color quality in the environment. What is phenomenologically manifest seems to be the world itself as having the properties red, round, sweet, and so on. The higher-order state, on HOROR, represents oneself as being visually presented with a property of the world. It does this by targeting the first-order seeing of red (which is itself a non-phenomenally conscious functional state) and describing it in a certain way by employing concepts to form intentional contents. This targeted first-order state, which is picked out by the pointer content, then becomes state-conscious. It may begin to have a functional impact on the system (since it has become available to the system, it may be further accessed by that system). In addition to targeting these first-order states, the HOROR is describing oneself as being in those very states. The HOROR furthermore describes those very states as being a special kind of state that puts one in a direct and unmediated relation to the worldly property—'a distinctly visual' relation to perceptible red.

We will discuss these issues in more detail in the section on introspection (3.7), but it is worth stopping here to emphasize the point. Sometimes critics of higher-order theories say, 'look, I'm not aware of any mental states or processes in ordinary perception; I'm aware of red out there!' Occasionally this will be accompanied by furious pointing to some red object in the environment. The response to this, it seems to me, is to point out that transparency claims are about what is phenomenologically manifest. The HOROR theorist agrees that this is what is phenomenologically manifest, at least in ordinary perception (I endorse a weak version of transparency, as discussed in section 3.4). The question, though, is what accounts for this being phenomenologically manifest? What explains why it is *these* things which are manifest in *this* way? Gesturing at the world is perfectly appropriate here. However, according to the higher-order approach that I'm developing, what accounts for one's phenomenal character, and therefore what is phenomenologically manifest, is the occurrence of this higher-order state that is about the first-order state. It represents you as being in the first-order state, and it also *describes* you as visually encountering a perceptible property. You deploy these concepts describing yourself as being in a state of being visually presented with a property in the external environment, and so that's the way you experience things.

That's what the content of these higher-order representations has got to be if you're going to make sense of what is phenomenologically manifest. If the higher-order state describes you as being in a state by using the concept of *mental red*, then it will seem to you as though you are in a mental state. It will not seem like you are seeing an object in the environment. At the same time, I think that this higher-order state counts as an awareness of the first-order state. The targeting relation is such that it picks out the first-order state, and the content that's descriptive says, 'the state that I'm referring to and describing in this way is the one that I'm in right now.'

The result of all this is that the HOROR is somewhat confused in the way it represents one's mental life. To have a phenomenally conscious perception as of a red tomato is to represent oneself as seeing a red tomato. This much all the higher-order camps agree on. The HOROR theory as I envision it goes on to take a particular approach to this content. One represents oneself as being in a mixed-state that is partially mental—the seeing part—and partially non-mental: the red part. One does this by becoming aware of oneself as being in the first-order state—all the while the first-order state is most likely not this way at all. The first-order state is likely a representation of the object's surface reflectance profile, or whatever physical property turns out to characterize objects we perceive as red. It is this physical property that the first-order state likely represents. This first-order mental state plays a certain role in the mental life of the organism. Yet I do not represent myself as being in a functional state representing a surface reflectance. According to the HOROR theory I am not representing myself as being in a state that merely tracks, or has the function of standing for, some physical property. I represent myself as being visually presented with a simple property of some external object.

It is for this reason that I do not think of the relevant HORORs as *re*-representing their targeted first-order states. By analogy, the first-order representation of red is not a re-representation of that property. Presumably physical red is a property of objects like surface reflectance profiles, but the mental states we deploy to represent those properties are just plain old representing them. They are not re-representing physical red.

3.2.3 Meeting the Meta Challenge

It is in this way that the HOROR theory meets the meta challenge we met back in Chapter 1. To remind ourselves, the meta-problem asks how a theory of consciousness accounts for our judgments about the nature of consciousness. In addition, it asks how some people could be led to think that it is not physical or presents a problem for science. Hopefully it is clear that if one had a HOROR as described above, then it would seem to one that one had a mental life that put one in direct contact with an external world populated with wonderfully primitive qualities. As I argued in Chapter 1, I take this to be a vindication of physicalism about phenomenal consciousness. We may take phenomenal red to be problematic because what is phenomenologically manifest is a simple qualitative property of the environment.

Chalmers mentions a view like HOROR in a footnote in the meta paper, "An interesting variant of higher-order thought theory that is driven by the meta-problem is primitive higher-order thought theory, which says that conscious states are the objects of primitive higher-order thoughts. A primitive higher-order thought is one that attributes primitive qualities and/or relations to a lower-order state" (Chalmers 2018, 38). In a way this is what the HOROR theory is doing. I do not, however, think that it is driven by the meta-problem. My desire is to capture what I think our ordinary conscious experience is like. What I care about is in some sense doing justice to what is phenomenologically manifest. It is a happy accident that the resulting view accommodates the meta challenge.

An issue with Chalmers' characterization of this kind of view is that he assumes that the phenomenally conscious states will be the *objects* of the higher-order representations, which in my language is the target of the HOROR. This makes the kind of higher-order theory that Chalmers suggests a version of what I call the traditional higher-order approach discussed in Chapter 5. I will wait until then to address the underlying assumption here.

3.3 Some predictions of the HOROR Theory

We saw in the previous section the way in which the HOROR theory proposes to address the meta-challenge. In this section we can think of ourselves as taking the first step toward addressing the Real problem from Anil Seth, which we also discussed in Chapter 1. The challenge, as we saw, was to predict and control the phenomenal consciousness of humans. What does that mean according to the HOROR theory?

3.3.1 Mismatch Cases on HOROR

The HOROR theory postulates two kinds of content, each with a different role to play, in the relevant higher-order states. Because of that there are now new ways that we can get misrepresentation cases depending on which aspect of the content is doing the misrepresentation. Consider the following cases,

1: the pointer content *accurately* points to a representation of red and the descriptive content represents one *inaccurately* as being visually presented with green
2: the pointer content *inaccurately* points to a representation of red and the descriptive content *accurately* represents one as being visually presented with green
3: the pointer content *inaccurately* points to a representation of red and the descriptive content *inaccurately* represents one as being visually presented with green
4: the pointer content points to a non-active/defective address and the descriptive content represents one as being visually presented with green

Let us now go through each of these cases.

In 1 above, suppose that one is being presented with a red rose, and a first-order state of seeing red is tokened in your mind. Suppose, then, that a HOROR representing one as seeing green targets this first-order seeing of red. The pointer content is hypothesized to target and possibly have certain functional effects upon the first-order states. This state will be routed for further processing, kept online, and so on, because of its being targeted by the higher-order representation. The targeted first-order state of seeing red is now state-conscious. But one will experience seeing green. One's phenomenal experience will be in every way indistinguishable from perceiving green because this is what it is to consciously perceive green. However, one will likely behave as though one is visually aware of red because of the enhanced functional profile of the first-order state being targeted by the HOROR.[7]

It may sound a bit odd to say that one is in a conscious-state of seeing red and consciously perceiving green, but that is only because

---

[7] One can imagine cases where this isn't the case. Perhaps the first-order state of seeing red is casually shunted off and doesn't have any noticeable effects on behavior, then the point in the text remains. However, this is presumably a rare occurrence.

of the ambiguity in what counts as a conscious state (section 2.3.1). One way we might make this point is by separating awareness from phenomenal-awareness (with a hyphen). To see red, or to be visually aware of perceptible red in the environment, and to have phenomenal-awareness, or phenomenal-seeing, of red in the environment are psychologically distinct. To see red is to be in a state that puts one in touch with the physical property that red objects have. This is the state that allows one to be 'informationally sensitive' to the environmental property in a way that allows one to think, reason, and act appropriately with respect to the property in question. To have phenomenal-seeing is for there to be something that it is like for one to see. The first-order state of seeing red cannot be phenomenally conscious on the HOROR theory. That is not the state that, when one is in it, there is something that it is like for one to be in it. On the HOROR theory that is just the occurrence of the HOROR itself. So, seeing red equals having the relevant first-order states/processes and this is distinct from phenomenal-seeing, which equals having the relevant HOROR.

What about case 2, where the targeting relation is inaccurate? This kind of case will amount to a more complex version of the previous case. Suppose that one is looking at a green leaf. If all goes well, one will thereby token a first-order representation of green (among other mental states and processes). Suppose that, as it happens, one also has a stray, perhaps weakly activated, representation of red around. One may then come to token a HOROR that targets this stray first-order state of red but describes it as a seeing of green. Once again, we have a case where there is a conscious-state of seeing red and a phenomenally conscious state of perceiving green. What it is like for one will be like seeing green, but the first-order state will come to have new functional properties because of being targeted by the HOROR.[8]

Then we have versions of 3, where both kinds of content are inaccurate. This is the most complex kind of case. Suppose that one is being presented with a purple grape and tokens a first-order seeing of

---

[8] The pointer content lists the address for the first-order red state. It will then be part of the accuracy conditions of that state that one be in the first-order state of red. In this sense the pointer content cannot be inaccurate unless one is not in the listed first-order state at all. However, the pointer is inaccurate in the sense that it is supposed to be targeting the green state.

purple. Suppose also, as before, that there is a stray first-order representation of red in one's mind. Let us just stipulate that the first-order purple state is caused by one's being visually aware of the grape and that the visual awareness of red is accidental. We can also suppose that the purple first-order state is very active, and the higher-order system attempts to label it as being a distinctly visual awareness of purple. Unfortunately, something misfires at just the right time. The HOROR that is produced tokens the address for red, not purple, and the descriptive content describes the addressed state as a seeing of green.

In this case the subject will experience green and most likely report seeing green verbally. As described so far there is no first-order representation of green in this subject's mind, but this is the way their mental life will seem to be. All the while they may behave as though they are seeing purple since we stipulated that this first-order state was very active due to being freshly caused by the physical stimulus. However, since the relevant HOROR targets the first-order representation of red, and not this first-order seeing of purple, and keeping everything else equal just to make this point, then the HOROR theory predicts that the first-order purple state will become less active, and the first-order red state may become more active. The subject may begin to act inconsistently as though they are seeing red or purple (all the while insisting that they are seeing green). If the targeting relation is psychologically real in the way posited by the HOROR theory, then we should be able to detect its functional effects. This may be one way those effects manifest.

Finally, there are versions of case 4. In these kinds of cases, one would list the address for a first-order state that was not at that moment active in the mind of the subject at all. In one case there would be no first-order state to be conscious, and so it would not be routed to working memory, selected for further processing, and so on. One would in effect be mailing a letter to an address that is non-existent. This will be reflected in the subject's behavior. They will not behave in a way that suggests that they are seeing the stimulus. Thus, there is no state that is state-conscious in this case. The pointer content tells us which first-order state(s) are being referred to, and in this case they aren't there. However, there is a state that is phenomenally conscious, and that is the HOROR itself. So even though there is no state-conscious state in this case, there is a phenomenally conscious perception of green (a phenomenal-awareness of green).

It turns out that each of the cases above will be phenomenologically indistinguishable (all other things being equal, *ceteris paribus, mutatis mutandis*, etc.). In each of the four cases above the subject will experience seeing green according to the HOROR theory. In fact, since on the HOROR theory the pointer content must be 'phenomenally silent,' varying the pointer content, though it will have functional consequences for the subject, will not affect the phenomenology of the subject in any way. In the limit one can imagine setting things up so that the pointer content points to a seeing of red and the descriptive content describes it as a hearing of an oboe. In that case one will consciously perceive the sound of an oboe (though one will not behave as though this is the case) and have a state-conscious seeing of red (one will behave as though one is seeing red). This would no doubt be subjectively quite surprising!

Accomplishing this would take a lot of effort and some very strange circumstances. Just owing to the highly interconnected nature of the brain, it is almost certain that in the typical case of ordinary day-to-day conscious experience, a change in the first-order states will cause a corresponding change in the higher-order representation. Likewise, changes in the content of the higher-order representation likely have top-down effects on the first-order states (Fleming 2020; LeDoux 2024). The result will likely be that our conscious experience closely follows our mental life, and vice versa. Still, these dissociations are possible, at least in principle.

We will explore these predictions at the neural level in the next chapter. Before doing so there is another issue to deal with, and that is the richness or sparseness of these contents.

3.3.2 Phenomenology: Sparse or Rich?

One issue that has come up in the context of higher-order theories is the richness of perception (Brown 2012a, 2015). We have discussed this previously a bit in Chapter 1 (section 1.1.3). We discussed inattentional blindness in that chapter, but it is also useful to consider change blindness. There you are, looking at the two pictures flashing in front of your eyes. To take one classic example, suppose that you are looking at a picture of a military jet on the tarmac. There are some soldiers lined up boarding the plane. One can see the military jet very prominently displayed in the center of the picture. One picture has a jet engine in your foveal area of the visual field, and the other does not. So, in effect, the jet engine is blinking in and out of existence right in front of your eyes. Yet many people fail to notice. When one is examining the pictures, looking for the difference between them (as one is instructed to do in these experiments), one gets the impression that there isn't a difference between the two pictures at all. In fact, one may begin to suspect that the psychologists are really conducting an experiment on patience. Did they really present two identical pictures without any difference, and now they are just waiting to see how long I will do this until I give up? That is, until you spot the difference! And then all you can see is the engine blinking: there, not there, there. How in the world could you have missed that?!

The question about the sparseness of perception can be put into focus by asking about your experience before you consciously noticed that the engine was the thing that was changing (or whatever example of change blindness one wants to use). The changing thing is right in front of you. You had plenty of time to look around. In fact, you were furiously searching the entire image for something changing. It seems safe to say that one must have seen the engine at one time, say T1, and then also seen the same area of the picture minus the engine at another time, say T2. One says that one did not see the difference in this interval. We can now ask whether one's experience, that is, whether what it was like for you to see these two pictures during the interval T1-T2, included the blinking engine. Were the engine and its absence phenomenologically manifest during this period?

Those who support the rich view of perception tend to think of things in the following way. One's experience captures all the details of the scene, at least for some brief limited window of time. So, much like a detailed image, one can focus in on it and examine the details anywhere one wants. The rest of the image remains there, just out of sight, waiting for us to examine it should we choose. When one shifts one's attention to some other area of the detailed image, the previous area remains as detailed as it was before, and so on. Just how rich perception is itself a matter of some dispute. There must be some lower bound just due to the physical nature of light and the eye, but at least intuitively it seems as though our experience is very rich in detail. On the rich view of perception, the engine was phenomenologically manifest at T1 and was not at T2, even if the subject did not notice. If they had been able to attend to that portion of their experience, they would have become aware of those elements of their experience. They just failed to notice what was phenomenologically manifest.

There are different ways in which one might hold a sparse view of perception. One way is to think in terms of an image on a computer screen. Suppose that one is viewing a zoomed-in portion of an image on the screen. To make it more specific let's say you are looking at a picture of a dog and have zoomed in on his neck to read the inscription on the collar. The portion of the image that one is viewing on the screen may be very detailed, but the rest of the image is not rendered off screen waiting for you to examine it. The file you have stored on your hard drive may have enough information in it to render a detailed image of the entire dog when zoomed out to its original size. So, what is on the screen is just a portion of the relevant file. In that sense it is sparse.

To use the jet-engine example from above, let's suppose that one is in fact in first-order states that encode all of the relevant details. One has alternating first-order representations of the engine as being there, and then not there the entire time (let's suppose). Now suppose that one came to have a HOROR to the effect that one was seeing the jet-with-its-engine. Then let's suppose that there is a highly accurate description of the jet engine in one's HOROR, and to make things simple let's suppose that none of these facts change for the duration of the time we are talking about. Of course, nothing is this simple, but let's just make this assumption to illustrate the point. Finally, suppose that this HOROR was targeting both states, but described them as just being one unchanging state. Given all this, the HOROR theory says we would have a case where the subject experienced no change even though the state-conscious states of which they were aware were in fact changing. This is a kind of sparseness relative to the first-order level even though the phenomenology can be very detailed. The jet engine with all of its detail may have been phenomenologically manifest, but the first-order states had detail that is missing from the higher-order representation. For lack of a better term, I call this relative-sparseness since it is sparse only relative to the content of the first-order state(s).

Another way perception might be sparse would be in terms of abstract or generic content. One might hold that what is phenomenologically manifest is just 'impressionistic sketches' that leave open what color something is, or how many fingers a hand has, and so on. In the previous case we were imaging that the 'zoomed in' portion of the 'mental image' was rendered in a great amount of detail, or at least enough for you to read the inscription on the dog's collar. Alternatively, we might imagine that instead of zooming in and getting the details of the collar's inscription, we may zoom in and find the zoomed-in portion blurry and distorted. The result may be that one can sort of tell that there are some letters on the collar, but one cannot make out what exactly it says. The image may merely represent something like 'there are some letters in a certain font here,' and correspondingly one may think that one can have sparse experience in the sense of experiencing vague 'letter-like' things as opposed to the detail mentioned before. Again, for lack of a better term, I call this absolute-sparseness. The term 'absolute' has many meanings. For my purpose I want to emphasize that the sparseness is not relative to the first-order content but is just sparse on its own.

This would give us an alternative interpretation of the change blindness scenario we were just discussing. In the previous case we imagined that the detail was in the first-order representations and that the higher-order representation just represented the two states as being an unchanging single state with a lot of detail. In this case we can imagine that the higher-order state represents the very same first-order states in a vague or generic way. Perhaps the area where the engine is located is represented in an indeterminate way that leaves open whether there is a shadow there, or a jet engine, or something else. One might have the following kind of representation,

I am seeing an airplane and its parts in great detail[9]

In this case one would experience some general or partial content but experience it as though it presented a great amount of detail; and that detail may or may not be actually represented in the first-order state-conscious states of the organism.

There can be mixtures of these as well. Someone might hold that in the center of our visual field there is relative-sparse content in the sense that there is a great amount of detail in the first-order states, but the content in the higher-order state is a detailed rendering of some smaller portion of it. Then, as you move out to the periphery, one might argue that you find more absolute-sparse contents in the sense that these representations assert general, or vague, or partial contents.

3.3.3 Rich and Sparse HOROR

What lessons can we draw from this general discussion of the richness of phenomenology and the different kinds of sparseness we may find? How does all of this apply to the HOROR theory?

What we want is a theory that can account for what is phenomenologically manifest to us. That is to say that the HOROR theory is a theory of phenomenology. So, if the typical experience of a person is rich, then we posit corresponding rich contents for the relevant HORORs. If the typical experience of a subject is sparse, then we posit sparse contents for the HORORs. We start with the phenomenology and then we theorize, not the other way around.

The primary objection against this way of approaching the theory involves either the fineness of grain of the first-order states, or alternatively the deficiency of concepts available for deploying in the higher-order states. We will discuss my reasons for thinking this is not a decisive objection in Chapter 4. In addition to this there has been

---

[9] As we have seen I think that the 'I am ... ' should be cashed out along the lines of 'The entity in which those very states are occurring is ...,' but for brevity I revert back to 'I am ... ' from now on.

healthy skepticism that the detailed rich contents posited by rich versions of HOROR would be found in the brain. If so, then so much the worse for rich versions of HOROR theory. We want a theory of phenomenal consciousness, and if this theory cannot account for a real aspect of phenomenal consciousness, then the theory should be modified so that it can account for that aspect, or it should be abandoned.

At the very least we can see that there are varieties of HOROR and that we want to distinguish rich versions of HOROR from sparse versions of HOROR. Let us think through a couple of examples from the HOROR perspective. Let's start with a kind of Sperling type case. Suppose that one is briefly presented with an array consisting of the following letters arranged in a block:

```
a     d     l
g     r     w
x     h     u
```

and then asked to name the letters from a cued row after the array had disappeared from the screen. The cued row could wither be the top, middle, or bottom. What is happening in the mind of the person?

Drawing on our discussions from the previous sections we can distinguish the following three cases,

> Case I: There are rich representations of the letters and their identities in a lower-order state (or set of states). There is a HOROR that targets that first-order state (or set of states) and accurately describes the subjects as seeing the following letters arranged in a block: 'a' in upper left, 'd' in upper middle, 'l' in the upper right; 'g' in the middle left, 'r' in the middle middle, 'w' in the middle right; 'x' in the lower right, 'h' in the lower middle, 'u' in the lower right
>
> Case II: There are rich representations of the letters and their identities in a lower-order state. There is a HOROR that targets that first-order state (or set of states) and describes the subject as seeing the letters 'r' in middle middle, 'd' in upper middle, 'l' in upper right, *and some other letters as well*, arranged in a block

Case III: there are sparse representations of the letters and their identities in a lower-order state. There is a HOROR that targets that first-order state (or set of states) and describes the subjects as being in a situation like either case 1 or case 2 above

The subjects in cases I and II have the same state-conscious mental states. Both are aware of themselves as being in the rich first-order state. However, the phenomenology of the two subjects will differ in the two cases.

The subject in case I will experience a rich and detailed phenomenology of the letters and their arrangement. The subject in case II will have a much sparser phenomenology. This will be filled out in detail where they are attending, giving them relative-sparse content as I defined it. There is more in the first-order state than is rendered in the higher-order state, but what is rendered by the higher-order state is in great detail. The rest is absolute-sparse content. Thus, subjects in case I and subjects in case II will be in different phenomenally conscious states even while being in the same state-conscious state, as discussed in section 2.2.[10]

The subject who was unable to secure the targeting relation to the appropriate lower-order states will have a different behavioral profile from the other subjects. Recall that the targeting content is postulated to keep the first-order state online, or route it to working memory, or other forms of processing that result in the control of behavior. It is in this way that the HOROR theory tries to capture the idea that consciousness is the gateway to cognition. Consciousness 'greases the wheels of access' via the targeting relation in the HOROR, but that does not mean that this shows up in the phenomenology.

Both case I and case II need to be distinguished from case III, where some of the sparseness is located at the lower-order level. We will discuss the empirical quest to find versions of these cases in Chapter 4. Before turning to that, though, we will round out our presentation of the HOROR theory with an account of introspection.

---

[10] This may be a case where the difference in what is phenomenologically manifest in these two cases is yet subjectively indistinguishable.

3.4 HOROR Theory for Introspective Consciousness

We will spend a lot of time with the traditional higher-order theory in Chapters 5 through 7, but we will jump ahead slightly here to talk about introspection on the HOROR theory. The HOROR theory, as I see it, is compatible with any theory of introspection that one likes. I have my preferences and will argue for them below, but this is another part of the theory that can be adjusted by those who may be likeminded but prefer a different account of introspection.

3.4.1 The Traditional Higher-Order Theory of Introspection

The way the traditional higher-order account of introspection works is as follows. Suppose that one is having an unconscious perception of something in the environment. Then, on the traditional view, one is in an unconscious qualitative state and a first-order perceptual belief to the effect that something is in the environment. On the traditional view, most clearly articulated by David Rosenthal, one is thereby aware of the object in the environment, but one is not consciously aware of that object. To be consciously aware of the object one must not only have the relevant first-order perceptual states but also token the appropriate THOT (traditional higher-order thought) to the effect that one is in the relevant first-order perceptual state. Then one is consciously aware of the object in the environment. On Rosenthal's account one's conscious states are directed at the world and its properties, which is just to say that it is the first-order states that are conscious according to the traditional view, as we will discuss in Chapters 5 and 6.

When one introspects, on the traditional approach, one's THOT itself becomes conscious in virtue of having a third-order THOT to the effect that one is in the second-order THOT. Rosenthal interprets this as a shift in the focus of one's conscious states (Rosenthal 2005). Before introspecting the focus of the subject's conscious states (which is to say the focus of their first-order states) was the world and its properties. Once the subject introspects, it is then the case that they are now consciously aware of being in the first-order state. Their awareness (which is the THOT) of the mental qualities is itself now conscious.

This is all commonsensical, and I do not disagree with the general idea that Rosenthal is trying to capture. The issue is in the way that the traditional approach implements these commonsense ideas. According to the traditional approach what it is like for me is completely determined by the relevant THOT. If so, then that will also be the case for the third-order THOT. It should determine what it is like for me according to the traditional higher-order view. In the case of introspection, it should be the case that what it is like for me when I introspect will be like having a conscious thought. It will be a thought that is phenomenologically manifest. Furthermore, the way in which it manifests is as a thinking of a thought, not the having of an experience. What this means is that from my subjective first-person point of view the thought 'I am seeing a red tomato' will appear. However, having a conscious thought and having an experience of introspective consciousness are not the same thing (Renero and Brown 2022).

As I see things, it is the case that sometimes when I am having ordinary conscious experience, I do find myself having these kinds of conscious thoughts. Yet, it is puzzling how this could be the case on the traditional higher-order approach. These THOTs are supposed to be the states that engender phenomenal consciousness (Berger and Brown 2021), but when they are conscious it seems to me like I am having a conscious thought, not an episode of introspective consciousness (cf. Gottleib 2015).

3.4.2 Introspection and Transparency

It seems to me that there is a sense in which I seem to be directly acquainted with phenomenal qualities in my introspective experience. Some may think this conflicts with their sense of transparency of the mental. I hope this is not the case because I share some affinity with a weak version of transparency.

To clarify things, I think it is useful to take David Chalmers' (Chalmers 2013b) distinctions from his response to a commentary by Benj Hellie. Hellie argues for an austere version of transparency and here is Chalmers' clarifying taxonomy, "The general form of a transparency thesis is that it is (i) difficult/impossible to stand in (ii) a certain relation to (iii) certain mental properties or entities. Perhaps the most important dimension of variation involves (iii): this may involve intrinsic qualities, the awareness relation, phenomenal character, mental states in general, and so on. The relation in (ii) may be attention, direct attention, awareness, introspection, and so on. The dimension in (i) can involve at least difficulty (call this prima facie transparency) or impossibility (call this absolute transparency)."

Chalmers continues this passage by applying this general form of a transparency thesis to specific defenders of transparency we find in the literature.

> Using this regimentation, we can talk of the prima facie transparency of awareness to attention (Moore), the absolute transparency of intrinsic features to attention (Harman), the absolute transparency of phenomenal states to direct attention (Tye), or the absolute transparency of phenomenal states to attention (Hellie). Other transparency theses might include the absolute transparency of experiences to thing-awareness (Dretske), and the absolute transparency of the self to introspection (Hume), and the transparency of belief to direct introspection (Evans). Perhaps one can assume that "absolute" and "attention" serve as default values, so that we can simply talk of Harman's thesis as the transparency of intrinsic features, Moore's thesis as the prima facie transparency of awareness, Hellie's as the transparency of phenomenal character (or just phenomenal transparency), and so on. (http://consc.net/papers/contents.pdf, 2–3)

I have always found these distinctions, and the discussion that follows it, to be helpful in thinking about these issues.

Especially enlightening is the discussion of phenomenal attention and the argument against absolute transparency theses. When I take off my glasses while I am reading the text on the screen, everything is suddenly blurry, and I attend to that blurriness almost involuntarily. But, as Chalmers notes, I am not representing anything in the environment as changing. I have an experience that is crisp and sharp of the letters on the screen followed by a fuzzy and blurry experience of the same letters. The difference is in how I experience what I am aware of in the environment, not in the things of which I am aware. It is a difference in what is phenomenologically manifest to me. This is a difference I can spontaneously attend to in some sense. When I take my glasses off, I become spontaneously aware of my phenomenal consciousness and its associated properties.

To see this, contrast this case of me taking off my glasses with the case of me before I knew that I needed glasses. I had always had very good vision, and yet as I aged slowly over time my vision was getting worse without my noticing it. In fact, in an ultimate *mea culpa*, while writing a book review, I complained that the printing of a certain article was poorly done because the text was blurry and hard to read. It was only years later, after getting glasses and rereading the relevant text, that I noticed that the 'blurry' passages were just printed in a font that was smaller than the rest of the text. The blurriness was entirely absent now that I had my glasses! I took my glasses off and the familiar blurriness re-appeared (as well as a certain sinking feeling of guilt about the review). So, the me-before-getting-glasses experience was as of a blurry page, but I mistakenly experienced that blurriness as attaching to the text itself. That is, I thought that I was having a sharp-experience-of-a-blurry-page rather than a blurry-experience-of-a-sharp-page.

In the former case, taking off my glasses leads me to spontaneously attend to what it was like for me, while in the latter case of having blurred vision without knowing I remained wholly focused on the external environment. If what it is like for me is absolutely transparent to attention, then it would always be like the latter case for me. Things would always seem as though they were happening in the external environment. There are two lessons we can draw from this. The first is that many, if not all, of the absolute transparency theses are plausibly false. The second is that introspective consciousness involves a kind of phenomenal consciousness. There is something that it is like for me to attend to what it is like for me.

Someone who wanted to defend the transparency thesis might object that the difference in the cases above is not in my experience but is instead in a post-perceptual judgment. In both cases, the objector supposes, I have the same stuff being phenomenologically manifest. In one case I judge this to be the world that is blurry and in the other

I judge it to be my experience that is blurry. In both cases I am making a judgment based on exactly the same phenomenal character. The difference in the content of the judgement, the objector continues, is explained by background differences in my cognitive states, what I believe, and so on. This may be one consistent interpretation, but I find it to be phenomenologically implausible. It certainly seems to me like something changes when I take off my glasses. It seems like my experience got blurry. It doesn't seem to me that world appeared to get blurry and then I reasoned my way to the belief that it must be my experience that was blurry. At the very least I would like a theory that allows that it is possible that we can attend to our experience in this way.

How does the traditional higher-order approach handle this kind of case? When I take my glasses off and spontaneously notice that my vision is blurry, according to the traditional higher-order account of introspection, I come to have a third-order THOT and thereby have a conscious second-order THOT. What it is like for me will be like consciously thinking 'my vision is blurry.' This may be a deliverance of introspection, as I do find myself thinking these kinds of conscious thoughts on occasion, however, these kinds of conscious thoughts seem to me to be the *result* of a kind of introspective experience whereby I attend to my own mental processes.

This seems to be a kind of introspective consciousness that cannot be captured by having a third-order THOT. The traditional higher-order view is compatible with the displaced perception model of introspection. At the very least some may want to supplement the traditional account in order to capture the kind of introspective consciousness we have been talking about.

3.4.3 HORIFIC: Higher-Order Representation Intentionally for Introspective Consciousness

Adriana Renero and I have developed an account of introspection for the HOROR theory that we called Higher-Order Representation Intentionally for Introspective Consciousness, or HORIFIC (Renero and Brown 2022). The kind of introspective consciousness that we are considering does not involve the introduction of a novel phenomenal quality at the first-order level. Nor is there the becoming aware of some new part of my first-order representations. There is the experience of focusing on the awareness of the mental quality that was already there. The change in one's phenomenal consciousness has to do with the attentiveness, focus, clarity, and sometimes deliberateness, with which one is aware of one's mental life. Since the HOROR theory is a representational theory of phenomenal consciousness, it seems natural to say this will amount to a change in the representational contents of the relevant HORORs.

In what way does one's higher-order contents change? Suppose that I am wearing my glasses and looking at a red ripe tomato in my environment, then according to the HOROR theory if I am having a phenomenally conscious seeing of the tomato, then I have a HOROR with something like the following content,

I am visually aware of a (perceptibly) red tomato

Then I take my glasses off and my attention spontaneously shifts from the tomato in my environment to my awareness of it. That amounts to a change in the content of the HOROR in something like the following way,

I am experiencing course-grained visual awareness of a (perceptibly) red tomato

In the case where I wasn't aware that it was my experience that was blurry, I might have a different HOROR.
Something to the effect that,

I am visually aware of course-grained (perceptible) red

So, in this case one will experience the world as being blurry, and in the other case one will experience one's experience of the world being blurry.

In both cases the pointer content of the relevant HOROR would quite possibly remain constant. In that case, then, one is aware of oneself as being in the same first-order state in all three cases. In the case of ordinary phenomenal consciousness, one is aware of that state as presenting a perceptible property to one visually, whereas in introspection one is aware of the state as oneself experiencing the visual presentation of the perceptible property.

That concludes my presentation of the HOROR theory. I think of this as an interesting and neglected version of the higher-order approach to consciousness, but I haven't yet argued for it. That is the job of Chapter 4.

4
HOROR in the Brain

Having arrived at this point we need to ask what reasons we have for taking the theory seriously. The HOROR theory occupies a point in logical space and, considering the shombie argument discussed in Chapter 1, may even be a possible candidate for a physicalist account of phenomenal consciousness in some possible world or other. What reasons are there, though, for thinking that the HOROR theory may be true in the actual world?

In section 4.1, I argue that the only reasons to take a theory of consciousness seriously are empirical. In section 4.2, I examine the question of how we should map our psychological states to neural states. In section 4.2.1, I examine the relation of HOROR theory to the prefrontal cortices. In section 4.2.2, I do the same with respect to the sensory cortices. In section 4.2.3, I take up the question of the neural coding of HORORs. In section 4.2.4, I look at the argument against conceptual representations based on fears that the cortex cannot handle the required amount of conceptual representations. In section 4.3, I put all this together and begin to spell out specific neural implementations of the specific versions of the HOROR theory. Of particular interest is the distinction between sparse and rich HOROR theories developed in section 4.3.1. Finally in section 4.4, I examine the existing empirical support for HOROR theory. I end the chapter, in section 4.4.1, by discussing the case for subjective inflation.

4.1 The Empirical Motivation for HOROR

Traditionally, those who defend higher-order theories start with what they call the Transitivity Principle. The basic idea behind this principle was floated by David Rosenthal in a paper defending materialism against dualist objections (Rosenthal 1980). It was subsequently developed in his 1986 paper "Two Concepts of Consciousness" (Rosenthal 1986) and has come to be thought of as the defining commitment of higher-order theories by most philosophers.[1]

As we have seen in the previous chapters, I interpret the Transitivity Principle as a claim about state-consciousness, not about phenomenal consciousness. I therefore deny that the Transitivity Principle can allow us to get ahold of the data that we want to explain. Also, as we saw in Chapter 2, the existence of the ascending road shows that more needs to be said than merely the Transitivity Principle in order to differentiate higher-order theories from first-order theories. I also deny that it helps us define the goal of a theory of consciousness. Even if one were to interpret the Transitivity Principle in terms of phenomenal consciousness (Berger and Brown 2021), I think it is very contentious to say that commonsense rules out the transparency of experience or prevents there being a kind of phenomenological overflow. We will discuss this in detail in Chapters 5 and 6, but for now we can say that I reject the traditional way of defending or arguing for the higher-order approach to consciousness.

While I do think that there is a commonsense platitude in the area, namely one that connects phenomenal consciousness to being aware of my own inner life (section 2.1.1), I also think there is a folk-psychological platitude that denies that and asserts something like transparency (when I try to become aware of my mental life I end up focusing on the world, not my mind). It is not clear that folk-psychology rules out phenomenological overflow either. Folk-psychology can be an inspiration for theorizing. That is what I take the Transitivity Principle to in fact be. It is a theoretical projection from folk-psychology. It can only be vindicated by passing the tribunal of empirical science.

As we saw in Chapter 1, I take the central challenge of consciousness science to be adjudicating between the *currently existing* theories of human phenomenal consciousness that are deemed to be 'contenders' by the scientific community. These theories may not be

---

[1] As far as I can tell, the phrase 'Transitivity Principle' does not show up until 2005 (Rosenthal 2005).

final. All of them may end up being completely misguided, or each of them may have only part of the story. That remains to be seen. What we do know is that there are a handful of significant ideas that have been worked out in enough detail that we can begin to see what kinds of predictions they may make. Unfortunately, many theories make the same predictions! What we would like to see is which predictions a theory makes that will falsify it, or at least challenge a central tenant of the theory, or at the very least distinguish it from other theories.

According to me, the only reasons for taking the higher-order approach seriously at all—any version of it—are the following:

A. The theory is consistent with what we know so far, which is to say there is a plausible interpretation of existing experimental results in terms of the theory
B. The theory makes testable falsifying/differentiating predictions and empirically 'passes' this tribunal in the sense of getting the empirical results that are consistent with the theory

In fact, I would say that these are the only reasons for taking any theory of consciousness seriously. Of course, this betrays my physicalist leanings, but for those who lean in the other direction we can say that these are the reasons for taking a proposed theory seriously as a theory of the neural correlates of consciousness.

A and B make no mention of the Transitivity Principle. There is no begging the question about transparency or phenomenological overflow. Nor are there grandiose claims about folk-psychology, or a priori conceptual analysis. There is just the workaday claim that the best reason to motivate a theory of phenomenal consciousness lies in passing empirical hurdles, which, in part, means making falsifying/ challenging predictions. This is why we should accept higher-order theories if we do. So, of course, folk-psychology and a priori reasoning can serve as a starting point for theorizing, but they do not give us the reasons to take a theory seriously. To paraphrase Hume, Nature retains the rights to foil our deepest theoretical desires. Much of what has been done in consciousness science up until now has focused on A. Someone proposes a theory of consciousness, say Global

Workspace Theory, and then one constructs an interpretation of existing experimental results in terms of it. We need to move beyond that strategy. It is time to start pitting the predictions of our contender theories against each other.

The problem with this has been that, up until now, the predictions have not been fine-grained enough to allow us to differentiate the various theories. At this point we are still arguing largely about whether the 'front' or 'back' of the brain is where we should be looking for the neural activity that underlies these mental phenomena (Odegaard et al. 2017; Melloni et al. 2023). Different theories can generally be divided into whether they think prefrontal areas are important for consciousness, but this is an incredibly coarse-grained way to classify theories. Different theories may agree that the prefrontal areas are required, and yet have very different interpretations of what activity in those areas is doing, or even which of the many different prefrontal areas are involved.

The HOROR theory predicts that the neural correlates of consciousness are the neural correlates of the HOROR, whatever that turns out to be. There is no direct implication from the HOROR theory to neural implementation because the HOROR theory is a psychological theory. Consciousness is a psychological phenomenon, after all. So, to make any kind of prediction about the brain, you need to connect the psychology to the neuroscience. To do that, one needs to specify a way in which the psychological level theoretical posits are implemented in the brain. To specify a *neural implementation* of a psychological theory is to give an account of how it is that the proposed neural machinery carries out the tasks/functions specified at the psychological level. We are not in a position yet to say what kind of code the brain may use to implement inner awareness, but can we say anything about the neural implementation of HOROR theory?[2]

---

[2] It is worth noting here that there may be versions of higher-order theory that deny that there is any neural implementation of the theory in the sense I mean. One could take the relevant psychological states to merely be theoretical posits that help us make sense of folk-psychological and laboratory data without actually being implemented in the neural workings of the brain. This would be a kind of operationalist account of the mind akin to Dennett's intentional stance.

4.2 Mapping Psychological States to Neural States

There is a tendency for people to conflate two senses of 'higher-order' in the debates about higher-order theories of consciousness. On the one hand there is an established neuroscientific sense of the phrase that is related to the processing hierarchy we think exists in the brain. A 'higher-order' area in this sense would be processing information about relatively high-level visual features, maybe faces for example. We typically divide the visual areas of the brain into 'primary' visual areas, V1, processing relatively low-level features of objects, all the way to higher-order visual areas processing information about fully formed objects, say the fusiform face area in the temporal lobe. One may also see the prefrontal cortex as 'higher-order' in this sense since it arguably sits at the top of the entire processing hierarchy (Passingham 2021).

However, as we have seen, this is not the sense of higher-order that we mean to invoke when discussing higher-order theories of consciousness. There 'higher-order' means specifically a kind of inner awareness of something mental as opposed to outer awareness of the world. Because of this ambiguity, a brain area can be higher-order in the hierarchical sense, say processing high-level visual features of a stimulus, but not higher-order in the philosophical sense, since visual features of a stimulus are non-mental stimulus items. Where, then, should we expect to find the neural activity associated with these states of inner awareness?

4.2.1 Inner Awareness and the Prefrontal Cortices[3]

Hakwan Lau argues (Lau 2022) that we have empirical reasons to think that metacognition and consciousness share overlapping neural circuits in the prefrontal cortex. Therefore, it's reasonable to think that maybe the prefrontal cortex is importantly involved in phenomenal consciousness. Lau has suggested dorsolateral prefrontal cortex and related areas in that general prefrontal area might be important (ibid.).

---

[3] this section draws from Brown Richard (2025) "How to Interpret LeDoux's Mltistate Heirachical Theory of consciousness" Cerebral Cortex, Volume 35, Issue 1, January 2025, Pages 84–87, https://doi.org/10.1093/cercor/bhae389

Joseph LeDoux on the other hand has argued we should look at other areas in the prefrontal cortex for largely anatomical reasons (LeDoux and Brown 2017; LeDoux 2019, 2024). Our experience is not just of shapes and colors, but also emotional, based on memory, and infused with a sense of self; that this is happening to me, now, that the red sphere is an apple, and so on. If we are to have more than merely sensory input, LeDoux argues, we need to look beyond areas that process sensory information to areas that process semantic and episodic memory as well. The areas in the brain associated with these processes feed into the prefrontal cortex, but not to the dorsal lateral prefrontal cortex. There is more input to ventral medial areas and the frontal pole. LeDoux suggests that these areas may form a 'higher-order network' (LeDoux 2024).

So, we have two proposals about where in the prefrontal cortex the relevant higher-order neural activity may be found. However, the prefrontal interpretation is not the only game in town. Rocco Gennaro is another higher-order theorist, and he thinks we shouldn't be looking at things related to abstract conceptual processing about our sensory processing (like LeDoux), or metacognition (like Lau), but instead things related to pre-reflective self-consciousness (Gennaro 2012). We will discuss Gennaro's version of the traditional higher-order theory in Chapter 6. For now, the important point is that if you're thinking in terms of self-consciousness, you're going to look at different areas in the brain. Areas related to self-consciousness include the medial and inferior parietal cortex, as well as the temporal cortex, posterior cingulate cortex, and the anterior cingulate (which many consider an honorary member of the PFC) (Gennaro 2012). But there may even be this kind of activity in the hippocampus (so-called allocortex) according to Gennaro.

Finally, there is Axel Cleermans' view that the relevant neural activity could be anywhere in the cortex because it is whole cortical higher-order learning that matters for consciousness (Cleermans et al. 2020).[4] This covers all the bases!

---

[4] Put into the language that we have been developing, I view Cleermans' SOMA account as a specific connectionist implementation of the traditional higher-order theories. By this I mean that the account appeals to non-conceptual meta-representations that are learned by monitoring the activity of various lower-order states.

The lesson from this is that it is currently a matter of some dispute which areas of the brain might be crucial for the kind of inner awareness we are seeking to understand. There is no strong link between the higher-order theory per se and the prefrontal cortexes. Each of the versions of higher-order theory mentioned above, with their posited neural implementations, provides an empirical hypothesis that should generate testable predictions.

Abstracting away from the specifics of the debate about higher-order theories, I think the jury is still out on whether prefrontal cortex is importantly involved consciousness. There are some reasons to think maybe it is involved (Michel 2022), and some reasons to doubt it (Kozuch 2021). The HOROR theory is consistent with both kinds of neural implementation and makes specific predictions about what we should find in each implementation scenario. This should be viewed as an unresolved empirical matter.

4.2.2 Perception and the Sensory Cortices

When you look at the other end of the spectrum, you get similar sorts of issues when you try to figure out where the first-order state is. If we set aside the question about which states are phenomenally conscious, we can ask the more general question of where in the brain we will find the first-order representational states.

Sticking, as we have been, to vision, should we look in V1? Do we require recurrent processing or feedback first? If so, is it specifically to V1 (Lamme 2018)? Or just in general (Block 2019)? Or perhaps first-order states are to be found at a more intermediate stage of the processing hierarchy (Prinz 2012). If so, then the states in V4 may be the relevant first-order states. Or one might take an even more global view of first-order states in that perhaps they are complex states comprising most of the visual cortex (Fleming 2020). An even more global view of the first-order states is to argue that they are the ones that are globally broadcast, or the ones that the Attention Schema models. If so, then we would expect to find states with first-order content in the prefrontal cortex. Joe LeDoux's multi-state hierarchical view is an example (LeDoux 2019, 2023). On his view the neural states in the frontal poles represent states in the non-granular areas of the prefrontal cortex, which count as the lower-order states of which we are aware (Brown 2024). Importantly, these lower-order states are found in the prefrontal cortex themselves. LeDoux has jokingly called this a HO HO version of HOROR theory (LeDoux 2024) because the states that are targeted by the relevant HOROR are themselves higher-order and found in the prefrontal cortex.

So far, we have seen there is debate about which brain regions we should expect to be involved in the various psychological roles we have been postulating. But it gets worse!

4.2.3 Neural Coding of HORORs

Even if we knew where in the brain to look for the relevant higher-order representations, we would then face the question of what kind of activity is important. We know something about which areas of the brain are active, but we do not know what that activity is doing. It is as though I am viewing thermal imaging of a restaurant from across the street. I can say where the cooking is taking place. I might even be able to determine whether the oven or stove is being used. If I could correlate that with what patrons were ordering, I might be able to make some guesses about what is being cooked in the kitchen based on my thermal imaging. But I would not be able to say anything about the recipe being used, what the cooks were doing, which pans were being used, and so on. This is the level at which most of our empirical science of consciousness has been based.

To illustrate these issues consider finding neurons in the prefrontal cortex that respond to faces in much the same way as neurons in the fusiform face area do. Suppose that we could use prefrontal neurons to 'read out' the content and 'decode' whether the face the subject was presented with was happy or sad from these prefrontal neurons. So, is this activity associated with first-order representations of faces? Or is it associated with higher-order activity related to our visual processing of faces? On one reading the activity is about some physical object (a face), while on the other it is about something mental, visual processing of the face. In short, is this activity, at the psychological level, a representation of seeing a face (and so higher-order)? Or just a representation of a face (and so first-order)? Or maybe something else entirely? We would need to know a lot more about the actual nature of neural coding and the exact kind of content, if any, this activity correlated with, to answer this question. We may eventually be able to do this sort of thing, but we are nowhere near being able to do that now. At this point we must take all the neural evidence with a grain of salt. That doesn't mean we can't conduct experiments and see where they point. We can and should. We should also be aware that we run the danger of stepping on our own feet with our lack of understanding.

There are several concrete examples of this playing out in the literature. One is Miguel Ángel Sebastián's (2013) use of the finding that prefrontal cortex is relatively deactivated during dream experience as an argument against higher-order theories. As discussed in Chapter 1, dreams are widely taken to be vivid phenomenal experiences. Sebastián argues that as a result we should expect increased activity in the relevant areas on the assumption that there are more representations when we have vivid conscious experience. I can see the intuitive pull of the idea that less blood flow amounts to less neural activity, which then amounts to fewer higher-order representations. Unless we know exactly what it is that neural activity is doing, I don't think we get anything more than intuitive pull from that consideration. If the HOROR theory is on the right track, then it makes a prediction about dream cases. If there is vivid phenomenal consciousness during dreams, then there should be some neural instantiation of a rich HOROR. To say more than that requires an understanding of how these HORORs would be coded at the neural level.

For another example, consider the question of whether the brain uses a neural code that allows for compositionality at the neural level for these higher-order states. Perhaps the higher-order states have components of their content encoded by separate neural codes, or perhaps they use repeatable or 'content-invariant' codes. For example, in the HOROR 'I am seeing red' and 'I am seeing green' is there a neural pattern of activity which is distinct for each of these representations? Or will there be elements which are 'compositional' in the sense that the same neural activity represents the same aspect of the higher-order state? 'I am seeing ____' is common between the two representations, and so maybe there will be some commonality in the neural code underlying them as well. It should be possible to empirically differentiate these views. We are seeing some movement in that direction and will discuss it in more detail in Chapter 7 (7.4.1).

Adding to the mess is that other theories posit a role for the prefrontal cortex. This is why in Michel 2022 he uses 'prefrontalism' to name the view that the prefrontal cortex is importantly involved in phenomenal consciousness. To adjudicate among theories that all invoke activity in the prefrontal cortex, we need to know more about how the brain functions. For example, many people take the 'global ignition' of neural activity to reflect some content entering the global workspace. But Steve Fleming (Fleming 2020) has suggested that perhaps this activity reflects a higher-order network back-propagating information to correct first-order states (as in his HOSS model discussed in Chapter 7). Even the recurrent processing/feedback some associate with first-order activity (Lamme 2018) has been hypothesized to reflect a higher-order process at the psychological level. For example, perhaps recurrent feedback in the brain reflects the higher-order state interacting with the first-order representations it targets (Gennaro 2012) instead of first-order processes.

The take-home message from all of this is that we are still in the very early stages of mapping our theoretical posits at the psychological level to neural functioning. No strong conclusions can be drawn about the neural implementation of the various theories we have discussed. Because of this, we cannot say which animals or creatures are capable of the kind of higher-order representations the HOROR theory postulates. The kinds of higher-order representations I am envisioning could, in principle, be had by any typical mammal or bird it seems. Could bees have higher-order representations? Possibly. To answer that question, we first need to understand how brains instantiate representations at all. Obviously, we cannot do that yet. But if bees are phenomenally conscious, then they are probably capable of higher-order representations as HOROR theory sees them. I see this as another reason that the science of consciousness is better off focusing on human consciousness rather than animal consciousness for the moment.

4.2.4 Higher-Order Non-Conceptual States?

Before moving on to discuss the way that I think we should proceed given the discussion of the previous sections, there is another lesson I think we can draw from this discussion. I have suggested that the relevant HORORs will have conceptual and pointer contents, but there is a widespread belief that this may pose too difficult a task for the cognitive machinery of the brain (Carruthers 2000; Gottleib 2022; Lau 2022). Considering this, some have proposed that the relevant higher-order states must have non-conceptual content (Sebastián 2022a). People can mean many things by 'non-conceptual,' but there is a somewhat standardized notion involving state-non-conceptual. What this means is that the state will have content that the organism lacks concepts needed to specify. Others have used this as an argument against views like HOROR altogether. I think we should be highly skeptical of these worries.

First, I do not see any reason to think that the conceptual HORORs pose too much of a burden on the brain. We are not able to say how it is that the brain encodes these kinds of higher-order states. Even the cutting edge in this is in the early stages (Frankland and Green 2020a). A recent idea is that one may represent linguistic conceptual items in a map-like manner (Frankland and Green 2022b), which may interestingly impact these discussions. We are in very early days here. These objections sound to me a bit like someone being skeptical that the brain generates and uses electrical currents because the propagation speed of the nerve impulse, or action potential, is much slower that the speed of electrical current through a wire (see Piccolino and Bresadola 2013 for an excellent overview of this scientific drama). Or someone who doubted that the synapse was truly a chemical event whereby the electrical current in the action potential triggers the release of chemicals known as neurotransmitters, on the basis that it was too slow to implement the speed at which we can react (see Vallenstein 2005 for an equally excellent overview of this equally fascinating scientific drama).

It turns out that the brain does generate and use electrical current. It does so in a uniquely biological way involving the entry and exit of charged ions (sodium, potassium, and calcium mostly, though there are others). It also turns out that these biologically generated electrical signals do in fact synapse and get translated into a chemical event that depends on the relatively slow process of diffusion. It also turns out that all of this is quick enough to explain our rection times. To establish this scientifically required very hard empirical work. It was well over two hundred years, and a lot of acrimonious disputes, from the discovery of 'animal electricity' to an understanding of the electrical and chemical aspects of neural transmission.

It should be further kept in mind that we are only about fifty years away from these findings being generally accepted in the scientific community. The optimism with which certain assumptions are made is a little baffling considering the history of our endeavor. The only thing one can conclude from even a cursory glance at the history of this stuff is that we should be humble in the face of our ignorance, yet bold in our attempts to chip away at that ignorance empirically. I do not mean to suggest that we will in fact find out that there are conceptual representations importantly involved in consciousness. My claim is that this is an empirical matter and that one cannot dismiss a theory of consciousness based on one's intuitions about what the brain should be able to do. It is reasonable to be suspicious, but these suspicions must be empirically grounded and empirically arbitrated.[5]

We have some ideas about how the brain may encode these things, but this is not known in enough detail to rule out a theory a priori. As we have seen in the previous chapter, I view all these as empirical challenges that await arbitration. How, then, should we proceed?

---

[5] We should note that the HOROR theory is compatible with state-non-conceptual content. All that entails is that there is some state that has content and that the subject fails to have the concepts needed to specify the content. Suppose one had a first-order representation of a specific shade of red, and that one did not have the concept for that shade of red but did have the concept for color more generally. Then one could have an experience of color by having a HOROR that deployed that concept, but since one did not have the concept for the specific shade of red, that first-order content is state-non-conceptual. This seems to me to be a plausible response to Ned Block's recent (2023) argument that children aged six to eleven months can discriminate colors but seemingly do not deploy color concepts or reason about colors.

4.3 How to Empirically Test HOROR

Given that we are uncertain exactly how to map these ideas onto the brain, does that mean we must give up on our empirical questions? I don't think so. There are two different strategies that I think might be helpful given our uncertainty about this mapping onto the brain.

4.3.1 Neurally Implementing HOROR

One important step lies in realizing that there are different versions of HOROR theory depending on how one navigates the choice points we have been exploring. Each of these versions should be developed to the point where it makes falsifying predictions. This is a bit laborious and time-consuming, but it is these individual implementations of the theory that ought to be tested.

One version of the theory, what we might call prefrontally implemented HOROR, or PFC-HOROR for short, claims that the relevant higher-order representations will be found in the prefrontal cortex. I view LeDoux's recent account (LeDoux 2024) as a specific proposal about the neural implementation of a version of HOROR theory, and thus as a version of PFC-HOROR. According to PFC-HOROR the relevant higher-order states, which are postulated to be identical to phenomenal consciousness, will be found entirely in activity supported by the prefrontal cortex. If so, then PFC-HOROR makes some definite predictions. For example, it claims that we will find activity in the prefrontal cortex that we can interpret as targeting some activity elsewhere (wherever the first-order states are) and we will also find activity that reflects the conceptual/intentional content of the HOROR. Ideally these two kinds of content could be varied. There may also be more specific versions of PFC-HOROR that specify specific prefrontal areas, such as the frontal pole, as being important (LeDoux 2024).

So, to recall our discussion from Chapter 3, if we varied the pointer content but not the intentional content, then we would expect functional differences but not phenomenological ones (granted that we kept that content the same). On the other hand, if we varied the intentional content but not the pointer content, then we would expect the experience of the subject to change while the functional profile of the first-order states remained the same. We might find out that there is no pointer content, that consciousness doesn't co-vary with activity in the frontal pole, that changing activity there did nothing to conscious experience, and so on. If so, HOROR as a category would not be falsified, but an implementation of it could be checked off as an uninteresting candidate.

One could also have a Parietal-hot zone implementation of the HOROR that would make different predictions about the relevant neural areas. One could even have a SOMA-like connectionist implementation of HOROR. What is crucial to each of the implementations of HOROR is that phenomenal consciousness just is the occurrence of the relevant higher-order representation of a representation. Where and how that kind of representation is implemented in the brain is a matter of empirical investigation. It cannot be derived a priori from psychological theorizing.

There are reasons for taking each of these implementation strategies seriously. First, as discussed in the previous section, it is an open empirical question whether, and to what extent, the prefrontal cortex is involved in phenomenal consciousness. I have some credence in PFC-HOROR, but what is crucial is that even if the prefrontally implemented version of HOROR is empirically falsified, we would still need to test these other implementations of the theory. What we really need is some definitive way of saying what the content of these neural areas is, but we are of course far from being able to do that.

4.3.1.1 Rich and Sparse Neural Implementations of HOROR

Once one decided on where one might expect to find the activity that implements the various mental states we posit, one would then need to determine the precise nature of the content of these psychological representations. We would want to focus on what has been called the rich-versus-sparse distinction in terms of phenomenology, which was discussed in Chapter 3. Probably, as discussed there, it will be the case that there will be a mix of relative-sparse and absolute-sparse contents in the typical case. These kinds of contents may come to the forefront in certain problem cases like change blindness.

Taking rich HOROR and sparse HOROR and taking them to be importantly realized in the prefrontal cortex gives us prefrontally implemented sparse phenomenology HOROR theory (Sparse PFC-HOROR—I think LeDoux's version counts as being in this category) and prefrontally implemented rich phenomenology HOROR (Rich PFC-HOROR—coincidently this is the view I am most attracted to in this region), respectively. Rich and sparse PFC-HOROR views may agree on their predictions about the first-order states. They could agree that holding the relevant HOROR constant and varying the first-order states would change the behavior of the subject but not their experience. They might even agree that holding everything else constant in the HOROR, and only varying the pointer content would have no effect on phenomenology but would affect the first-order states (if we let it).

The two versions of the theory would disagree about the kind of content one would expect to find in the higher-order states. Rich PFC-HOROR predicts that you would find activity in the prefrontal cortex that, if we knew the language of the brain, we would see that the content is very rich and represents all, or most, of the content in the targeted first-order states. Sparse PFC-HOROR would expect different activity corresponding to the sparse contents. My money is on rich PFC-HOROR as a proper contender, but there is room for disagreement. The important point I want to emphasize is that when one is aiming to test HOROR theory using the tools of cognitive neuroscience, one strategy is to aim explicitly at rich or sparse versions of PFC-HOROR.

4.3.2 Computationally Implementing HOROR

Looking at specific neural implementation proposals is one way to empirically test higher-order theories. There is another way to do so that does not rely on tying the relevant psychological states to any particular neural area. To do so we would need to find a way to isolate the computational and structural elements of the proposed higher-order states.

This strategy would involve identifying elements of these states that we might look for in a 'real-estate' independent way. We have already discussed, in section 4.2.3, the question of whether the brain uses an atomistic or compositional code for the relevant HORORs. This involves the question of whether there are unique sets of neurons, or a unique code among the same neurons, which encode any particular HOROR. So, if I have a HOROR to the effect that I am seeing green vividly, and one that I am seeing green faintly, will there be distinct sets of neurons for each? Or will there be some commonalities corresponding to the compositionality of the representation? Depending on the answer we end up with atomistic HOROR and compositional HOROR.

This distinction can be combined with the implementations we met in the previous section. We would then end up with atomistic-sparse PFC-HOROR theory versus compositional-sparse PFC-HOROR theory, versus atomistic-rich PFC-HOROR and compositional-rich PFC-HOROR and so on. I am aware of the terminological mess here. I view it as the unfortunate cost of precision, but I am open to better terminology!

I think there are also ways we might try to test for the atomistic versus compositional distinction without specifying an implementation of the theory. One way we might do this is with multivariate pattern analysis on fMRI data. We will discuss the details in Chapter 7 section 7.4.1, but the basic idea is to train neural decoders to decode one of these elements and suppress the other. To take one quick example, suppose we have someone looking at colors and in an fMRI machine. We might then train the decoder on the resulting data to decode the color and ignore that it is seen, or to decode that it is seen and ignore the content. We might then be able to isolate some neural signature correlated with subject's experience and provide some evidence for or against the claim that it had compositional or atomistic structure, without caring too much where the signal is coming from.[6]

With all of these distinctions in place we can now ask how the project of empirical adjudication is going.

---

[6] I really would love to talk more about the details of the proposed experiments here instead of referring the reader to section 7.4.1, but unfortunately, I can't do that. The details involve the Templeton-funded Adversarial grant that is looking at several different versions of higher-order theory. Since the main ones, HOSS and PRM, are not properly discussed until Chapter 7, it is best to wait to discuss the details.

4.4 The Status of the Current Empirical Case for and against HOROR

Currently many theorists comb through the empirical literature to marshal support for or against their theory. Many other theorists run empirical labs that aim to support one particular theory, using a particular methodology. The predictable results being that each lab seemingly confirms their theory's predictions (Yaron et al. 2022; Cleermans 2022). How has HOROR faired in this endeavor? Since many of the distinctions we have made are not (yet) present in the literature, it is hard to say if the theory has explicitly been tested. However, the central prediction of any kind of HOROR theory is that there can be cases of mismatch between levels of content and that the phenomenal properties are to be found at the higher level, not the lower. There have been some attempts to produce evidence for or against this claim, but they are currently not convincing.

Change blindness was used by Dretske (Dretske 2007) as an argument against the traditional higher-order thought theory early on, in many ways giving us the first argument for phenomenological overflow. In the original presentation we consider two pictures rapidly changing where there is some difference between the two pictures, say a spot is missing in one or a leaf on a tree, or some such. The subject says they do not see the change (until they do), but, as we discussed previously (1.1.4), the question remains: was the change phenomenologically manifest? Dretske argues that the answer is yes because one was looking at the screen and searching for the difference. It seems implausible that you would have missed it the entire time. One must have consciously seen the change but just not been aware of it. Thus, he reasons, we have a conscious experience that we are not aware of, and higher-order theories are false.

This is not the right way of putting things on the HOROR theory. As we have seen, HOROR theory dictates that one will have some pointer content that targets the states representing the changing feature. The HOROR will also describe those states while attributing being in them to the subject. Those first-order states will thus be conscious in the sense that they are the ones that you are aware of yourself as being in, but the way in which you are aware of them may gloss over the fact that they are changing (recall the discussion from the previous sections).

Thus, Dretske's argument equivocates in that the subject is in a phenomenally conscious state without being aware of it (the HOROR) but also in a state-conscious state because of being aware of it (the first-order state-conscious state). If one's first-order mental life includes representations of the changing feature, and one's HOROR targets both of those first-order states and describes them as just one where they are the same and nothing is changing, then one would have exactly the phenomenon of change blindness. One would experience no change even though the states representing the change were state-conscious. This is just one interpretation of how we might account for these experimental results on the HOROR theory.

Block has continued this challenge (Block 2011b), but the same basic reply can be given. Block's updated version of the argument invokes paradigms that use a Sperling-like partial-report paradigm (Sperling 1960) mixed with a change-blindness scenario. In these kinds of cases subjects are presented with two arrays of objects, usually ordered as though at the hours on a clock, separated by an inter-stimulus interval of varying lengths. The first array of objects, for example, may contain rectangles oriented in particular ways, or various objects like faces, houses, and cars. The change-blindness aspect consists in the fact that one of the items changes during the inter-stimulus interval. The Sperling-esque component is introduced by cueing subjects during the inter-stimulus period to the place whether the change might occur. For example, suppose that at the 5 o'clock position in the array is a picture of a motorcycle that is briefly displayed (along with the other items). The picture is then taken down and replaced with a blank screen. At some point an arrow will appear and point to the (now empty) 5 o'clock position cueing the subject to attend there. After this, the new array of objects appears on the screen and subjects are asked if the object at the cued location is the same, or different as from the first array. The object they are being asked about may still be a motorcycle, or it may have been replaced with a house or tree, and so on. Doing this makes the subjects much better at detecting the change than if the cue came after the inter-stimulus period, and so after the presentation of the new array.

These results have been used by Victor Lamme (Lamme 2018) and Ned Block (Block 2007) to argue that the subjects have rich phenomenally conscious experience of the contents of the pre-cue array before they were cued. The function of the cue was merely to direct attention to the already existing bit of phenomenal consciousness on their view. They continue to reason that in the cases where the cue wasn't present there was also conscious experience of the pre-change item. The reason that the subjects fail to notice this without the cue, on Lamme and Block's account, is that the second array over-writes the content so that when the subjects 'go to check what's there' they find the post-change item only. But, the reasoning goes, when you have the cue, which crucially appears before the second array does, then you can direct your attention to the phenomenally conscious state stored in memory and 'read off' what is there. You can also report what the pre-cue item was.

This is the rich phenomenology interpretation of these results. There is also a sparse phenomenology interpretation. On the sparse phenomenology interpretation, the subject does not have a rich and detailed experience of the pre-cue stimulus item. They have a rich and detailed experience of where they happen to be attending (say), but not of the entire scene. Once the cue arrives, then the subject can direct their attention to the unconsciously stored set of items. At this point those items can be consciously recalled.

Block has argued that there is a very strange consequence of sparse views in that they are committed to the claim that the cue somehow promotes, or 'catapults,' an unconscious state into a conscious state. This may be a legitimate criticism of certain responses to Block's argument, but it is not a criticism of the PFC-HOROR theory. As we have seen this implementation of the HOROR theory predicts that phenomenal consciousness just is the occurrence of the relevant HORORs and that those can be found in the prefrontal cortex. If one thinks that the phenomenology of perception is rich, then one can posit a prefrontally implemented rich version of HOROR theory. If so, then Block and Lamme's challenge boils down to the empirical question of whether we have any evidence to think there may be these kinds of rich HORORs in the prefrontal cortex. There is surprisingly little empirical work on this, and what little there is seems mixed and hard to interpret

(Raccah, Omri, Ned Block, and Kieran C. R. Fox 2021; Michel and Morales 2020; Mathias 2022).

Recently a group of scientists and philosophers, of which I am a part, supported by the Templeton World Charity Foundation's Accelerating Consciousness Research initiative, have tried to think of a set of experiments that might actually test the rich PFC-HOROR theory. In one set of experiments (Konig et al. 2023), they are using a traditional change-blindness paradigm combined with a Sperling-like retro cue. The hope is to minimize as much post-perceptual cognitive processing as possible. To do this they are trying to control for attention and working memory. In this setup subjects are shown an array of a few objects separated by a blank interval and then another array where one of the things may be different, as explained before. There is behavioral evidence that subjects are able to do this task very well when the cue shows up during the inter-stimulus interval and that they cannot do it very well if the cue shows up only after the second array is displayed. One hypothesis is that subjects have rich detailed experiences of the items in the pre-cue array (the first one) and that this is overwritten by the arrival of the second cue.

One might think this because in cases where subjects do notice that there is a change, they are able to say what item was there before the change (Lamme 2018). That is, they say 'yes, that item changed. It was a fish not a house,' or whatever. This suggests, according to Lamme, that the subjects have conscious experience of the pre-cue item and just cannot access it once the second array is displayed. This interpretation is often thought to be at odds with the higher-order theory, but if rich PFC-HOROR theory is on the right track, then it could be the case that subjects do in fact have a phenomenally conscious experience of the pre-cue item. This would be due to their having the right kind of higher-order representation that represents them as seeing the pre-cue item. This HOROR may come to be lost once the second array shows up. If this was the case, then we should expect to find some evidence that these kinds of HORORs were in the prefrontal cortex. To do so the experimenters propose putting people in the fMRI scanner while doing these tasks and seeing whether the activity of prefrontal or sensory cortices better correlates with what we take the subjects to be perceiving.

These experiments are interesting and hopefully will reveal something that will advance the discussion in this area. However, the experiments depend on an explicit assumption. It is the performance of subjects in a behavioral task with a retro cue that is used to infer what their conscious experience might be in a different fMRI trial without a retro cue. In the Sperling-esque change-blindness experiment subjects perform in a behavioral task that includes the retro cue. Based on their performance there the researchers say that in the fMRI cases where the retro cue is not presented, the subjects still had a rich conscious experience of the pre-cue item. In the pre-cue condition subjects are reliably able to notice the change and can tell you what the pre-change item in the first array was, but on conditions where there is no pre-cue and where the subjects fail to notice the change, can we say that we should expect that they had a detailed conscious experience of the pre-change item in the first array? The experimenters above reason that we should say yes because we *could have* presented the pre-cue and the subjects *could have* told us what the pre-change item in the first array was. It would have to be some mysterious effect of the cue on the first-order state that accounted for why in one case we have reason to think there was a detailed conscious experience and in the other we do not.

I find this argument somewhat convincing and have tentatively endorsed the predictions made by the rich PFC-HOROR (Koenig et al. 2023). However, it is also the case that, according to HOROR theory, the first-order state is state-conscious, it is the one you are aware of (the one that is targeted by the targeting relation). The theory allows that you may be aware of it in various ways that do not capture all of its details. So, one could opt for a sparse PFC-HOROR and still avoid Block's criticism. If the relevant rich first-order states are state-conscious, then there are at least two things we can say about the situation. The first is that the relevant first-order states will be the ones that it seems to you that you are in. It will be, from your point of view, as though you were in those states. The second is that there will be some targeting relation that has functional effects on the targeted states (but is not part of one's phenomenology).

Now suppose that the relevant first-order state(s) is(/are) that of seeing an array of figures arranged in a circle. Suppose further that the first-order states/processes one is in capture as much detail of the relevant stimulus as they can. Then, when one has a sparse HOROR targeting those states, they will be held online, routed to working memory, and so on, but one may experience simply seeing a few distinct letters and "some other letters in great detail as well." Then the cue shows up and your attention is directed to that part of the stimulus' first-order representation. At that point one's higher-order awareness is still targeting the same sate (the same state is state-conscious), but it is now describing it in a more fine-grained way as having these specific features at this location, and so on. Thus, the same state is state-conscious in both cases. Even though one's phenomenology has changed from sparse-where-the-cue-points to rich-where-the-cue-points, no new state has been made conscious on this view. There are just different contents in the relevant HOROR, which itself targets the same set of first-order states/processes. The reason there are different contents in the HOROR is simply that the cue has directed your attention to that area. One has the relevant first-order state already there (it is the state-conscious state) and that allows the HOROR to 'read off' the content and represent it.

Alternatively, one might have a 'super-sparse' view on which the cue does not affect what is phenomenologically manifest at all. This would require that the first-order state is what is allowing the subject to perform the task without any change in what is phenomenologically manifest. The cue may simply tap into the unconsciously stored first-order representations in a way similar to one interpretation of blindsight. The subject may have no conscious experience of the pre-change item and yet still be able to perform the task.

Putting my cards on the table, I have always found the rich view of conscious perception to be very intuitive. It does seem to me as though much of the detail of the world is phenomenologically manifest. I am also very sympathetic to PFC-HOROR. This makes me very partial to a rich PFC-HOROR view. For maximal completeness here, I am also partial to the compositional version of HOROR making my preferred package of views a *rich compositional PFC-HOROR*. However, if the empirical results came back suggesting that there were not these rich contents in the prefrontal areas, but we did find them in the sensory cortices, what should we conclude? Well, we should probably conclude that the rich PFC-HOROR theory was in trouble (how much trouble depends on the details). But this would not by itself count against versions of rich HOROR that posited a different neural implementation, like rich parietal-HOROR, and so on. Nor would it challenge sparse PFC-HOROR theories. Nor would it, all by itself, challenge the compositional version of HOROR. There may be other reasons for ruling out these versions of the theory, but we should be careful to note that the proposed experiments discussed above are aimed specifically at rich PFC-HOROR and don't tell us much about the other versions.

4.4.1 Subjective Inflation

In previous work (Brown 2012c; Lau and Brown 2019), I argued that we had some empirical support for the key claim of the HOROR theory in the work of Hakwan Lau. That paper was written in 2011 before I had officially solidified my thoughts into something like the HOROR theory (Brown 2015), but I did have the key idea that misrepresentation cases were a kind of surprising prediction that higher-order theories make (Brown 2012c). If we could find cases where there was more to the subject's phenomenology than could be reasonably accounted for by the subject's first-order states, then we would have some strong empirical evidence for the claim that higher-order states made some crucial contribution to phenomenal consciousness. This evidence would be especially strong in that it would be a test of a prediction of the theory rather than a *post hoc* confirmation of the theory. The ideal way to do this, as we have seen in the previous chapter, is to keep the first-order states constant somehow and then try to vary the phenomenology of the subjects. Then one could try to locate the neural correlates of the difference between the case where the subject did not experience the stimulus but had the first-order state and the case where the subject has the first-order state and experiences it.

The ideal case is difficult to produce with our current technology and understanding of the brain, but Hakwan Lau had devised a way to attempt a less ideal version of the ideal test. Could we keep the first-order states the same and have *any* difference in phenomenology? If so, then that difference must be attributed to the higher-order state. But as we have seen, saying what exactly these states amount to in the brain is rather difficult. When I first met Hakwan in 2010 or so, he presented himself as a former first-order theorist/global workspace *aficionado* who had been disillusioned by Blindsight and yet convinced by empirical data that the prefrontal cortex must play some role in producing consciousness. He had arrived at this conviction because when he had set out to control for task performance by matching d' (pronounced 'd prime,' this is a measure of how well the subject performs at some task and is taken from signal detection theory; Green and Swets 1966), he found that there was activity in the lateral prefrontal cortex that varied more reliably with the subject's subjective reports about seeing the stimulus (Persaud et al. 2011; Lau and Passingham 2006). This lingering affinity for first-order theories shows up in Lau's defense of a version of the traditional relational higher-order view (Lau 2022), and we will discuss it in detail in Chapter 7.

Here I want to focus on the question of whether finding that activity in prefrontal areas correlates with subject's visibility reports counts as evidence that there is phenomenology that varies independently of the first-order states. The relevant empirical findings have come to be known as *subjective inflation*, and they seem to be a robust behavioral finding (Tian and Maniscalco et al. 2023). In the areas of one's visual field that one is not attending to, one seems to make more liberal judgments both about whether one has seen anything at all and about whether a stimulus is more visible. One is more likely to say that they have seen something in the periphery even when nothing is presented there, and even when one is doing fine on the task in the centrally attended part of the visual field (Rahnev et al. 2011; Knotts et al. 2020). There are different ways that one could interpret these behavioral findings (Lau and Brown 2019). One could think that the subjects are correct, and their conscious experience is indeed inflated. In that case when the subject says that something is highly visible in the unattended region, they must have a HOROR that represents them as seeing something. This HOROR itself could be rich or sparse as we discussed in the previous sections. Another response is to take the phenomenological difference to be located at the first-order level, while the higher-order state points to it. We will discuss that option in Chapter 7, when we go through the details of Lau's Perceptual Reality Monitoring model.

What we need to focus on here is something that all versions of higher-order theories will agree on. This is the claim that subjective inflation is really a phenomenological finding. The alternative view is that what they have shown is that there is a cognitive judgment or belief that is issued after phenomenal consciousness is formed. This cognitive belief can be wrong about what is happening at the phenomenal level. On this debunking account the person is not experiencing any subjective sense of inflation (rich or sparse). Instead, they have just a mistaken belief that they experienced something.

Block has objected (Block 2019, 2023) that one would find the phenomenological interpretation of subjective inflation plausible only if one already accepted that the phenomenology was indexed to the higher-order states. If one did not assume that, he argues, then one would more plausibly think that the prefrontal activity was related to the subject's report on the task and not to the subject's phenomenology.

I think that ultimately Block's argument in his reply to subjective inflation is that since we have two models that both predict the same pattern of results, we cannot use the pattern of results as evidence for one model over the other. The two models are

(I) a first-order view where difference in task performance is indicative of a difference in conscious experience and difference in report is indicative of cognitive effects without necessarily effecting phenomenology

(II) a higher-order view where difference in task performance is not indicative of a difference in conscious experience and difference in report is indicative of an effect on phenomenology

The question then comes down to which of these two models we should prefer. Lau's results can be seen as attempting to secure option (II), while Block is arguing for option (I). There is no difference in the task performance, so why not think there is no difference in what it is like for these subjects? The problem with this is that all we have at this moment is that some activity in the PFC seems to be correlated with the subjects reporting that something they failed to detect is more visible. Does this show that this is a phenomenological difference?

I had previously thought that the case was stronger than I do now. Lau's group tried to control for this by offering feedback and training to the participants and noting that the training did not get rid of the effect. Even when the participants knew that they were likely getting it wrong they still tended to make more liberal judgments while not attending. This means that even though they were doing the task equally well and had received feedback and training on how to do the task and were given strategies and so on, subjects still say that the stimulus is more visible while doing no better (or worse) at the task. One might reasonably assume that something that resists training in this way would be phenomenological. If it were truly related to merely reporting, then one should be able to develop cognitive strategies that would allow one to overcome them. But true phenomenal illusions cannot be overcome in this way. No matter how much training one gets, the two lines in the Muller-Lyer illusion will look the same length and so on.

I still think that this argument makes it reasonable to say that these results put pressure on first-order views (Knotts et al. 2020), but they do not really offer the test of the empirical predictions we were hoping for. We have not yet found a generally convincing case of a mismatch case where people agree that the mismatch is phenomenal rather than informational. On the other side we have another problem. There is an argument from Lau and colleagues that matched d' means that the first-order states have been matched. That is to say that since we have matched performance, we have matched first-order states. The reasoning behind this is straightforward. D' is a measure of how much information is in the system and if there is an equal amount of informational sensitivity to the environment then that suggests that there are the same first-order states. But there is a problem here in that to get the results, that is to get matched performance on the task but a difference in these other judgments, they need to manipulate the stimulus. In one experiment they masked the stimulus, in the other they had to increase the contrast of the stimulus. So, when subjects say that the unattended stimulus is more visible, it may be because they have changed the first-order representations. Equivalent d' does not mean equivalent first-order states from this line of critique. If the stimulus has been changed, the argument goes, then the first-order representation it causes will be changed as well.

Lau has responded to this criticism in section 2.12 of his recent book (Lau 2022). The basic gist of his response is to acknowledge that these confounds exist, but then to argue that these confounds are better in some sense than the previous ones. The reason being that we have some idea that these confounds are there. Of course, changing the physical stimulus will result in a difference in first-order representations! But that is something that is obvious and therefore is something that we may be able to control for. If, on the other hand, we have a confound that we, or even worse the entire profession, are unaware of, then we are in worse shape. Lau's take on the situation is that there is a major confound that has been largely unacknowledged. This is the performance confound, which takes performance on some tasks to indicate that the subject has phenomenally conscious experience of the states that allow them to perform the task. Since no one acknowledges this confound, it is never controlled for. As a result, a lot of results are misinterpreted on Lau's view.

If this is right, Lau reasons, then introducing some easily spotted and controllable confounds to take the place of an unacknowledged and uncontrolled confound then counts as making progress. That is, if once one has controlled for the obvious confound, one still gets a disassociation between performance and subjective experience from the experiments, then that is good evidence. So, while it seems reasonably clear we haven't seen a true empirical test of the predictions that higher-order theories make about mismatch cases, the predictions that each side makes in the relevant cases are reasonably clear.

Taking all of this into consideration, the group I discussed in the previous section has also devised a set of experiments to carefully test whether first-order signals can be dissociated from subjective experience (Tian and Maniscalco et al. 2023). The basic idea is to us a stimulus that is composed of a texture-defined figure. In these kinds of figures the background may be composed of diagonal slashes in a left-to-right orientation. One can then compose a figure by having an area composed of slashes of a different orientation. One can vary these stimuli in all sorts of ways, allowing one to really test whether the first-order signal is varying with the subjective inflation. To do this, the researchers have come up with a clever idea. This is to compare the fMRI signals of the texture-defined figure with fMRI signals of just the background without the figure. Subtracting out the difference will allow them to isolate the first-order recurrency signal that is correlated most directly with what many would take to be the first-order state. We can then determine whether this signal is the one that co-varies with subject's reported phenomenology. If it didn't it would strengthen the argument from subjective inflation to some sort of higher-order theory (Brown 2012c; Lau and Brown 2019).

All the projects discussed in this chapter are in the early stages. It is very exciting to see that we may have some resolution to these issues within the foreseeable future.

5
The Traditional Higher-Order Approach to Consciousness

We have now set out the HOROR theory as I see it and given some indication of the empirical status of the theory. Overall, I think it is safe to say that it is so far consistent with what we know, hasn't been falsified, but also hasn't passed any major empirical hurdles directed directly against it. Though, as we also saw, there are some in the works as I write this. Hopefully we will begin to see results soon.

I have also been at pains to indicate that the HOROR theory is a non-traditional higher-order theory. I officially split my credence among various views and so do not take there to be any reason to strongly prefer non-traditional theories. I do, however, think that no matter whether traditional views turn out ultimately to be correct, the way in which the traditional approach sets up the problem in the first place is not the best way to do so. In this chapter I will try to set out what exactly the traditional higher-order approach is committed to, as well as the reasons why I think that setting up the debate in these terms isn't helpful.

The issues seem straightforward but turn out to be surprisingly convoluted. Higher-order theories have traditionally been presented as having a completely different goal than what we have been exploring. It is only antecedently that these theorists try to connect their goals to those of the larger profession. This has led to a great deal of insular debate and confusion. People are confused over what higher-order theories are trying to do, and the way in which they attempt to accomplish this goal. So, let's (re-)start at the beginning.

As I have been using the term, the 'traditional' approach to higher-order theorizing about consciousness is characterized by commitment to the following two claims:

1. The Transitivity Principle fixes the data a theory of consciousness needs to account for
2. The mental state that there is something that it is like for one to be in is the first-order state[1]

As we have seen, the HOROR theory rejects both as stated and accepts modified versions. It is finally time to look at the reasons why this is the case.

In section 5.1, I show that what I called 1 and 2 above do typically figure in how the theory is presented. In section 5.2, I present a new taxonomy of higher-order theories based on my distinction between relational and non-relational readings of the Transitivity Principle. In section 5.3, I go over my reasons for denying that the Transitivity Principle should be used to define what higher-order theories are.

5.1 The Traditional Higher-Order Approach and the Transitivity Principle

If one were attempting to learn about the higher-order theory, then one might consult various reference guides. For example, one might turn to the entry in the *Stanford Encyclopedia of Philosophy* on higher-order theories of consciousness (Carruthers and Gennaro 2020). We read the first sentence, and it says, "Higher-order theories of consciousness try to explain the difference between unconscious and conscious mental states in terms of a relation obtaining between the conscious state in question and a higher-order representation of some sort (either a higher-order perception of that state or a higher-order thought about it). The most challenging properties to explain are those involved in phenomenal consciousness." The first thing we notice is that higher-order theories seemingly are aiming at explaining the difference between unconscious and conscious mental states. That seems to be the goal of these kinds of theories according to the entry.

---

[1] Or content if they aren't separate states.

This automatically and immediately commits the theory to the existence of unconscious mental states. We are then told that the way in which these theories do this is by positing a relation that obtains between the conscious state in question, which would be the first-order state (where, to remind us, first-order states are representations of things that are not themselves mental), and the higher-order representation about it. The idea here is that you have the two states related in a certain way, and that results in the first-order state becoming conscious.

This way of presenting the aims of the theory and how it proposes to accomplish these aims is very common. That's why I call it the traditional view. So, for another example, if we went over to the *Internet Encyclopedia of Philosophy* and looked at their entry on higher-order theories of consciousness, we would find this entry written entirely by Rocco Gennaro. The key sentence is this one, "Conscious mental states arise when two unconscious mental states are related in a certain way, namely, that one of them (the [Higher-Order Representation]) is directed at the other ([Mental state]) (Gennaro 2022)."

This overall idea is sometimes referred to as the Transitivity Principle (TP):

(TP) A conscious state is a state whose subject is, in some suitable way, aware of being in it.

As we can see the pattern here is basically the same as the *Stanford Encyclopedia*. We have the two mental states, a relation between them, and one of them rendered conscious as a result. I suppose we should expect this similarity given that we have one of the same authors!

The Transitivity Principle, as previously mentioned, was introduced into the discussion by David Rosenthal, who is the originator of the higher-order thought approach. What would we find if we looked for a freely available introductory text where he sets up the aims of the theory. What we find here is an article on *Scholarpedia*, which is somewhat like *Wikipedia* but written by experts. This one is written by David Rosenthal and Josh Weisberg (Rosenthal and Weisberg

2008). The first sentence says, "Higher-order theories of consciousness seek to explain what it is for mental states to be conscious as against occurring non-consciously by appeal to other higher-order mental states that represent one as being in the states in question." The language here is not as straightforward as in the other examples, and there are important difference between these theorists that we will explore in due time. Before doing that, we can see common themes from the other two entries.

For one, the goal of a theory of consciousness is to explain the difference between conscious and unconscious mental states in terms of our being *conscious of* that mental state. Rosenthal is very clear about this in his recent writing (Rosenthal 2022), saying, "Explaining consciousness requires saying how conscious and unconscious states differ. And because a state's being conscious is a mental property, we must specify that difference in distinctively mental terms. The Transitivity Principle offers a satisfying proposal. It's not obvious what credible alternative there might be that's also cast in distinctively mental terms" (251). This shows that the traditional theorists agree that a mental state is conscious when one is conscious of it. Later in this article they introduce the Transitivity Principle, saying higher-order theories "all embrace the idea that a mental state is conscious when the subject is appropriately conscious *of* that state" (op. cit.). This partially lines up with the previous way of putting things, but it does mask some divisions in the way these theorists think about the Transitivity Principle, which we will explore in the next section.

So now we can see that these theorists are committed to 1 from the previous section, which was that the Transitivity Principle fixes the data for a science of consciousness. We have seen that the primary goal of a theory of consciousness, according to the traditional approach, is to explain the difference between a mental state when it occurs unconsciously, and that same mental state when it occurs consciously. The very meaning of 'unconsciously' in these characterizations is given by the Transitivity Principle. That is to say that what it is for a state to be 'unconscious' is just for one to be unaware of it as occurring, as opposed to there being nothing that it is like for one to be in that state, or something else. Thus, according to the traditional higher-order approach, the very data that a theory of consciousness needs to account for is determined by the Transitivity Principle itself.

Is the traditional approach committed to 2 as well, which was that it is the first-order state which is conscious? It is easy to see that it is. There are numerous places in Rosenthal's writing where he says things like the following, "There being something that it's like for one to have a sensation of red, for example, will consist in one's being conscious of that sensation as a sensation of red" (2005, 4). This seems to me to indicate that Rosenthal takes the sensation of red, the first-order state, to be the state that there is something that is like for one to be in. Some might not think that this kind of passage shows what I think it does. Perhaps it should be taken as suggesting that the first-order state is the conscious state but not the state that there is something that it is like for one to be in.

I think Rosenthal makes this the most clear in his recent writing (Rosenthal 2022) where he says, "being aware of a first-order state explains why it subjectively appears that one is in that state, so that there's something qualitative it's like to be in it" (252). For the traditional view, it is the first-order state that is conscious, and it is the first-order state which there is something that it is like for one to be in when it is conscious. These sentiments are echoed by every traditional higher-order theorist (for a representative sample see Kriegel 2009; Gennaro 2012; Berger 2014, 2017). It is, according to the traditional approach, the first-order state itself that is like something for one to be in, and the explanation of that is given in terms of the Transitivity Principle.

The Transitivity Principle, then, is at the heart of the traditional higher-order approach. However, what seems to have gone largely unnoticed, until relatively recently (Brown 2012b), is that there is a disagreement between these traditional theorists. This disagreement was largely unnoticed because it involves an ambiguity in the Transitivity Principle itself. One can see the beginnings of this disagreement in the quoted texts above. The introductory text from Rosenthal and Weisberg is subtly different from that of Carruthers and Gennaro. This difference reflects more than mere linguistic style. It reflects a fundamental fault line in traditional higher-order theorizing. We will draw this out in the next section.

5.2 Relational versus Non-relational Readings of the Traditional Transitivity Principle

The Transitivity Principle, which says that *a conscious state is one that I am aware of (myself as being in)*, appears to be straightforward, but there are many choice points before one gets a workable theory of consciousness from this principle. As I am using the terminology, all the traditional higher-order approaches endorse the Transitivity Principle. There are at least two distinct readings of that principle, and so there are two distinct versions of the traditional approach.

The first reading is what I have called the *relational* reading (Brown 2012b, 2012c, 2015). Relational versions of the traditional higher-order theory interpret the Transitivity Principle in a relational sense. When these theorists say that a conscious state is one of which you are aware, they mean to be talking about a property of the first-order state that is a result of one's being in an awareness relation to that very state. The first-order state being a component of this relational structure is what explains it being a conscious state. They, so to speak, want to know what the difference between a conscious state and an unconscious state is *from the first-order state's point of view*. Their answer, as we have seen, is to posit a higher-order representation that is directed at, or related to, the state that previously was unconscious. As a result of being *targeted* by the higher-order representation, and thereby entering into the awareness relation to it, the first-order state is rendered conscious. On relational versions of the traditional higher-order approach, the explanatory goal of a theory of consciousness is to account for state-consciousness, and they posit a higher-order awareness as the suitable way in which we are aware of our own mental states.

Relational versions of the traditional higher-order approach thus accept the following two claims:

(a) The first-order state is the conscious mental state (because of being the target of a higher-order state)
(b) What it is like for the subject is to some degree determined by the first-order state's content (the first-order state is phenomenally active)

The Transitivity Principle commits them to (a), and the relational reading of the Transitivity Principle commits them to (b).

Relational versions of the traditional higher-order approach seek a kind of reconciliation between purely first-order accounts and higher-order views. They endorse the Transitivity Principle, and so argue that a mental state is conscious only when one is suitably aware of it. They also want to argue that what it is like for you, specifically whether it is like seeing red, or rather like hearing a trumpet, or like being nervous, is accounted for by the state of which you are aware. The first-order state's content is itself phenomenally active on the relational reading. This means that the first-order content determines, or accounts for, part of what is phenomenologically manifest in one's stream of consciousness.

Non-relational versions of the traditional higher-order theory are easy to mistake for the relational versions because they both accept the traditional Transitivity Principle. What is distinctive of the non-relational versions of the higher-order approach is that it gives a non-relational reading of the Transitivity Principle. This means that they deny that the first-order state that is targeted by the higher-order representation determines what it is like for the subject (while also affirming that this first-order state is the state-conscious state). The first-order state of which we are aware will be phenomenally silent and will not determine or account for a phenomenologically manifest aspect of one's stream of consciousness according to non-relational versions of the traditional higher-order approach. To put this in the terms above, traditional non-relational higher-order theories accept (a) but reject (b). It is because these views accept the Transitivity Principle that they are committed to (a). This is why this kind of view is a traditional view. These kinds of views are non-relational because they reject (b). The first-order state is not phenomenologically manifest, and its content is not phenomenally active. The first-order state is conscious, but phenomenally silent on traditional non-relational views. There has been a lot of debate about how a theory could consistently accept (a) and deny (b), and we will turn to that in the next section.

The distinction between relational and non-relational traditional higher-order theories is partially inspired by thinking about the debate in the philosophy of perception more generally. There, much of the debate has been between so-called naïve realists, who model perception as some kind of directly revelatory relation that puts us in touch with the properties of the world as they really are, versus the representationalist, who models perception as a representation of the properties in the environment.[2] Relational versions of the traditional higher-order approach are somewhat similar to the naïve realist approach in that they tend to view the 'awareness' relation as something direct and intimate in a way that prohibits misrepresentation, which reveals the nature of the first-order states. Non-relational versions of the traditional approach view 'awareness' in a distinctly representational rather than in a revelatory relational way. They are thus more akin to representational views in the philosophy of perception.

This analogy is not perfect, but it does help us to see this overlooked distinction. It also lets us see one of the main problems with relational views. The first-order states must be thought of in way that is similar to the way in which naïve realists think about physical objects. The first-order mental quality that represents red, for instance, will have to be qualitatively red in an 'inner-awareness-independent manner,' and this pushes you either away from relationalism or toward a first-order view of the mental qualities. We will come back to this argument in Chapter 7.

Each of the two major branches of the traditional higher-order theory can be further divided into at least two more subsections. On the traditional non-relational side, we have what I will call pure non-relational versus mixed non-relational views. On the traditional relational side, we have what I call spotlight or 'light switch' views (a kind of pure-relationalism) versus joint-determination views (a kind of mixed-relationalism). To see the differences among these various ways of thinking about the Transitivity Principle, it is useful to start with cases of misrepresentation.

---

[2] I mean to side-step the issue of direct realism, on which both naïve realists and representationalists may agree. Direct realism is just the denial of indirect realism, which is the claim that we are aware of the worldly properties indirectly via being aware of an inner state.

5.2.1 Misrepresentation and the Different Versions of Relational and Non-Relational Theories

We have discussed the issue of misrepresentation from the HOROR perspective extensively in Chapters 3 and 4. In this section we will discuss it from the point of view of the traditional higher-order theory. I think this is a really important issue and hasn't received the attention it deserves. What I mean by this is that it is often thought of as an objection to the higher-order approach in general, but, on my view, it is an empirical prediction of the theory, one that is particularly ripe for testing as it is very counter-intuitive. Any evidence for it would constitute strong evidence for the higher-order approach. As we saw in the previous chapter this hasn't been done yet. Hopefully we will see some progress on this soon. However, most philosophers view the possibility of misrepresentation as a devastating objection to non-relational versions of the traditional higher-order approach (cf. Neander 1998; Levine 2001; Gennaro 2012).

Since traditional higher-order theories, in all their forms, postulate two distinct states (or at least two contents), the problem of misrepresentation of the targeted state by the higher-order state immediately becomes a consideration. Most of the differences among these kinds of theories becomes evident once one begins to think about misrepresentation. So, we will start there. Misrepresentation can come in two kinds. One, following tradition (Neander 1998), we'll call 'radical misrepresentation,' and the other, in a slight departure from tradition, 'garden-variety misrepresentation.'[3]

Radical misrepresentation occurs when the higher-order state represents you as being in a first-order state that doesn't exist, which you're not in at all. Garden-variety misrepresentation mis-describes an existing state incorrectly. So let us suppose that one is in a first-order state F, but the higher-order state H represents F as being F^*. This would be a case of garden-variety misrepresentation. If H represents

---

[3] Weisberg, following Neander, calls this 'mild misrepresentation' (Weisberg 2011), but I want to emphasize that this kind of misrepresentation occurs all of the time on the typical non-relational views, so I gave it a name that emphasizes that.

you as being not in F or F^*, but instead in a state you are not currently in at all, say G, then that is radical misrepresentation.

Let us start by thinking about radical misrepresentation. To simplify things let us suppose that one has a higher-order state representing that one is seeing red, but one is having no first-order visual states at all. To help us, we can invent a hypothetical 'brain clamp' that can hold the activity of some brain areas constant (akin to a voltage clamp). Then we can imagine 'clamping' the first-order activity at a minimal level and then stimulating the higher-order representation area to get the appropriate higher-order state. This is, of course, not actually possible, but it allows us to think about cases of radical misrepresentation. To make this more concrete let us suppose that we have our volunteers from the previous chapter, Alvin and Simon, both having the higher-order representation that would occur when typically experiencing red. In Simon we have brain clamped his first-order activity so there is no first-order representation of red. Further suppose that we haven't done this to Alvin. What is it like to be these two subjects according to the traditional higher-order view?

There are at least four ways one could respond to cases of radical misrepresentation.

1. One could deny that there is any conscious experience in cases of radical misrepresentation.
2. One could say that there is a partial or degraded conscious experience in these cases.
3. One could say there is (or could be) a typical conscious experience in these cases.
4. One could deny that there ever are any cases of radical misrepresentation.

One way to hold 4 is to suggest that every case of radical misrepresentation can be thought of as a case of garden-variety misrepresentation. There might always be some existing state which can be thought of as being misdescribed rather than some non-existing state being the target. Perhaps when H represents you as being in G it is really misrepresenting you as being in F. This will become a major issue in

Chapter 6. In our case of Alvin and Simon, we have avoided this with our hypothetical brain clamp. So, we can set aside option 4 for now.

If 1 is true, then Simon has no experience at all while Alvin has the usual experience of red. In 2 Alvin and Simon will both have conscious experience, but Simon's will be very different from Alvin's. Alvin will see red as usual, and Simon will have some other kind of experience. In 3, Alvin and Simon have the same conscious experience. As we will see in the next two sections, the different versions of traditional higher-order theory will align with different subsets of these three options.

5.2.2 Two Versions of Non-Relationalism: Pure and Mixed

Take traditional non-relationalism first. One option for this kind of view would be to endorse option 3, perhaps even with enthusiasm. If the contents of the higher-order states are the same, and they are the sole determiner of what it is like for one, then the default position would seem to be option 3. Of course, if the contents of the higher-order states were themselves sparse or degraded then the non-relationalists might take option 2, but we are setting that aside for the moment. We can call non-relational views that take option 3 pure non-relational views. According to pure non-relational versions of the traditional higher-order approach, what it is like to be Simon will be the very same as it is for Alvin (granting that we have kept their higher-order contents identical). Simon and Alvin will differ in other psychological ways, but not with respect to what it is like for them. Combining this with (a) from the previous section, which says it is the first-order state which is conscious, gives us the view that, even in cases where the first-order state is completely absent, I can be in that conscious mental state. Furthermore, what it is like for me to be in that completely absent mental state will be as the relevant non-relational higher-order state describes.

On the other hand, a traditional non-relationalist might try to take option 1. To do that would be to deny that Simon has any conscious experience even though he and Alvin have identical higher-order states. To attempt this, the non-relationalist needs to move from a pure version of the theory to a mixed version of the theory. Mixed non-relationalism allows a relation to the first-order state to play a role, but only in such a way as to continue to deny (b) from the previous section. Recall that (b) was the claim that the first-order state or content is phenomenally active and plays a role in determining what it is like for one. I call these kinds of views 'mixed non-relational' views. Mixed non-relational views thus hold that there needs to be some relation between the first and higher-order states/contents for there to be a conscious state at all, but what it is like for the subject to be in that conscious state is completely determined by the higher-order content.

This allows us to see that much of the debate among various higher-order theories has been between pure non-relational views (Rosenthal 2005; Weisberg 2008) and mixed non-relational views (Kriegel 2009; Gennaro 2012). The various relations that were postulated were there to block the implication of the pure non-relational view that there could be non-existent conscious states. For those interested in the argument between these versions of the theory, I go through the details in Chapter 6. I give my reasons for thinking that these views are inadequate but also argue that these are largely empirical issues.

5.2.3 Two Versions of Relationalism: Spotlight and Joint-Determination

Relational views must take a different approach to the problem of radical misrepresentation. Because they accept (b), the claim that the phenomenology of the subject depends on the content of the first-order states, the relationalist can take either option 1, and deny that there is any conscious experience in these kinds of cases, or take option 2, and argue that there is a partial or degraded conscious experience in these cases.

Relational theories have some reason to prefer 1. After all, if the first-order state is made conscious by being related to the higher-order state, and if the first-order state is itself entirely responsible for the specific way that one's experience is for one, then in the case where that state is absent, there will be nothing that it is like for one to have the relevant higher-order state. This would amount to saying that while what it is like for Alvin is seeing red, there is nothing that it is like for Simon. I have called these kinds of relational higher-order views Split-Level in past writing because the phenomenal content is all at the first-order level while the 'consciousness making' aspect is at the higher-level (Brown 2019). The higher-order content on this kind of view is a mere phenomenally silent spotlight that shines a light, so to speak, on the states that are already there.

Because of this it might be better to call this the 'spotlight' or 'light switch' view. What it is like for one to be in some conscious state is determined by the properties of the first-order state, and the higher-order spotlight is hypothesized to let you experience what it is like to be in those first-order states. The higher-order state 'illuminates' what is already there, or in some sense allows one to 'see' (i.e., become aware of) it in the same way one might come to see an object in a room once one shines a light on it. Or perhaps it is more like plugging in a nightlight. The first-order state becomes 'illuminated from within' once it is 'plugged into' the higher-order state. Whatever metaphor one prefers, the net result is that the first-order state's content becomes phenomenally active. Its content is then part of what is phenomenologically manifest to the subject.

Spotlight views attempt to take a divide-and-conquer strategy with regard to phenomenal qualities. On these kinds of views, one must give an independent account of the qualitative aspect of the mind. The higher-order element is postulated to allow one to experience the qualitative content. So, one has the qualitative redness of red and the higher-order pointers simply 'turn on the lights' allowing one to be aware of the mental quality, which, following the Transitivity Principle, allows one to experience it. This view is inviting in that it attempts to preserve the intuitive idea of the traditional Transitivity Principle while also preserving the intuitive idea that one's first-order states provide a lot of mental content that might not need to be represented at the higher-order level. It is also appealing in that the higher-order state itself does not contribute to what it is like for you. It merely allows there to be something that it is like for one. In this sense spotlight views are a form of pure relationalism. All the higher-order state does is to activate the first-order qualities.

Of all the various rivals I feel the strongest pull to spotlight views. However, I am reluctant to endorse them because I cannot see how they could explain how it is that the first-order state becomes phenomenologically manifest without having to commit to what I view as an implausible view of the mental qualities. As mentioned above and argued for in Chapter 7, I agree that there must be some kind of indexing or pointer contents in the relevant higher-order states, and that this pointer content must be phenomenally silent. I have made extensive use of this phenomenally silent content in my formulation of the contents of HORORs in Chapter 3. What I cannot quite understand is how this phenomenally silent pointer can make an unconscious qualitative red state into a phenomenally conscious red experience. How does one cash in the metaphors of 'turning on the lights' or 'shining a spotlight' in a naturalistically acceptable way? I will save discussion of this issue for Chapter 7, but I think we both know what I am going to say. I am skeptical but will wait for the empirical results.

Alternatively, a relationalist could argue that (2) is the best route. If one thinks that the first-order state and the higher-order state are both phenomenally active, then one might hold that when there is just the higher-order part, one has a conscious experience that is partial or degraded. This would precisely be because one is just having half of the typical content. If phenomenal consciousness typically consists in two phenomenal aspects related to each other, and one only has half of that, then one will have just part of the experience (Lau and Brown 2019). I call these kinds of relational views joint-determination views. Joint-determination versions of relational higher-order theories hold that some aspect of the phenomenology is 'carried' by the first-order state but also some aspect is carried by the higher-order element as well. The two together jointly contribute their contents to the stream of consciousness. For example, a first-order state representing red in the environment would all by itself be unconscious, but when the appropriate higher-order state targets it and enters into the correct relation with it, then one experiences redness. The redness would be contributed by the first-order state, but the higher-order component contributes as well in some way, perhaps in indicting how vivid the first-order state is (Lau and Brown 2019). We can view this as a mixed-relationalism.

So, according to the joint-determination view, there is something that it is like to be Simon even without the first-order state. It will not be like seeing red, since the first-order state is missing. As a result, the 'redness' isn't there to be phenomenologically manifest. It will still be like something for him because the higher-order content is itself phenomenally active and contributes part of the phenomenology typically present in the stream of consciousness. Simon will perhaps experience *vividly seeing something or other* without experiencing any particular thing being seen vividly. So, Simon might say, "I see something," when asked, but not be able to tell you anything further about what he saw. Neither would he be able to correctly behave as though he were seeing red.

Joint-determination views face a difficulty right away in that if they allow that the higher-order state has phenomenally active content, then it is because of something other than by our being aware of it. The higher-order component is only conscious when there is a further third-order pointer pointing at it. And if so, joint-determination views reject the Transitivity Principle, at least for components of phenomenology contributed by the higher-order state itself. Some version of non-traditional account must be given to supplement the joint-determination view, at lease for the part of phenomenology that is captured by the content of just the higher-order state. There must be an aspect of phenomenal consciousness that cannot be accounted for by being the target of a pointer. This in turn weakens the rationale for accepting the joint-determination view (Lau and Brown 2019).

Joint-determination views also face the same difficulty in explaining how it is that the first-order states contribute their contents to one's phenomenology and become phenomenologically manifest. For those interested in the details I have tried to make this argument in Chapter 7, but just as before I ultimately think that these are empirical issues. The benefit of all this research is in clarifying what the various theories are empirically committed to so that we can try to sort them in terms of plausibility.

So, though I very much see these all as empirical issues that are yet to be resolved, thinking about radical misrepresentation suggests that a non-traditional mixed non-relational higher-order theory is an interesting version of the theory. That is, of course, exactly what the HOROR theory we developed in Chapters 3 and 4 is.

5.2.4 The Kinds of Higher-Order Theory

Putting these distinctions together we see that we can have at least six general kinds of higher-order theory.

First one must decide whether the theory in question accepts the traditional Transitivity Principle. If so, then the theory is traditional. If not, the theory is non-traditional. Non-traditional higher-order theories take the higher-order state itself to be the phenomenally conscious state and separate state-consciousness from phenomenal consciousness (as discussed in Chapter 2). Non-traditional higher-order theories come in pure and mixed versions. The HOROR theory is an example of a mixed non-traditional higher-order theory, and possibly the first one to be explicitly non-traditional. There are others that are beginning to explore non-traditional higher-order theories (Gottleib 2022; Sebastián 2022b), and we can see that there are different versions depending on how one treats the higher-order representation (as discussed in Chapter 3).

The HOROR theory does postulate relational and non-relational contents in the relevant higher-order states, but the relational content is phenomenally silent. So, the HOROR theory is a mixed non-relational theory in the relevant sense, namely that it rejects (b) above. The first-order states have a functional role to play in the animal's mental life, and reference to them is essential to determining who the subject of the experience is and what they are aware of via inner awareness, but these first-order states have no role to play in the phenomenology of the subject. There is the possibility of a pure non-relational version of HOROR where there is no targeting relation. I will argue in the next chapter that we have reasons for postulating one, but once again, this is largely an empirical issue.

As I defined things, there doesn't seem to be space for a non-traditional relational higher-order theory as that would amount to accepting and rejecting the Transitivity Principle (that is accepting and rejecting that a conscious state is one I am aware of).[4]

If one accepts the traditional Transitivity Principle, then one must decide whether it is to be interpreted relationally or non-relationally. Here we have pure non-relational and mixed non-relational views. Pure non-relationalism posits only descriptive contents in the higher-order states and no relations between levels of content. Mixed-relationalism adds in a relation to the first-order states while denying that these states are phenomenally active. If one prefers relational views, then there are spotlight and joint-determination views. As we have seen these can be thought of as pure and mixed version of relationalism.

The taxonomy has a nice symmetry to it. Pure non-relationalism denies that a relation between higher- and lower-order levels plays any role in phenomenal consciousness. Only the higher-order content is phenomenally active on pure non-relationalism. Pure relationalism, on the other hand, asserts that the relation between these levels does all of the work. Only the first-order content is phenomenally active on pure relationalism. Mixed non-relationalism allows that there is a relation between levels but agrees with the pure non-relationalist that only the higher-order state plays a phenomenally active role. Mixed-relationalism allows that both levels of content are phenomenally active. Pure non-relationalism and mixed-relationalism share that the first-order state can be absent and still result in conscious experience, because the higher-order element is phenomenally active. Pure relationalism and mixed non-relationalism have in common that the first-order state is required to have a conscious state.

We will discuss the current versions of higher-order theory and how they fit into this taxonomy in Chapters 6 and 7. Before doing so I want to turn to justifying the claims I made earlier about the traditional way of presenting the higher-order approach to consciousness.

---

[4] Maybe one could envision a view where the higher-order state had to become related to a first-order state in order for the higher-order state to become phenomenally conscious. I can almost make out such a view in my mind, but it is very strange!

5.3 Reasons for Non-Traditionally Presenting Higher-Order Theories

The organization of this book reflects my belief that the traditional way of presenting the higher-order approach to consciousness in terms of the Transitivity Principle is somewhat outdated and unhelpful. Ultimately, whether any of the versions of higher-order theory discussed in this book can give us a satisfactory account of the nature of phenomenal consciousness is perhaps a vexed question that many will feel uneasy about. However, whether any of these accounts gives us a grip on the neural correlates of phenomenal consciousness is a question that, at least in principle if not soon, we could answer empirically. But even if one of these traditional views turns out to be correct, I still think that presenting higher-order theories as those which accept the Transitivity Principle (i.e., presenting them in the traditional way) is a mistake.

The first and most obvious way that presenting higher-order theories as those that accept the Transitivity Principle is misguided is that there are versions of the theory that do not accept the Transitivity Principle. The consequence of defining higher-order theories in that way would amount to excluding non-traditional theories. But it is hard to see what reason someone might have for saying that the HOROR theory isn't really a higher-order theory. One might suggest that we could modify the Transitivity Principle in some way to include all the higher-order views discussed in this book, but I don't see any way of doing that. Instead, it seems to me that what unifies them is their allegiance to the idea that inner awareness is required or important for phenomenal consciousness as discussed in Chapter 2. They then vary precisely on how they account for that kind of awareness. Certainly, the Transitivity Principle is an important way in which theorists have attempted to interpret what it means for there to be inner awareness, but it is not the only way to do so. Those who endorse the Transitivity Principle should be recognized as traditional higher-order theorists.

Secondly, and related to this, is that unless one is very careful in the way one presents the Transitivity Principle, it is easy to think that the view must be relational. In fact, I would say that most people interpret it in this way. It takes a lot of work to get people to see how one could accept the Transitivity Principle in a non-relational way (as evidenced by the next chapter!). But as we will see in the next two chapters, these two kinds of higher-order theory are very different from each other, and a lot of confusion in the literature can be traced back to people not clearly distinguishing the two kinds of views.

I also think that my way of taxonomizing the theoretical landscape makes sense of the kinds of theories that we find people holding. In the next two chapters I will turn to categorizing the various versions of traditional higher-order theory that people defend and making good on some of my claims to have arguments for preferring a non-traditional mixed non-relational higher-order theory like HOROR. Before doing that, I think that there are at least three other reasons for moving beyond the traditional approach.

5.3.1 Does the Transitivity Principle Fix the Data for a Science of Consciousness?

The first reason that I am hesitant to endorse the traditional approach is due to its insistence on a special status for the Transitivity Principle itself as fixing the data relevant for the science of consciousness. As discussed in Chapter 2, I agree that there is some common-sense appeal to something akin to the Transitivity Principle. As also discussed there, I think this has to do with the common-sense appeal of the notion of inner awareness playing some important role with respect to the mind and consciousness. However, I do not think that this is the way to fix the data for the science of consciousness.

Philosophers like Weisberg and Rosenthal start with a common-sense platitude and then try to regiment it into the Transitivity Principle. That is where they go wrong. There is nothing in the folk-psychological platitude about awareness of mental states. There is just the claim that consciousness is a kind of inner awareness. Even worse are philosophers like Gennaro who claim that the Transitivity Principle is an a priori conceptual truth about conscious states (and he uses this to mean phenomenally conscious). Gennaro is quick to admit that seemingly a priori conceptual truths can be refuted by empirical work (2012, page 29), but is the claim that a conscious state is one I am aware of even seemingly an a priori truth about consciousness? I find that hard to believe.

Some people do find the Transitivity Principle intuitive, some even strongly so. Many others do not. For one thing there seems to be another folk platitude to the effect that one is conscious of just the things in the environment, not of one's inner representations of the environment. It seems somewhat arbitrary to select the one of them as the foundational platitude for the science of consciousness. One of the problems with doing so is that it rules out that there are phenomenally conscious states that you don't know that you have by definition (Brown 2014). Whether there is more to our conscious experience than what we can report is an empirical matter and should not be settled by how one fixes the data, unless it really were the case that it was obvious, or a truism, or a priori, but that hardly seems to be the case. People disagree on the status of the Transitivity Principle, and it might be the case that there are conflicting platitudes in commonsense thinking about the mind and consciousness.

I am not suggesting that something like the Transitivity Principle is known to be false, far from it! I am merely saying that the Transitivity Principle is an empirical conjecture about the nature of consciousness and does not enjoy a special status. In particular it does not fix the data for a science of consciousness without considerable support. One has to argue that this fixes the data for a science of consciousness. I haven't seen anything except appeals to its folk-psychological credibility or a priori status. I want empirical reasons to believe the Transitivity Principle.

As I argued in Chapter 1, what fixes the data for the science of consciousness, or at least for what I called the central challenge of consciousness science, is phenomenal consciousness. This is because what we are trying to explain, predict, and control is what it is like for one to be. The traditional higher-order approach seems to want to re-orient the science of consciousness to 'states of which we are aware' rather than 'states which there is something that it is like for me to be in.' We will come back to this consideration in just a moment.

5.3.2 The Commitment to Unconscious Mental States

The above considerations seem to me to be enough to suggest we look for an alternative way to introduce the theory, but there is another reason to briefly consider. If you set up the goal of a theory of consciousness as explaining the difference between a conscious mental state and an unconscious mental state, then you have begged the question against the claim that there are no unconscious mental states. There are some theorists, for example Ian Philips (Phillips 2021a), who argue that perception always being conscious perception is the default view. There are even some higher-order theorists, for example Joe LeDoux, who think that emotions are always conscious—but nonetheless they are just higher-order states (LeDoux and Brown 2017). I think it is a mistake to say that the goal of a theory of consciousness is to explain the difference between conscious and unconscious mental states because we're not sure if there really is such a difference (Peters and Lau 2015). Conceptually I think we can make sense of there in principle being one (or not), and it is easier to present higher-order views as starting with an unconscious first-order state and then saying that this is not enough for consciousness. Still, it is an empirical question that is ultimately unsettled.

I certainly would not want it to be the case that if we found out that there were no unconscious mental states that meant higher-order theories were false. That's not a way to falsify the general approach. It may be a way to falsify certain versions of the theory, but not the entire approach or class of theories. Therefore, I don't think it's essential to understanding what the theory is (note that if there are unconscious mental states then the higher-order theory has an advantage in explaining their existence).

Rosenthal (in personal communication) has seemed to suggest that higher-order theories really are just those that accept that there are unconscious mental states, even unconscious qualitative states like pain and anger. For Rosenthal, a pain or an experience of blue will have a qualitative component that we have been calling its qualitative character. Many theorists assume that qualitative character must be phenomenally conscious, as discussed in Chapter 1. Rosenthal, and others, have spent a great deal of time arguing that pains and other mental qualities can occur unconsciously (Rosenthal 2005, 2010a; Pereplyotchik 2017). What they mean by this is that the pain can occur, and be qualitative, without any kind of higher-order awareness of the pain. Importantly they also mean that this qualitative state is not phenomenally consciousness when there is no higher-order awareness. These states are genuinely qualitative according to the Rosenthalian approach, and still there will be nothing that it is like for one to be in these qualitative states when they are unconscious.

But this way of distinguishing higher-order theories from first-order theories does not seem right to me. Suppose it turned out, for whatever reason, that qualitative states are wired up in such a way as to always have a higher-order awareness occur. We may imagine a law of nature that necessitates a higher-order awareness every time there is any kind of first-order awareness. Suppose also that this higher-order awareness plays the relevant role in making the first-order state conscious. If so, there would never be any unconscious qualitative states, but a higher-order theory would still be true. Alternatively, suppose that the states that are unconscious are not properly qualitative. Perhaps it is better to think of them as merely non-conscious information processes and not truly mental states at all, let alone nonconscious qualitative mental states. One could think of the first-order mental states that we attribute to ourselves as being a kind of false theory that we apply to our own mind. Again, this would be a view where there were no unconscious mental states, but a higher-order theory was true. This would be a kind of internal version of Dennett's intentional stance where the higher-order system itself takes the intentional stance toward the lower-order processes. Even if seeing or pain were somehow inherently always conscious, it still might be because we are aware of the seeing (Caston 2002).

Given all of this, I don't think it makes sense to define higher-order theories as those that posit unconscious mental states and then try to explain the difference between those and the conscious ones.

5.3.3 Is the Explanatory Target the Same as Other Theories of Consciousness?

Finally, there is the issue of how state and phenomenal consciousness relate to each other. If the goal of a theory of consciousness, according to the traditional approach, is to explain state-consciousness, and yet I have argued that the main goal of a theory of consciousness is to explain phenomenal consciousness, then what is the relation between these two? Are they trying to explain the same thing or are these different phenomena? This has led some to question whether the traditional higher-order approach to consciousness even aims to explain the same phenomenon as the other theories of consciousness (Farrell 2018).

As we discussed back in Chapter 2 (2.3.1), some traditional theorists have tried to reconcile these notions by explicitly connecting the Transitivity Principle to phenomenal consciousness. For example, Berger and Brown (2021) acknowledge that the traditional version of the Transitivity Principle says that a state that one is not aware of being in is not a conscious state. They then point out that one can also say that a state one is not aware of being in is not like anything for one to be in. This allows the Transitivity Principle to be explicitly connected to phenomenal consciousness and results in the claim that if one is in a phenomenally conscious mental state, then one is aware of being in that state (in some suitable sense). If so, this line continues, then the traditional approach holds that it is the first-order state, the targeted state that one is aware of, which is the phenomenally conscious state. Likewise, Rocco Gennaro says, "when I am in a conscious mental state, there is something that it is like, for me to be in that state from the subjective or first-person point of view" (Gennaro 2012, page 6). For these traditional theorists, then, explaining the difference between a conscious mental state, and that same mental state when it is unconscious, amounts to explaining why there is something that it is like for one to be in that mental state at one time, and nothing that it is like for one to be in that mental state at another time. So, for those theorists, state-consciousness is phenomenal consciousness.

This allows those theorists to speak the same language as other theorists, but we have already seen the problems with the attempt to identify state-consciousness and phenomenal consciousness. Before that can be done, we need some empirical reason to think that the Transitivity Principle is correct, and we have not yet seen that kind of evidence.

Rosenthal, on the other hand, has been somewhat ambivalent about phenomenal consciousness. The issues there are tricky, but it is enough to note that even on Rosenthal's view it will be the case that the mental state that there is something that it is like for one to be in will be the targeted first-order state. Whether he wants to call that state phenomenally conscious seems like a terminological issue. Whatever the case with that terminological issue, the above claim is enough to put that version of non-relational theory at odds with the HOROR theory.

In the next chapter I will argue that a pure non-relational theory has trouble with saying which states are the conscious states a subject is in. In fact, the argument serves two purposes. On the one hand it, to me, establishes the need for some kind of pointer content in the higher-order states. On the other hand, it substantiates the claim that the Transitivity Principle doesn't capture what is at issue in the debate. As we will see, once one sees what a conscious state is on this kind of pure non-relational view, we see that state-consciousness is a very odd kind of thing! It can occur even without there even being a first-order state present!

Making sense of this wildly counter-intuitive claim is the job of the next chapter.

6
Non-Relational Versions of Traditional Higher-Order Theories

In this chapter, I will argue that the purely non-relational versions of the traditional approach have a problem specifying which of one's various mental states is the state-conscious state. Since non-relational higher-order theories are traditional in the sense that they aim to give an account of state-consciousness, this puts the theory in some hot water. Mixed non-relational views, which aim to establish some sort of substantial targeting relation between first-order and higher-order states/contents (with identity being the strongest relation), may solve the problem of which state is the conscious state, but require implausible and ad hoc assumptions. I will aim to turn these various differences into possible empirical predictions. In the next chapter we will turn to relational versions of the traditional higher-order thought accounts. There are a substantial number of philosophers who defend versions of non-relational traditional higher-order thought theory. Pure non-relationalists include David Rosenthal (2005) and Josh Weisberg (2011), as well as others (Pereplyotchik 2013; Berger 2014; 2017; Shargel 2016). Mixed non-relationalists include Gennaro (2012) and Uriah Kriegel (2009).

In section 6.1, I begin by closely examining David Rosenthal's Higher-Order Thought Theory. This is the most well-worked-out version of traditional pure non-relationalism. In section 6.2, I turn to examining mixed-non-relationalism. There are two current versions in the form of Uriah Krieigel's self-representational view and Rocco Gennaro's Wide Intentionality View. These views attempt to rule out misrepresentation while also holding onto the claim that the higher-order state determines what is phenomenologically manifest. In section 6.3, I compare these traditional versions of non-relationalism with the HOROR theory, which is a non-traditional mixed non-relationalism.

6.1 Pure Non-relationalism: Higher-Order Thought Theory

David Rosenthal's version of higher-order theory is a non-relational version of higher-order theory. Many people find this surprising because they take his endorsement of the Transitivity Principle to indicate a relational reading of the theory. This is mistaken. Rosenthal has said in many places that his is not a relational theory, but here is one where he is particularly clear, "Since there can be something it's like for one to be in a state with particular mental qualities even if no such state occurs, a mental state's being conscious is not strictly speaking a relational property of that state. A state's being conscious consists in its being a state one is conscious of oneself as being in. Still, it is convenient to speak loosely of the property of a state's being conscious as relational so as to stress that it is in any case not an intrinsic property of mental states" (2005, 211).

It seems to me that it is precisely this loose talk that has led to confusion about Rosenthal's version of the theory. Many readers of this kind of passage take Rosenthal's 'loose talk' of relationality to indicate more than just a denial of the first-order account of consciousness, or more than merely emphasizing the non-intrinsic nature of consciousness on his version of higher-order theory. They take it instead as the much stronger claim that the relational reading of the Transitivity Principle is what Rosenthal has in mind.

As we can see, this is not what Rosenthal has in mind. Instead, what Rosenthal is doing is offering a good old-fashioned philosophical *analysis* of the concept of 'conscious state.' For mental state F to be conscious is just for there to be an appropriate non-relational THOT (Traditional Higher-Order Thought) in one's mind. The occurrence of an appropriate non-relational THOT is what being in a conscious state consists of on Rosenthal's account. What it is like for one to be in F is wholly and completely determined by the occurrence of the non-relational THOT representing oneself as being in F. When the relevant non-relational THOT occurs in the appropriate way F is thereby conscious—by definition—and there is something that it is like for one to be in F, whether F exists in the mind of the organism at that time or not.

There are two major problems with this view, which we will explore in the following sections.

6.1.1 Radical Misrepresentation: Not Enough Conscious States

Let us start with the case of radical misrepresentation. Recall that the Transitivity Principle says that a conscious state is the one that I am aware of myself as being in. We are considering a case where there is no first-order state for one to be aware of being in. So, which state is the conscious-state on pure non-relationalism? The usual answer is that it is the first-order state that is described by the descriptive content of the higher-order state. It is the state that 'fits' or satisfies the descriptive content of the relevant THOT. In the case of radical misrepresentation there is no first-order state that fits the description. So, the state you are aware of yourself as being in is a purely notional non-existent state and that, we are told, is the conscious state you are in. Go ahead and read that again. I know, I also was struck with a case of the *Incredulous Stare* when I first heard this as well. How could there be state-consciousness when there is no existing conscious state?

This is a well-known problem for non-relational versions of the traditional higher-order thought theory (Rosenthal 2005; Kriegel 2003; 2009; Mandik 2009; Weisberg 2011). Consider our two subjects Simon and Alvin from the previous chapter again. Let's vary their experience this time. Alvin has both the first-order representations of the blue sky and the higher-order representation of himself as being in that state. Simon just has the higher-order state and so is in a case of radical misrepresentation. Uriah Kriegel then presents a dilemma for the non-relational theorist. Either (a) what it is like for the two subjects is the same, or (b) what it is like for the two subjects is not the same. Non-relational theorists reject the possibility of (b), so that leaves them with (a).

Here is what Kriegel says, citing a passage from Rosenthal that is similar to the one we have been talking about,

> Let us start with (a), since this is the horn Rosenthal (1990 [/1997 paper in Block, Flannigan, Guzedere]: 744; emphasis added) embraces explicitly in print:
>> Strictly speaking, having a HOT [higher-order thought] cannot of course result in a mental state's being conscious if that mental state does not even exist... Still, a case in which one has a HOT along with a mental state it is about may be *subjectively indistinguishable* from a case in which the HOT occurs but not the mental state. If so, folk psychology would count both as cases of conscious states.
>
> The problem with this response [Kriegel continues] can be set out as follows: the combination of higher-order representationalism and (a) is inconsistent with the following obvious truism:
>> (OT) For any subject S and time t, there is something it is like to be S at t iff there is a mental state M, such that (i) S is in M at t and (ii) M is conscious at t.
>
> In other words, [Kriegel continues] if higher-order representationalism takes the first horn of the dilemma, it entails that OT is false. I take this to be an unacceptable consequence. (2009, 130)

OT here is a formulization of the commonsense claim that phenomenally conscious states have got to exist. HOROR theory satisfies OT, but not everyone thinks that OT is an important truism. Traditional pure non-relationalists tend to reject it straightaway (Berger and Brown 2021).

As an example, Josh Weisberg (2011) responds to this challenge in the following way.

> The subject can be in a conscious state that does not exist because all there is to being in a conscious state is being aware of oneself as being in that state. "Being aware of oneself as..." introduces an intensional context. Conscious states are simply objects of representation, and as such they need not exist. In the same way that I can be aware of the yard as containing a deer, even though no deer exists in the yard, and in the same way I can be aware of myself as being hungry, even when

the biological state of hunger doesn't exist in me (I've just eaten a big meal, say), I can be aware of myself as being in a mental state that I'm not in fact in. And since that is all that's required for being in a conscious state according to the TP, I can be in a conscious state that does not exist. (419)

Non-relational versions of the higher-order approach are representational theories of consciousness (Berger and Brown 2022), and so they invoke the non-existence aspect of representationalism (Pautz 2020). The reason that these non-relational theorists reject the existence claim is precisely because of their analysis of the Transitivity Principle.

When pressed on this issue at the 2012 Towards a Science of Consciousness conference in Tucson, David Rosenthal responded to Ned Block by saying, "one of the things you can do in philosophy, and you're doing it now [Ned] it seems to me, is make things that aren't paradoxical sound paradoxical and people have been doing this in philosophy for millennia" (link here: https://www.youtube.com/watch?v=_ormMOouRKs; go to the fifty-minute mark). Rosenthal's point is that all this talk about non-existent mental states will only seem paradoxical if one formulates the issue in a way that makes it seem paradoxical. According to Weisberg and Rosenthal's background theory of intentionality (Rosenthal 2005, ch. 3), which they are assuming, saying that you're in a conscious state that doesn't exist simply means that you are in the higher-order state, and that this higher-order state has descriptive content that describes you as being in a first-order state (as usual). As luck turns out, the first-order state isn't around. What's so strange? Rosenthal and Weisberg are quick to stress that it doesn't mean there's literally a non-material ghostly thing floating around somewhere non-physically. This is quite confusing to the ordinary theorist who is just trying to figure out what the theory says (!!).

While we can grant this stipulative philosophical point to Rosenthal and Weisberg, it does highlight three important facts about his theory. The first thing to note is that saying that there can be conscious states that don't exist certainly does lead people to believe that there are conscious states with no neural correlates.[1] This is especially true of the

---

[1] As one participant in a seminar once memorably shouted out upon hearing this during Rosenthal's presentation, "he's worse than a dualist!"

casual reader, for example a scientist whose aim is to empirically test the theory. Since the theory is cast in terms of the Transitivity Principle and that says that the conscious state is the first-order state this will naturally lead to the view that we should be looking for the neural correlates of the first-order state. This, of course, delivers exactly the wrong result for the traditional pure non-relational view.

The second important point that all of this shines a light on is that to accept non-relational versions of the traditional approach, one must also accept a view of intentional/conceptual content that allows one to make sense of ascribing properties to non-existent targets. This is an absolutely crucial component of the THOT theorist's account. This can be done, as Rosenthal and Weisberg's work has shown, but it should be made clear that the background theory of intentionality is somewhat controversial. For those who prefer alternative approaches to mental representation, there may be real costs associated with allowing non-existent mental states being conscious. At the very least this highlights that the pure non-relational version of the traditional theory is not obviously compatible with some theories of intentionality, contrary to what its advocates have suggested (Weisberg 2011).

Another point is worth stressing here. Once one finds out what it really means to be in a conscious mental state according to non-relational versions of the THOT theory, one may wonder why it is that we are still calling this a theory of *state* consciousness. There is not really a mental state that is conscious in any real sense in the case of radical misrepresentation. There is the appearance of being in a conscious mental state, which the theory *identifies* with being in a conscious mental state. One cannot help but feel as though the theory was originally cast as a relational version of the theory, and then got switched to a non-relational version when no one was looking (Block 2011a). Whatever the case may be, the possibility of radical misrepresentation shines a stark light on the theoretical costs of non-relational versions of the traditional approach. One needs to *already* have accepted the background account of intentionality that makes all this non-absurd to find any plausibility in it at all. This fact about traditional pure non-relationalism like Rosenthal's THOT theory is often obscured. If one is friendly to that way of thinking about intentionality, then the traditional non-relational versions of traditional higher-order thought theory may be for you. The rest of us may want to look elsewhere.

6.1.2 Garden-Variety Misrepresentation: Too Many Conscious States

It is a cornerstone of non-relational higher-order theories that a first-order mental state can be conscious in some respects but not others (see chapter three and four). Rosenthal (2024) goes so far as to suggest, "a refined version of the Transitivity Principle. The Transitivity Principle holds that a state is conscious only if one is aware of it. On the refined version, a state is conscious in respect of specific mental properties only if one is aware of the state in respect of those mental properties" (21).

To illustrate consider a typical case on the traditional higher-order thought view. One has a red47 mental quality, let's suppose, but no THOT to the effect that one is in that state. Then, according to the traditional higher-order thought theory, it is not like seeing red for one. Suppose one then has a THOT that one is seeing red47, or something in that range. Then it will be like something for one in a very specific way. It will be like seeing a very specific shade of red and will be more like this or that other shade of red and less like that and the other shade of green, and so on.

Now suppose that one moves one's eyes, or something, and so becomes aware of that red47 state in a less fine-grained way, maybe as red but not a particular shade of red. Then that red47 state is conscious in respect of its color, but not its specific shade. What it is like for you changes correspondingly. It will be like seeing some red color without specifying what shade of red it is. In all three cases the very same first-order state is involved according to the non-relational THOT theory. It is first unconscious, then conscious in respect of its detailed properties, and finally conscious only in respect of its general properties. In the second stage the relevant THOT is accurate, and in the third stage the THOT generates a case of garden-variety misrepresentation. It is not as though the THOT is entirely inaccurate. One is seeing a particular shade of red, and so it is true that one is seeing some shade of red or other. It is just that the THOT does not represent as much detail as it could. So, this is an example of relative-sparse content (discussed in Chapter 3).

This is why I call these kinds of cases garden-variety misrepresentation because arguably it is ubiquitous on an account like Rosenthal's. He wants to capture the sense that any given mental state can occur consciously as well as unconsciously and indeed consciously in different respects. But how can we square this way of talking with the analysis of what a conscious state is given in the previous section? There we found out that to be a conscious state was simply to be the state that fits the description deployed by the THOT.

So, in the case where I am in a first-order state of red47 and have a THOT to the effect that I am seeing red47, we can make a reasonable case that the first-order red47 state is the descriptive target of the THOT. But when the content changes to the more generic 'I am seeing red' (or a new THOT is tokened with that content), what reason is there to think that this THOT is misdescribing the original red47 state? Taking its content at face value, it seems like it is describing a mental state that doesn't currently exist. If it were accurate, then the creature in question would be in a first-order state of seeing generic red in the environment. But we have stipulated that this is not the case. So, it seems very reasonable to say that this higher-order state is about some non-occurring first-order state. What reason is there to take the THOT to be describing the red47 state, as opposed to the notional generic red state, or any other state of the mind of the individual?

One could argue that the red47 state does fit the description of generic red in that it is red. But it is a specific mental quality, and the higher-order state is here representing it as a generic red, isn't that a case of misrepresentation? If the organism is capable of being in a first-order state that would make the higher-order state accurate, then the higher-order state is misrepresenting its target. One possible response is that it is always the notional state, which is the conscious state, but it seems very puzzling to say that a theory of state consciousness is a theory of notional states being conscious.

The basic issue in this case is that we need some way in which to specify which first-order state(s) are the ones being described. 'Fitting the description' seems to leave too many borderline cases. Without any kind of relational content in the THOT, it starts to seem arbitrary which first-order state (if any) counts as the conscious state.

The previous puzzle involved one mental state transitioning from conscious in respect A to conscious in respect B. There is another puzzle in the other direction, so to speak. Ned Block (2023) has made a similar argument. He says,

> to see the problem, consider a [THOT] to the effect that I myself am seeing green. Let's say that this thought lasts two seconds and that there are two perceptions of green that occur at different times during those two seconds. Suppose further, that if we had asked the subject to press a button when they saw green, the time of the button press would pinpoint one of the perceptions as conscious but not the other. Note that what I am supposing here is that a certain counterfactual is true, not that the subject was ever asked to press a button when seeing green. The point of making this evidence counterfactual is that it provides evidence that one but not the other perception is conscious without elaborating the example in a way that would make it part of the example that the identifying information made it into the HOT. I am supposing that the HOT does not contain any information that would decide between the two perceptions. So the two perceptions equally satisfy the HOT, but only one is conscious, thus revealing an inadequacy in the HOT theory. (424)

I am very sympathetic to this argument. However, I think it has a flaw that the previous version I presented does not.

The problem with Block's version of the argument is that he stipulates that a behavioral task would have indicated one of the first-order perceptions was conscious. The obvious problem here is that someone like Rosenthal may say that the button push was caused by the unconscious perception. Why think that the (presumably) first-order state that is causally responsible for my button pushing is the one which is conscious? Counter-factual or not, this is actually question begging against Rosenthal's view. It does seem like it makes intuitive sense to say that one of the perceptions of green was conscious while the other was not. But must we say that?

When Block first presented a case like this during a presentation that Jake Berger and I gave (for Berger and Brown 2021), we suggested that both of the states may be conscious in Block's case.[2] Rosenthal (personal communication) seemed to agree afterward. From his theoretical standpoint it does make some sense. Neither of the two first-order states contribute to one's phenomenology according to the non-relationalist. What it is like for you is as the THOT represents your mental life to be, and the states that are conscious are the ones that meet the descriptive satisfaction conditions of that THOT's content. So, both states count as being conscious in the sense that they each fit the description equally well. None of this will make any difference to the mental functioning of the animal. All we are arguing about, it would seem, is purely a matter of how to use various words after all the real theoretical work has been done. Once you have made it that far into pure non-relationalism, it starts to seem that what we are doing is just trying to find some interpretation on which there is a first-order state we could say is conscious, in which case it sounds like a mental state's being conscious, for Rosenthal, is not really a property that matters or plays any role.

To some theorists this may be liberating. For those who think of phenomenal consciousness as a psychologically real property of the mind, it is a reason to look for some relational component of the higher-order state that allows us to say which first-order state is conscious. This is exactly the lesson that the HOROR theorist draws from this dispute. We saw in Chapter 3 that there were a couple of candidates for what kind of phenomenally silent content may play this role. Block does mention a view like this (425). However, he does not recognize that one can distinguish phenomenal consciousness from state-consciousness in the way we did in Chapter 2. Once one makes the distinction between phenomenal consciousness and state-consciousness Block's objection, which amounts to a case of radical mismatch, is not a problem for HOROR.

---

[2] In Berger and Brown 2021 I am exploring what a traditional pure non-relationalist should say to various objections. As I have said in various places, I split my credence between these views. I may have personal preferences, but my ultimate desire is to see all of these views worked out in enough detail that we could see what kind of empirical challenges we can throw at them. The argument I gave in the text is one I came up with after our presentation, and before I read Block's new book (Block 2023).

It seems like we are left with a proliferation of conscious states. One could say any of one's mental states were the conscious state, or none of them. To put it in another way, pure non-relational versions of higher-order thought theory don't have any non-question-begging way of saying what the non-relational THOT is about. It has descriptive content that can be satisfied in many ways. Without some kind of relational content to secure reference to the first-order states/processes, there is no non-arbitrary way of saying which states of mine are conscious. As I have stated repeatedly throughout the book, this is my primary reason for thinking that there must be some kind of relational content in any successful higher-order theory.[3]

6.1.3 The Self

It is often held by non-relational theorists that the self is always around to be represented and so there can be no radical misrepresentation there. But the details of the self-content on non-relational theories are sketchy indeed! Are there really no cases where the self isn't around on traditional non-relationalism?

Rosenthal (2011b) has noted that it is tempting to think of the mental analogue of 'I' referring to the subject as the thinker of the relevant non-relational THOT. On that tempting view the relevant THOTs would have something like the following as its content,

the thinker of this very thought is seeing red

---

[3] This issue generalizes quite a bit. Consider one more set of cases that are slightly more radical.
Case 1: One tokens an appropriate non-relational THOT perfectly describing a state one had yesterday when one doesn't have it now
Case 2: Same as case 1 but one also has the first-order state again along with the THOT
If the THOT in case 1 is arrived at in the usual way, what prevents it from being the case that the non-existent state that one had yesterday is the conscious state? In case 2 what rules out both the states being conscious? One may be able to tell an ad hoc story about why it is or isn't the case that one or the other of these mental states is conscious, but as far as I can tell that is the best that can be done. Without any relational content in the THOT, one is free to say whatever one wants about which state is conscious. Perhaps in every case it is both the tokened first-order state and the notional intentional state which are conscious; why not?

This can't be exactly right, though. One cannot explicitly think of oneself as the very person who is thinking the higher-order thought, as that would make one aware of the higher-order thought, which would make it conscious. Rosenthal denies that this typically happens. He has instead argued that the relevant THOT refers to the subject implicitly. So how does one manage to implicitly refer to the self as the thinker of the higher-order thought? Rosenthal's idea is that the 'I' refers to the self in virtue of a disposition that one has to answer the question 'who is having this thought' with 'I am.' This rarely comes up, on Rosenthal's rendering of the situation. If it ever did, and if the relevant THOT was itself conscious, we would answer in the way above. That is enough, on Rosenthal's view, to secure refence to self. The disposition is a part of mental reality, and even if one's THOT is never itself conscious, it can still manage to refer to the subject in virtue of the disposition being there.

Timothy Liang and Caleb Lane (2009) argue that the case of somatoparaphrenia presents a counter-example to Rosenthal's account. They present the case of FB, who had alien limb syndrome and denied that her left arm belonged to her. When touched on this arm she denied feeling it. But when told that researchers were going to touch the arm of her niece, FB reported feeling the sensation. Lane and Liang argue that this is a straightforward case where FB is not aware of the sensation as belonging to herself. If we take her at face value, she seems to be having the paradoxical experience of feeling a sensation that isn't her own.

Rosenthal (2010b) responds that there are two ways in which we can have mental ownership. One is as having the subjective sense that it is one's own experience. The other is a subjective sense of bodily location. Rosenthal uses phantom limbs as an analogical case. When one is missing an arm but has an experience as of clenching one's fist, one experiences a subjective sense of having a sensation located in one's hand and knuckles. One experiences the sensation as belonging to oneself, but being located on a part of your body that does not exist. So too, Rosenthal urges, FB is conscious of the touch as belonging to herself (which results in there being a conscious state on Rosenthal's view). She is also, according to him, conscious of that sensation as having a subjective location on her niece's arm instead of her own arm.

Rosenthal interprets the case as FB having something like the experience of *FB (herself) feeling something touching her niece's arm*. Her THOT, on his account, would be something like

I, myself, am feeling a touch on my niece's arm

On this interpretation it is her, FB, who is having the strange experience of feeling something that is happening. It is just that she experiences it subjectively as having a location on someone else's body. It is still her (FB) who is feeling it, not her niece, according to Rosenthal's interpretation. On Lane and Liang's interpretation, FB does not experience the sensation as being hers. She experiences it as belonging to her niece, not simply as something of hers that happens to be located in a strange place (i.e., her niece's arm).

Lane and Liang respond that even if we accept Rosenthal's interpretation, which is somewhat controversial, it still does not establish that the subject can never be wrong about who the thinker of the thought is. Rosenthal says we have a disposition to identify ourselves as the thinker of the relevant higher-order thought. Yet couldn't FB respond to Rosenthal's question about who is it who is aware of the touch by saying that it is her niece who is aware of the sensation? I take Lane and Liang to be arguing that this is a reasonable and plausible interpretation of these kinds of results, and I think they are right.

Gennaro suggests (Gennaro 2020) that perhaps these kinds of cases can be interpreted as subjects having an ordinary experience of the touch sensation in addition to a conscious belief that the sensation belongs to someone else. This interpretation is a possibility, but all of this is speculative and awaits further empirical work.

Thus, as in the case with conscious states, we see a similar problem with the self. It seems that on pure non-relationalism it is always arbitrary what the state refers to.

6.2 Mixed Non-Relationalism

The above results for a purely non-relational view have led many philosophers friendly to the higher-order approach to search for a way to preserve the basic insight of the traditional non-relational approach while prohibiting radical misrepresentation. Recall that as I use the terms what makes a higher-order view traditional is that it accepts the Transitivity Principle, which says that a conscious state is one we are conscious of. Mixed non-relational versions of the traditional approach agree that conscious states are ones we are aware of, but also that they have a complex structure where one part of the state represents the other part. As a result, the state ends up representing itself, or aspects of itself. Mixed non-relational versions of this kind of view hold that what it is like for the subject is determined by the higher-order content of the complex state. Even in cases of garden-variety misrepresentation, where there is a mismatch between higher-order and first-order contents of the same state, what it is like for the subjects follows the higher-order content. Because of this, these kinds of views are non-relational as I use the term. One's phenomenology is completely determined by the higher-order content, and the other components of the view are merely aimed at securing a first-order state. The first-order contents, on mixed non-relational views, are phenomenally silent. In other words, the idea is to try and solve the problems discussed in the previous section by finding a relation that requires a first-order state to exist to satisfy the requirement that there is some first-order state be conscious.

6.2.1 Self-Representationalism

Kriegel has argued for what he calls a self-representational view where the state we are conscious of and our awareness of it are the same state. Thus, Kriegel's self-representational view accepts the Transitivity Principle and qualifies as a traditional higher-order account on my way of using the terms.

Kriegel's account is also non-relational as I use the term. While Kriegel wants to argue that what he calls 'targetless' higher-order states can't occur, he allows garden-variety misrepresentation. Here is where he explicitly endorses this, "So, if a mental state misrepresents itself to be F when in reality it is G, where F and G are schmalitative properties, then self-representationalism's verdict is that the state is merely schmalitatively G but qualitatively F. For what it means for a state to be qualitatively F is that it represents itself to be F." (Kriegel 2009, 207). A 'schmalitative' property for Kriegel is a first-order representation of F or G. He is here using the term 'qualitative' for the phenomenologicaly manifest aspect of phenomenal character. It should be clear from this that Kriegel's theory is committed to the claim that it is the higher-order content of the state that determines what it is like for one.

Kriegel argues that when we have a targetless higher-order content there will be no conscious state on the grounds that there will be no complex state formed—hence, no first-order state of which we are aware. Yet, as others have argued it is not clear why this should be so (Weisberg 2011; Levine 2010). Because Kriegel's case is more stipulative, and Rocco Gennaro actually tries to argue for this conclusion in more detail, I will save discussion of this issue until the next section. To give a sneak peek of what I will argue there, I think that non-relational theories are committed to the view that targetless higher-order states can occur and that in such cases there will be a notional first-order state that the theory says is the conscious state. Ultimately, working through all this lets us see the differing empirical predictions each theory makes.

Kriegel's argument for self-representationalism is his 'epistemic argument' (2009, 121). His starting point is not just the Transitivity Principle, which says that conscious states are ones we are aware of, but also the stronger claim that we are *consciously* aware of our conscious states. We might call this the Strong Transitivity Principle or STP:

STP: If a mental state is phenomenally conscious then I am in some suitable sense *consciously* aware of being in that state

Kriegel argues from STP to self-representationalism, but why should we accept STP? He argues that we have phenomenological evidence for STP. We can tell by introspection that there is a kind of inner awareness on his view.

More strongly Kriegel argues that if we have any evidence for the Transitivity Principle it must come from direct phenomenological evidence, and this commits us to STP. As he puts it (2009, 118),

If conscious states are not always consciously represented, however, then there cannot be *direct* phenomenological evidence for their always being represented (at all). For, in that scenario, even if all conscious states are represented, at least some are unconsciously represented. Since their representation is unconscious, there will be no direct phenomenological evidence of it. The evidence must be different. I will now consider four possible alternative sources of evidence: indirect phenomenological evidence, a posteriori experimental evidence, a priori conceptual-analysis evidence, and philosophical principles. After arguing against each possibility, I will conclude that, if there is *any* evidence for the proposition that all conscious states are represented, it must be direct phenomenological evidence. Since the only way there could be direct phenomenological evidence for all conscious states being represented is if all conscious states were *consciously* represented, I will conclude that all conscious states are consciously represented.

As we can see it is commitment to STP that distinguishes traditional self-representationalism from THOT theories. This is a substantial difference, but it does obscure their allegiance to traditional non-relationalism. Where they differ there is on their theory of intentionality that gives us the pure and mixed versions of non-relationalism.

Many people do not find the phenomenological evidence that Kriegel appeals to. One of them is Gennaro, who we will discuss in the next section. I have denied the traditional Transitivity Principle and of course deny STP as well. I do accept a notion in the vicinity. I argued in Chapter 3 that subjective character may be phenomenologically manifest in virtue of being a phenomenally active component of the relevant HOROR. This does not amount to STP, though. I find it to be the case that sometimes I am aware of my phenomenally conscious states, and sometimes I am not. I think that the HORIFIC account of introspection offered in Chapter 3 (section 3.4) can account for the cases where we are consciously aware of our conscious experiences, by in effect representing that it is so.

As I argued in Chapter 4, I explicitly opt for Kriegel's 'a posteriori empirical evidence' as a reason to motivate any theory of consciousness. Kriegel's objection is that there was not any evidence at the time that this might be the case. I don't see why that should count against this being a reason to take the theory seriously. I do agree, though, that there is no empirical evidence for the Transitivity Principle, either strong or weak. Lacking evidence simply means there are no empirical reasons to accept the theory. I think it is useful to explore theoretical space even if one cannot connect it to empirical results right away. Either way, it is important to note that what Kriegel is looking for is something that supports STP. As I have argued in the last chapter, I don't think this is what supports these kinds of theories. Only the cumulative empirical case matters.

6.2.2 The Wide Intentionality View

Rocco Gennaro's version of mixed non-relationalism is called the Wide Intentionality View. Gennaro argues that we have a higher-order 'metapsychological' state (the MET as he calls it), and this gets bound up with a first-order mental state M to form the CMS (conscious mental state). The CMS is a complex of M (the world-directed part) and MET (the part representing one as being in M). On Gennaro's view the CMS has the structure where the MET represents M, but MET and M are part of one complex mental state that is conscious. Gennaro wants to deny that the MET is itself conscious (as opposed to Kriegel, who argues that the whole complex of the first-order content bound to the higher-order content is itself conscious, though in a peripheral way). The MET is, on Gennaro's view, a state-unconscious part of a conscious state. In the language I have been developing, it is a phenomenally silent aspect of the CMS. Gennaro thus rejects STP as well.

Gennaro (2012) attempts to argue for option 1 that we previously discussed (as opposed to Kriegel, who basically stipulates that this is the case). Recall that option 1 stated that in cases of radical misrepresentation there was no conscious state. Gennaro is explicit about this saying, "if there isn't a match (that is, an accurate representation) between a [THOT] concept and the content of a lower-order state, then it seems perfectly appropriate for the [THOT theorist] to hold that something like [the claim that there is no conscious state] is a legitimate possibility" (61).

Gennaro considers many empirical cases and ends up 'clarifying' his view as follows (180), "(2") Whenever a subject S has a [higher-order thought] directed at [an experience] e, the content c of S's [higher-order thought] determines the way that S experiences e (provided that there is a full or partial conceptual match with the lower-order state, or when the higher-order state contains more specific or fine-grained concepts than the lower-order state has, or when the lower order states contains more specific or fine-grained concepts than the higher-order state has, or when the higher-order concepts can combine to match the lower-order concept)."

So, Gennaro allows all kinds of garden-variety mismatch between the higher-order and lower-order states. In each case he argues that what it is like for the subject is given by the higher-order content. So, when the higher-order states are more general, the experience is more general (160). When the higher-order concepts are narrower, the experience is narrower as a result (179). In each case the way that the experience is for the subject is determined by the higher-order content. But when the first order-state is completely absent, or when the higher-order state can't be matched in some way, as perhaps a first-order representation of red that was bound to a higher-order awareness of hearing a trumpet, then he claims that there is no conscious mental state at all.

In this way Gennaro seems to attempt to walk the line between what I have called joint-determination views and traditional non-relational views. Joint-determination views are discussed in detail in Chapter 7, but recall that we introduced them in Chapter 5. These kinds of views hold not only that the first-order states exist but also that they make a genuine contribution to the phenomenology of the subject. Gennaro seems to endorse a kind of joint-determination because he insists that the first-order state must exist and that there must be a conceptual match (in some sense) between the two states. Then the first-order state, by virtue of its relation to the higher-order state, becomes conscious. Gennaro also seems to want to endorse key aspects of non-relationalism in that he insists that what it is like for one is completely determined by the conceptual content of the MET (i.e., the appropriate higher-order state). But when one follows the line of reasoning started here all the way to the radical misrepresentation cases, Gennaro insists that there is nothing that it is like for the subject.

There is no conscious mental state. Thus, on Gennaro's view there is a kind of joint-determination—both states are needed, and they must match in some sense—even though the phenomenology is not really jointly determined by both states.

Consider one of the empirical cases that Gennaro uses to make his argument, that of visual form agnosia. Visual form agnosia is an unfortunate condition where someone is unable to recognize what an object is on the basis of looking at it, though they may be able to use the object if asked to reach for it. Take a case where someone is looking at some object, a whistle is the classic example, and yet the subject fails to recognize that it is a whistle. Gennaro suggests an interpretation of this kind of case (2012, 159) where the higher-order content includes things like the color and shape of the stimulus, but not that it is a whistle. So, there is a partial match between the first-order and higher-order levels. Up until this point there is no real difference between this and the pure non-relational views. Once there is no first-order state at all Gennaro rejects non-relationalism. So, what is Gennaro's reason for rejecting non-relationalism?

Gennaro says, objecting to basically Rosenthal's version of non-relationalism (discussed in previous section), "The main problem is that one wonders what the point of having both a lower-order and a higher-order [mental state] is if only one of them determines the conscious experience. Moreover, higher-order thought theory is supposed to be a theory of (intransitive) state consciousness; that is, the lower-order state is supposed to be the conscious state" (60). As we have already seen in the previous chapters, the non-relationalist has an easy answer to the 'main problem.' They posit different roles for the two states. One is tied to behavior and the other is tied to phenomenology. Isn't a version of this also true on Gennaro's account? Isn't the first-order, world-directed content of the CMS responsible for button pushing and so on, and the higher-order MET content of the CNS responsible for what it is like for one?

Gennaro also makes it clear that he thinks in terms of traditional higher-order thought theory in that he takes it as obvious that the first-order state must be the conscious state. Setting aside the issue of HOROR and what the goal of higher-order theories ought to be, Gennaro here has offered no reason for rejecting traditional versions of non-relational theories. As we saw in the previous section, Rosenthal and Weisberg have been defending a traditional version of non-relationalism that claims the lower-order state is the conscious state (in a non-relational way), and that there are different roles for first-order and higher-order states.

Gennaro goes on to say that non-relational theories are implausible because, "Since the higher-order thought is itself unconscious, there would not be a conscious state at all unless there is also an accompanying lower-order state. We would merely have an unconscious higher-order thought without a target state, which by itself cannot result in a conscious state" (61). Gennaro is indeed unhappy with the non-relational reading of the Transitivity Principle, but these are not good reasons for rejecting it. It is only if one has rejected the non-relational reading of the Transitivity Principle that one would be allowed to say that there would be no conscious state without the lower-order state. The traditional non-relationalists like Weisberg and Rosenthal have offered an analysis of what it means to be in a conscious mental state in a non-relational way. As we have seen, I disagree with it, but it is not clear why Gennaro does.

What we can conclude from our discussion of Gennaro's view is that his view seems to imply non-relationalism and that the kinds of cases he appeals to do not really get at the main issue. To make the case for Gennaro's 2" empirically, one would need to find cases where there was a kind of radical misrepresentation, and then show that in such cases there was no conscious experience. The kinds of cases that Gennaro adduces all have in common that the relevant first-order states are present and that there is a posited higher-order awareness of those states. In fact, Gennaro's clarified view seems very close to Rosenthal's refined Transitivity Principle. The basic idea behind both is that it is the way in which one represents one's mental life that determines what it is like for one to be in the first-order states.

6.3 Comparing HOROR and Traditional Non-Relationalism

When I first started thinking about these issues, I interpreted myself as someone who was trying to formulate David Rosenthal's higher-order thought theory in terms that an opponent like Ned Block could accept. It had seemed to me that a lot of the discussion between the two camps had been at cross-purposes. I would find myself saying the following kinds of things all the time. "What Rosenthal really meant was," or "putting it in your terms, his point is..." So, at first, I thought that the HOROR theory was just a terminological variant of the traditional higher-order thought theory (and Rosenthal has occasionally suggested something like this as well in personal communication).

However, as I thought through the issues, I gradually came to see the distinction between relational and non-relational versions of the theory as well as the differences between versions of traditional and non-traditional non-relational views. I think it is reasonably clear from what has been argued so far that the HOROR theory is distinct in many ways from the Traditional Higher-Order Thought theory, but it is useful to emphasize some key points.

6.3.1 Rejecting the Transitivity Principle Is Bad, M'kay?

In his most recent discussion of these issues Rosenthal says that I am confusing a state's being conscious with a necessary condition for consciousness. (Rosenthal 2022, 251). And I do say that the phenomenal character of an experience is given by the 'seeing red' part of the HOROR, and this is pretty much saying that the seeing of red is a conscious state, right? It will appear to the subject as though they are seeing red, and so shouldn't the conscious state be the first-order state?

Rosenthal makes his cases, saying, "There is no qualitative consciousness without a [Higher-Order Awareness]. But one is rarely aware of any [higher-order] state. So there's rarely anything it's like to be in a [higher-order] state, and [higher-order] states are almost never conscious" (251). According to this objection, a higher-order representation is necessary for one to be in a conscious state, but since one is not (typically) aware of the higher-order state, one should not think of that state as a conscious state. One should think of the conscious state as the one you represent yourself as being in, even if it is notional; oh no, not this again!

This objection clearly assumes that the Transitivity Principle is a necessary condition for a state to be conscious—as do other objections that object to the higher-order state itself being the phenomenally conscious state. As we have seen, I gave a HORORibly simple argument that the higher-order state is the phenomenally conscious (but not state-conscious) state in section 2.3.2. A phenomenally conscious state is one that, when one is in that state, there is something that it is like for one. It is the state that, when one is in that state, there is subjective and phenomenal character. The HOROR is the state that, when one is in it, there is something that it is like for one to be in it. Rosenthal is right that when one has a phenomenally conscious experience the state that one subjectively appears to be in is state-conscious, but it is not phenomenally conscious. One can be in that first-order state, in just the same way that one is when that state is state-conscious, and yet there be nothing that it is like for one. This is just what happens when the first-order state occurs unconsciously on the THOT account. That means that the first-order state is not the one that, when it occurs, there is something that it is like for one to be in it.

This is related to the challenge that Chalmers presents from the meta-problem of consciousness first encountered back in Chapter 1. HOROR theory is somewhat like the kind of view he looks at that claims that phenomenal consciousness is associated with certain higher-order processes (3.2.3). The challenge is that intuitively we think of what it is that these states are representing as being the conscious states. Chalmers seems to be implying that he assumes that this is part of the ordinary notion of phenomenal consciousness. That is, that the ordinary notion of phenomenal consciousness assumes that it is the first-order states that should be the ones that are phenomenally conscious. But it is not clear to me that this is part of folk-psychology. Certainly, it is part of commonsense that there is something it is like for me to see red, but where in that is there anything about it being some first-order representation of red that gets the job done? Any intuitiveness attached to this must derive from what is phenomenologically manifest. Since this can be explained by the HOROR theory, it cannot be used as an argument against that view.

I will also note that even though on HOROR it is the higher-order state that is phenomenally conscious, it is not the case that I am typically aware of being in this higher-order state. I am aware of red, in the world. On the view of introspection discussed in section 3.4, this is exactly what we would predict. When we introspect, on my view, we experience ourselves as experiencing being visually presented with a primitive property of the perceptible environment. It never seems to me that the higher-order state is conscious, that is a theoretical claim that comes at a much later point once one begins trying to make definite the vague claim that inner awareness is an important part of phenomenal consciousness. In this way HOROR theory can agree that it doesn't seem to us that we have these kinds of higher-order representations. Even so, there are reasons (empirical reasons to be exact) for taking this hypothesis seriously. So, I don't think we need any conceptual re-engineering to take the HOROR theory seriously.

Rosenthal presses his challenge saying that without the traditional Transitivity Principle phenomenal consciousness remains unexplained (ibid.), however it is unclear what this could mean that doesn't assume the Transitivity Principle. The HOROR theory does attempt to explain phenomenal consciousness. As we have seen in our discussion in Chapter 2, I accept a modified Transitivity Principle I called HTTP (2.3.1.). HTTP says that a phenomenally conscious state is a state of inner awareness. As I have argued, I don't think we should take the HOROR theory seriously because it has its roots in commonsense. There is a commonsense platitude, involving inner awareness, that suggests itself as a platform for further theorizing, but I don't think it leads to the Traditional Transitivity Principle. Still, it is perfectly fine to say that the difference between a state-conscious mental state and a state-unconscious mental state involves that state being the target of a higher-order representation.

More importantly for my purposes is that the commonsense distinction allows us to say that when we are in no way aware of ourselves as being in some first-order state, there is no phenomenal consciousness. When there is no inner awareness there is no phenomenal consciousness. So, we can still capture the commonsense idea that some states are not phenomenally conscious and its relation to higher-order awareness.

I conclude that there is no challenge to the HOROR theory from these objections.

6.3.2 Differing Empirical Predictions?

We have now seen the various versions of the traditional non-relational approach and the reasons that I prefer the HOROR theory. As I have said all along, I think all of the issues are empirical. We can view each theory as making a prediction about empirical cases of misrepresentation. As many philosophical reservations as I have about traditional non-relational views, if the data supports that kind of theory, then I will support it.

We can see that all the disputes in the previous philosophical literature about higher-order theories ultimately boil down to different versions of mismatch cases. Rosenthal (2005) classically argued for his view using wine tasting. When we drink wine, we may learn to appreciate new tastes in the wine's taste that we hadn't previously had concepts for. This amounts to the empirical prediction that acquiring a new concept and deploying it in the relevant higher-order state will result in new phenomenal character while the first-order state remains unchanged. The first-order theorists countered that it is possible that the higher-order state changes the first-order state or produces a new one with that mental quality. Similarly, when Rosenthal discusses dental fear, he has in mind a mismatch case. In that case one is having a first-order sensation of vibration + anxiety. Yet one's higher-order state represents that as your being in pain. Rosenthal predicts that in this case one experiences pain, not vibration with a false belief.

The HOROR theory and traditional pure non-relationalism have in common the claim that first-order states can be state-conscious in various respects. As we have seen the pure non-relationalism of the higher-order thought theory does not have any non-question-begging way to say which state is the conscious state. The HOROR theory avoids this issue by postulating phenomenally silent relational content in the relevant HORORs. So HOROR predicts, while traditional higher-order thought theories do not, that there should be a component of the higher-order state that serves to identify the first-order state to which the description is being applied. If this turned out to be incorrect, then one could opt for a pure version of HOROR depending on what background philosophical theory of intentionality one was partial to. The remaining issue would be over whether the view should be traditional or non-traditional, and that brings up the issues about intentionality again. These philosophical issues are interesting, but I think they go beyond what is empirically testable.

Pure non-relational theories therefore make the prediction that there can be radical and garden-variety misrepresentation, but also asserts that the first-order states are the conscious ones. This is confusing in that they also assert that the neural correlates of consciousness will be the neural correlates of the higher-order state. So pure non-relational views like Rosenthal's HOT theory will identify the neural correlates of consciousness with the neural correlates of the higher-order state just as HOROR does. That is, if one is experiencing seeing blue on traditional pure non-relationalism, then one should be looking for the neural correlate of the higher-order state, not the neural correlate of the first-order state. If so, then one cannot empirically distinguish pure HOROR theory from non-relational HOT theory in this way. The real difference between them lies in the background theory of intentionality. One could have a version of HOROR that invoked Rosenthal's theory of intentionality, but traditional non-relationalism only works with Rosenthal's theory of intentionality. Any reason to be skeptical of a pure kind of holism about meaning is a reason to be skeptical of traditional non-relationalism.

Mixed non-relational theories make the prediction that there may be garden-variety cases of misrepresentation but that there cannot be cases of radical or targetless misrepresentation. Kriegel goes on to make somewhat speculative, but more specific suggestions about the neural correlates of his kind of theory.

> In any case, the [Cross-Order Integration, which is later called Self-Representationalism] hypothesis for the NCC is based on the idea that the same sort of synchronization we have focused on may unify a first-order representation with a representation of that very representation. If the brain harbored two synchronized representations, one in V4 representing redness and another in (say) the [dorsal lateral prefrontal cortex] representing increased firing rate in V4, at the personal level we would experience ourselves to have a single representation that folds within it both an awareness of red and an awareness of that awareness. That is the sort of cognitive character that,

according to self-representationalism, distinguishes conscious states from non-conscious ones. (246)

It also follows from this that if we had two synchronized representations, one in V4 representing blue and the other in the prefrontal cortex representing the firing rate for red, then Kriegel's view predicts that the subject would experience red. Furthermore, if you blocked the activity in V4 but nonetheless preserved the activity in the prefrontal cortex, then Kriegel's view predicts that even though there is a higher-order representation of seeing red, there is no red phenomenology. I am not aware of any direct test of these ideas, but they are testable at least in principle.

Overall then we can see that Kriegel's self-representationalism is not that different from a prefrontally implemented version of HOROR (discussed in Chapter 4), albeit without the additional claim that these representations must be synchronized and without the denial that there would be phenomenology in the targetless case. Thus, there seems to be a resolvable empirical issue between these kinds of theories. What happens in cases of radical misrepresentation might be a way to test between these views with the ultimate aim of consolidating them.

Gennaro takes a different interpretation of the neural implementation of his theory. Gennaro argues that "we can thus think of reentrant feedback as an unconscious [Higher-Order Thought] or MET [Metapsychological state] directed at a lower-level mental state M. M will not become conscious without a MET. However, M may persist unconsciously during the feedforward sweep." On Gennaro's hypothesis, then, we should expect the neural correlates of a phenomenally conscious state to involve reentrant feedback loops between areas of the brain associated with self-consciousness and first-order content areas like V5. Gennaro cites possible candidates for the self-consciousness aspect as the medial and inferior parietal cortices, the temporoparietal cortex, the posterior cingulate cortex, and the anterior cingulate cortex (281). Gennaro offers this explicitly as an alternative to long-range temporal synchrony, though he does suggest (301) that we might explore how these two approaches could work together.

This debate is interesting for many reasons. One of them is that it really highlights that we are not sure how these various theories are related to one another. Might Lamme's theory that reentrant processing is required be a neurological implementation of Gennaro's version of higher-order theory? Is synchrony between areas required or something else, perhaps an index or pointer as suggested by HOROR and other more relational theories? Is a pointer, as postulated by HOROR, dependent on neural synchrony in any way?

The remaining disputes among these various higher-order theories await empirical adjudication. Most of the remaining disputes involve how tightly connected the two different levels of content are. The exciting thing is that there is a real chance that we could see some progress in consolidating these ideas, though of course background philosophical disputes will remain (as on which theory of intentionality one prefers, etc.).

Interestingly it has recently been suggested that perhaps these kinds of mixed non-relational views need to move to something that allows the first-order state to directly contribute its content to the higher-order state (McClelland 2020). Perhaps something like mental quotation would better capture the core claim of these views? That brings us to relational versions of the traditional approach.

7
Relational Versions of Traditional Higher-Order Theories

Higher-order theories have gained in popularity as of late. The interesting thing is that many of the 'new' varieties that have appeared in the last ten to twenty years have been relational versions of the traditional higher-order approach (Picciutto 2011; Sauret and Lycan 2014; Coleman 2015; Fleming 2020; Lau 2022; Giustina forthcoming). Many take it as something akin to obvious that the first-order state must somehow be involved in the 'final product' of the higher-order process. Relational versions of the tradition higher-order approach typically search for something besides representation to model inner awareness.

All relational versions of the traditional approach are united by two claims. One is the Transitivity Principle, that a conscious mental state is one of which I am, in some suitable way, aware of (myself as) being in. The other is that the Transitivity Principle should be interpreted relationally, which amounts to the claim that the state of which I am aware must play some role in determining the overall phenomenology of the subject. The question then becomes one of finding the appropriate relationship that might exist between first-order states and the higher-order states that target them. The motivating idea behind the relational versions of the traditional approach is that the first-order states themselves becomes conscious, and that this is a substantial change in the state that in some sense allows it to become phenomenologically manifest.

Relational versions of the traditional higher-order approach somewhat resemble naïve realism in the philosophy of perception in the sense that the mental qualities that we are aware of have their qualitative aspects even when we are in no way aware of them. This is for me a major reason for being skeptical of relational theories.

Consciousness as Representing One's Mind. Richard Brown, Oxford University Press.
© Oxford University Press 2025. DOI: 10.1093/oso/9780197784006.003.0008

As with non-relational theories, there are many varieties of traditional relational higher-order theories. These kinds of theories are especially inviting in that they propose the possibility of having the best parts of both higher-order and first-order theories. Consciousness requires a kind of inner awareness as the traditional higher-order approach requires, but it also requires first-order content of the right kind, as first-order views require.

While not exactly higher-order theories in the sense invoked here (i.e., in the sense of attempting to explain phenomenal consciousness), it is helpful to start with views that invoke acquaintance before turning to specific versions of relational higher-order theories. In section 7.1, I begin by discussing a related view that appeals to acquaintance and non-physical qualia. This will set the theme for our discussion. In section 7.2, I examine several versions of pure relationalism, what I have called spotlight views. As of now I am aware of five such views. (1) Mental Quotation (discussed in section 7.2.2), (2) non-representational intentionality (what I call 'Attentional Sifting') (7.2.3), (3) dual-content theory (7.2.4), and the latest addition, Perceptual Reality Monitoring (7.2.5). Afterward we turn to the comparatively few versions of the joint-determination view. A classic version of the view is the traditional higher-order perception theory (7.3.1). We then discuss a more recent version of this kind of view, which is called the Higher-Order State Space model (7.3.2). Then in the final section, 7.4.1, I discuss the ways we might empirically differentiate these views.

7.1 Hellie and Chalmers: Qualia + Acquaintance

I think Benj Hellie is the first to introduce higher-order acquaintance as a model of the relation between higher-order and first-order states (in Hellie 2007). In his words, "According to Acquaintance Theory, to have F as the phenomenal character of one's experience is to bear acquaintance (a [non-intentional/non-representational awareness relation]) to an instance of F-ness" (305).

This kind of view is interesting. There is much to discuss and think about in Hellie's excellent paper. It is arguably one of the first instances of the ascending road we discussed back in Chapter 2. For the most part I will sidestep a discussion of the details. What matters for now is that it is clear on such a view that the thing one is related to is an instance of F. So, if I have redness as the phenomenal character of my experience, then I am, on this account, acquainted with an instance of redness. The thing with which I am acquainted is itself a qualitative property, and my acquaintance with it is nothing more than a kind of non-intentional/non-representational awareness of the redness that the state has. The qualia F-ness will have its properties whether one is acquainted with them or not. It follows on this view that the redness one is acquainted with was already there in the first-order state. It is the phenomenal redness that explains my acquaintance with it.

So how, on this view, does the redness of the first-order state become phenomenologically manifest? The obvious answer is that it does so by *being red*, in the very way that you experience the redness when the state is conscious, even when one is not experiencing it. The red quale is qualitatively red independently of any inner awareness. Importantly, the way in which it is qualitatively red is the same as it must be when I am aware of it. It is already an instance of phenomenal red, it just isn't something you are aware of until you have your non-intentional/non-representational awareness of it.

Interestingly David Chalmers (2013b) also endorses a variant of this kind of theory. For instance, here is what he says in his response to Benj Hellie (again in *Analysis*), "I think the most plausible line here is that phenomenal awareness is an acquaintance-involving relation by its very nature: in virtue of the nature of awareness, to be aware of x entails being acquainted with one's awareness of x.[4]" He goes on to say in the footnote, "[4] This is a relative of higher-order representation theories of consciousness, and especially of the Brentano-style self-representational views of consciousness that have become popular in recent years (see e.g. Kriegel and Williford 2006). The key difference with standard versions is that I understand the background awareness as Russellian instance-acquaintance rather than as a standard form of representation (this immediately avoids all objections from higher-order misrepresentation as well as from over sophistication). My version of the view is also nonreductive, in that the awareness relation is irreducibly a phenomenal relation" (Chalmers 2013b, 5). Chalmers' view is that phenomenal properties, like phenomenal red, consist in phenomenal awareness of Edenic (primitive) qualities, and that this kind of awareness is by its nature reflexive.

The Chalmers/Hellie view is a kind of ultimate spotlight view. All that inner awareness does is to shine the light on what is already there. One then becomes directly aware—acquainted with—the qualitative property as it was already. It is important to note that Chalmers' acquaintance view is doubly non-reductive. The redness of the red phenomenology is non-physical, but so also is the awareness relation. Both the redness of red and the awareness of that quality are modeled by Chalmers as irreducibly phenomenal/qualitative properties/states. To be aware of the primitive Edenic redness of the apple on his view is also, and thereby, to be aware of your awareness. An argument that Chalmers gives, which I find convincing, is that our ability to pay attention to our phenomenal properties is best explained by a constant background acquaintance with these properties. That seems to be best explained in terms of a general background acquaintance with our awareness of Edenic red. This allows us to focus in on various aspects of what it is like for us.

This inviting and elegant picture clearly and explicitly commits us to non-physicalism. As I have said in Chapter 1, I take physicalism to be the default view until there is some reason to doubt the shombie argument (discussed in the Appendix). I don't completely reject non-physicalism. I have some small credence allotted to various non-physicalist views, but I think we have enough reason to be hopeful for an account that is compatible with physicalism. So, is there some way to get the benefits of the Hellie/Chalmers picture without committing us to some form of non-physicalism? Unfortunately, if one succeeds in finding a version of this kind of view a physicalist can accept, it then threatens to collapse into a first-order view or inflate into a non-relational view.

7.2 Contemporary Spotlight Views

There have been many attempts to find an appropriate relation that may be naturalistically acceptable and still deliver the benefits promised by acquaintance. They all either collapse into a first-order theory, or end up as a kind of non-physicalism, or they merely stipulate that the relevant relation works. If experimental evidence forces us to accept this, then we will do so. It would come, in my opinion, at a heavy cost.

7.2.1 Acquaintance + First-Order Representations

Anna Giustina has recently offered the most direct attempt to get a naturalized version of the spotlight view (Giustina forthcoming). Giustina argues that the acquaintance view is preferable to self-representational views like those of Uriah Kriegel discussed in the previous chapter.

Giustina is very clear that she has a relational spotlight view in mind. It is worth quoting a passage from her recent paper that develops her view. She says,

> First-order representation is what constitutes qualitative character. However, by itself, first-order representation is not sufficient for consciousness (for consciousness also requires *subjective* character). Acquaintance is what makes the first-order representation conscious and it is that in virtue of which conscious representation has subjective character. The first-order representation is the *terminus* of the acquaintance relationship—it is that which one is acquainted with.
>
> By being acquainted with the first-order representation, the subject becomes aware of the experience's qualitative character. By being the terminus of acquaintance, qualitative character is not merely *in* the subject (like unconscious representation such as subliminal perception), but also *for* the subject. To use a metaphor (to be taken with a pinch of salt!): acquaintance *illuminates* first-order representation, thereby making the subject aware of it; this is what makes the first-order representation conscious. Without acquaintance, first-order representation is, so to speak, "in the dark"—it is unconscious. When it becomes the terminus of acquaintance, first-order representation "comes to light" and is thereby "revealed" to the subject—it becomes conscious.

This is perhaps the clearest statement of the spotlight version of relational higher-order theories. Unfortunately, I do not think there is enough salt to make sense of the metaphorical talk of a state 'coming to light,' or becoming phenomenologically manifest as I would put it.

As Giustina notes, this commits the view to the possibility of unconscious qualitative states. These unconscious qualitative properties are the first-order representations of redness and other such properties in the environment. On Giustina's view, acquaintance with first-order representations is a genuine cognitive achievement. The acquaintance relation allows us to find out about the state that is illuminated and to know about the properties it had *before we were acquainted* with it. The inner spotlight of acquaintance does not create or bring into existence the phenomenal property. It merely shines a light on something which was already there. This allows us to experience its content.

But this makes it clear that the unconscious qualitative state postulated has its properties in what we might call an 'inner awareness independent' manner. This is exactly what we found on the nonphysical versions of the acquaintance view. When I have an experience of a red object on those views, I am thereby acquainted with something which was like *this* (gesturing at the qualitative redness which is phenomenologically manifest), before I was aware of it. A mental quality being independent of inner awareness means that the redness of red is qualitatively identical in cases where it is phenomenally conscious and in cases where it is phenomenally unconscious.

In versions of this kind of view that take qualitative redness to be a primitive and irreducible notion, we can make sense of how it is that the postulated inner awareness makes us aware of *that*. The way in which the redness of the first-order representation becomes phenomenologically manifest is simply my becoming aware of what was already there. If my inner awareness is of a primitive qualitative red, then we can understand why it is *like seeing red* when I am aware of that state. But on the naturalized version of the spotlight view, how can the first-order qualitative state have the qualitative properties unconsciously? If one endorsed the ascending road, one would then need a first-order account of phenomenal consciousness and then a higher-order account of inner awareness.

To put this challenge in another way, if it isn't an irreducible phenomenal property, or a first-order phenomenal property, then what is it, other than mere stipulation, which allows the first-order representations + acquaintance view to conclude that the very same first-order state when we aren't acquainted with it is unconscious in the phenomenal sense rather than merely the state-conscious sense? If the first-order representation is robust enough to account for what it is like for me when I am aware of it, then why isn't it the case that the acquaintance relation merely makes me aware of *what it is like* for me to have the first-order representation? Proponents of the view want to cast it as my becoming acquainted with a perfectly naturalistically acceptable representation. When I do so, according to them, I simply become aware of the representation. My challenge is to ask: Why aren't they becoming aware of what it was like for them? How do they, besides stipulation, rule out phenomenological overflow in these situations? If there was something that it was like for them to have F before they were acquainted with it, then the acquaintance does not explain what it is like for me. Therefore, it does not explain phenomenal consciousness.

This seems like a fundamental challenge for any kind of spotlight view. Can the relational versions of the higher-order approach give an account of unconscious qualitative character that doesn't commit them to a first-order view, or some kind of non-physicalism, but also allows us to understand how that content could become phenomenologically manifest? Giustinia cites others as holding the unconscious qualitative state thesis as well, so let's look at those views.

7.2.2 Mental Quotation

Another way in which theorists have sought to capture the core claims of acquaintance-type theories, but in terms that are more naturalistically acceptable, is by taking quotation as a model.

Vincent Picciuto (2011) introduced the quotational model and suggested the quotational higher-order state has something like as the following as its structure,

The state: <blank>
Or perhaps 'this state: <blank>'

On Picciuto's view the actual first-order state is what is placed in the <blank> and thus gets displayed to the subject.

Sam Coleman (2015) introduced a similar model he called the Quotational Higher-Order Thought (QHOT) theory. The basic idea for Coleman is that these QHOTs have something like

> This state is present: "*insert actual state here*"

Both of these views are inspired by the so-called *phenomenal concepts strategy* introduced by David Papineau (2002). On Coleman's model the first-order state is 'displayed' via a mechanism that 'quotes' it. Though there are differences between these two kinds of quotational views in the details, they are similar enough for us to make the point that we want to make, and I will use QHOT to refer to both kinds of quotational views.[1]

The first thing to note about the QHOT view is that it is not clear how such a theory could be implemented in the brain. What would it mean for a sensory state to be embedded or quoted in this way? I am

---

[1] Coleman gives a nice breakdown of the technical differences in footnote 81 of his paper, which I quote below:

> Picciuto (2011) develops a superficially similar HO account of consciousness, 'the quotational view' (QV). Though QHOT theory and QV agree consciousness involves embedding a sensory state in a HO state, they differ in crucial respects:
> i. For Picciuto *phenomenal concepts* are implicated in consciousness, not just in thoughts about experiences as per the Papineau/Balog account. But QHOTs may not be conceptual at all, and certainly don't involve phenomenal concepts (concepts of phenomenal states). If there are no phenomenal concepts (as Tye 2009 argues) then QV fails, whereas QHOT theory is untouched. ii. Picciuto understands his HO quotational structures as 'demonstratives' which *refer* to embedded sensory states and *represent* them as states of the subject. QHOTs demonstrate sensory states but are not demonstratives, nor do they refer to embedded sensory states, and they do not represent them (let alone as states of the subject)—but simply *present* them. iii. Picciutto says quotational embedding 'activates' a sensory state, suggesting an intrinsic modification, like acquisition of an 'inner glow.' On QHOT theory awareness is held just to *consist in* a sensory state's mental quotation, with said state intrinsically unaltered. Piciutto's talk of activation recalls constitutive HO accounts, with associated problems. iv. On QV the quotational HO structure is 'part of' the 'conscious state' (§5.3), meaning we are conscious of the quotational element. On QHOT theory we are conscious only of what the QHOT embeds, i.e. the sensory state. The QHOT itself is not conscious.

not saying we can't make sense of this but only that we need some kind of account of how it is to be implemented if we are to empirically differentiate these kinds of theories from other versions of the relational approach.

The second thing to note is that the view is just as committed to the mysterious unconscious qualitative states that are independent of inner awareness. It thus owes us an account of what these unconscious qualities are and how it is that they become phenomenologically manifest. How does the unconscious first-order state's content become phenomenologically manifest? Either something must happen to the first-order state when it is quoted, or it must remain unchanged. Either way we are left with a mystery. Interestingly, there is evidence of this tension in the two different presentations of the quotational view (see footnote 1). Picciuto seems to think that embedding a sensory state into a higher-order quotational frame 'activates' the first-order state. The metaphor is a bit like plugging in the nightlight as opposed to shining a light on what is there. The nightlight is dark before you plug it in. With this metaphor in mind one can seemingly avoid the implication that the first-order representation of red has its properties in an inner-awareness independent manner. But if the first-order sensory state is dark, by which I mean phenomenally silent, at some time, then how could quoting it cause it to be phenomenologically manifest? No explanation is given of this. How could presenting something that is dark light it up?

On the other hand, Coleman insists that the quotational frame presents the sensory state as it is, intrinsically unaltered. Coleman's view is committed to the inner-awareness independence of the first-order qualitative states. Thus, this view is a bit like naïve realism from the philosophy of perception. Instead of the claim that the mental qualities are 'mind-independent' as on Naive realism does, Coleman's quotational model requires that the mental qualities are 'inner awareness independent' in that they can exist in just that way when we are in no way aware of them.[2]

---

[2] This difference may also be related to the fact that one of these is a spotlight view and the other is a joint-determination view. I will ignore this distinction for now so as to keep the quotational views both in this section.

But what could it mean for qualitative red to be just as qualitatively red when I am in no way aware of it? Coleman has an answer to this challenge. He goes on to argue for a version of pan-quality-ism, namely that there are unconscious qualities akin to the redness of red, that are fundamental to reality (Colman 2022). This allows him to unabashedly endorse the QHOT view. If the qualities are fundamental to physical reality, then they are surely the way that they are independent of inner awareness! This is an interesting view, and some people think there may be reasons to take it seriously. However, it is debatable whether this is a kind of physicalism. In addition, the reasons given for taking pan-quality-ism seriously turn mostly on the same a priori arguments we dealt with in Chapter 1. It seems that the notion of unconscious qualitative character at play in Coleman's picture shares more with Hellie and Chalmers' notion of a non-physical qualia.

The general lesson we seem to be drawing is that there is a dilemma for relational enthusiasts. The unconscious qualitative states must have their 'what it is like' properties either independent of inner awareness or not. If they do, then the view threatens to collapse into a first-order view. Those on the ascending road will not mind, as they already recognize that consciousness must be a first-order phenomenon. This is to give up on the higher-order approach. If they don't have their 'what it is like' properties independent of inner awareness, then it looks kind of like magic is at work. I would think we would need some strong reasons to think non-relationalism isn't a viable approach before we were moved to conclude that the qualities of which we become aware are a fundamental aspect of reality. Is there any way of making sense of unconscious qualitative states that still allows them to become phenomenologically manifest to the subject with some very thin notion of direct acquaintance-like awareness?

7.2.3 Attentional 'Sifting'

Sauret and Lycan (2014) propose a model whereby attention is the mechanism via which we become aware of our mental lives. As they put it, "Attention is not an internal monitor. But, attention does seem to play an important role in internal awareness. Attention, like an internal monitor, can be voluntarily controlled. When asked to focus on a portion of one's phenomenological field, people naturally initiate this process by directing their attention inwards. The tight connection between internal awareness and ordinary attention suggests a simple hypothesis: attention is the mechanism that enables subjects to become aware of their mental states." Here the authors argue that there may be some non-intentional form of inner awareness. They invoke analogies like that of a funnel or a sieve. These kinds of devices seem to be directed at things, the way a funnel will be directed at whatever it is funneling something into, but they do so in a decisively non-intentional way. This attentional process does not employ concepts describing the targeted states, nor does it have any kind of satisfaction conditions.

If this is correct, then the attention view is a version of traditional higher-order theory that accepts the Transitivity Principle but seeks to implement it via a non-cognitive non-intentional mechanism. Sauret and Lycan make this move explicit when they go on to discuss Lycan's (2001) famous argument for higher-order theories. We previously discussed this argument in Chapter 2 (2.3.2), but they remind us of it quickly,

> (i) A conscious state is a mental state whose subject is aware of being in it; (ii) the 'of' in 'aware of' is the 'of' of intentionality; (iii) intentionality is representation; (iv) thus, awareness of a mental state is a representation of that state; and (v) thus, a conscious state is a state that is itself represented by one of the subject's mental states.

They go on to say,

> The problematic move occurs in the second premise. The 'of' in the phrase 'aware of' is not the 'of' of intentionality. Instead, it is some other non-cognitive, non-representational relation. Ultimately, [the tenability of the view that attention is the mechanism that enables subjects to become aware of their mental states] will depend on whether its proponents develop a plausible theory of what this awareness relation amounts to. But we see no reason to doubt that

they may do so – there are multiple candidates for what that relation might be. It may be some variety of the acquaintance relation (Gertler 2011; Tye 2009), or perhaps the non-cognitive 'awareness-access' relation suggested by Block (2007) in his response to Levine's (2007) commentary.

I think this is an extremely important point that generalizes to all relational higher-order views. Until one is able to actually define a relation that avoids the dilemma presented in the previous section, relational theories are more of a wish list than an actual theory. They, it seems, exist in a semi-fictional state as a placeholder so that theorists can avoid non-relational versions of higher-order theory.

We have seen that there are reasons for doubting Block's notion of awareness-access in Chapter 2 (2.1.1). So far, we have also found reasons to doubt the alternatives. Being dissatisfied with ideas people have currently been able to come up with does not mean there isn't something waiting for someone to discover. It could be out there. It is important to emphasize, though, that so far, we haven't found an alternative to intentional/conceptual representation.

Sauret and Lycan cite Michael Tye's account of the acquaintance relation. This is interesting in that Tye has recently argued that this notion of acquaintance must be fundamental and so non-physical (Tye 2021). He argues that this notion is a fundamental notion of what it is likeness so that in a typical conscious experience we have a representation F, and consciousness*, which on his account is what makes the representation of F into an experience. He then argues that this is fundamental and that even quarks have this property (but without content). Though Tye thinks of his view as a first-order account, one could see it in terms of an account of acquaintance and so higher-order.

It may be the case that some notion of an acquaintance-like relation can be found that enables us to simultaneously understand how it is that it could be naturalistically implemented and see how the first-order states that it makes us directly, non-intentionally, non-representationally aware of could thereby become phenomenologically manifest. That could happen. But at this point what we have is promissory notes and a wish list.

7.2.4 Dual-Content Theory

Peter Carruthers defended a version of higher-order theory that he called the dual-content theory. In Carruthers' view first-order states consist in analog content, which for him means that these contents will be more fine-grained than any concepts that the subject possesses (so state-non-conceptual). Like many relational theorists Carruthers is motivated by ruling out misrepresentation cases. This first-order analog representation of red will become phenomenally conscious when that state becomes available to a higher-order thought generating system (in a proposed theory of mind module). In virtue of being in this memory store, this first-order representation comes to acquire a new 'seeming' content. So, if the first-order state was an analog representation of red, then it now acquires the content 'seems red.'

This 'seems red' content is added to the first-order state because that state is related to a potential higher-order thought (Carruthers 2005). The analog first-order state is disposed to cause higher-order thoughts about itself. Because of that, this state comes to have a new content, that it seems red. The basic idea is the same as the relational higher-order-thought view, in which a first-order state is rendered conscious by its being related to a higher-order thought. It is just that in this case the higher-order state is dispositional and not necessarily actual. When the higher-order thought is itself conscious, on Carruthers' view, it will be moved into the short-term memory store and thereby acquire a dual content as well.

To make this work Carruthers appeals to a kind of consumer semantics where a state's content is determined, at least in part, by how downstream consumer systems use that content. If a system is disposed to use the content to categorize and conceptualize its first-order states, then that first-order state thereby acquires a new (analog, non-conceptual) content. When pressed on what it means for a state to be disposed to cause a higher-order thought, Carruthers appeals to the Global Workspace theory. If a state is broadcast to a wide variety of systems, including a theory-of-mind system, and if a version of consumer semantics is correct as noted above, then all of the globally broadcast states will acquire this dual content. This makes the dual-content view a synthesis of the global workspace view and higher-order views as noted in this first chapter.

This view is interesting, but it has never attracted any proponents. Part of the reason is that there is no empirical evidence for the kind of dual contents that the theory proposed (Carruthers 2019, 94).

7.2.5 Perceptual Reality Monitoring

Perhaps the most well-worked-out version of a spotlight view is Hakwan Lau's Perceptual Reality Monitoring (PRM) view (Lau 2022). Lau attempts to provide a spotlight model that makes use of unconscious qualitative states but in a way that reduces those qualitative states to their functional role in the mental life of the subject. The spotlight, on Lau's view, is a contentless pointer that refers to the unconscious mental quality thereby rendering it phenomenally conscious.

Suppose one is viewing a ripe tomato. Then, on Lau's view, there will be a sensory representation of the tomato characterizing it as round (spherical), red, over there, and so on. From the brain's point of view, Lau reasons, this neural signal representing the tomato may be noise, internally generated (as in imagery), or a veridical perception. Every signal in the brain must be sorted into these three categories. So, there must be some system in the brain/mind of the person that is monitoring these neural signals and 'deciding' whether they are noise or veridical representations. This higher-order system does this by indexing the relevant first-order states with an address (Lau 2022). What one then comes to experience is the content of the indexed first-order representation, in this case the red ripe tomato. When the first-order state is pointed to, and the system indicates that it is veridical, the first-order state's content becomes phenomenologically manifest. PRM is motivated by a strong desire to have all of one's phenomenal character located at the first-order level with the higher-order pointer merely allowing one to experience what is there.

What about the objection from unconscious qualitative character? Lau adopts a version of the Quality Space Theory that Rosenthal presents (Rosenthal 2005; Berger 2014; Renero 2014; Young et al. 2014; Berger and Brown 2022) as a model the first-order mental qualities. On this kind of view qualitative properties are those properties of the subject that allow it to discriminate sensory stimuli. So, if a creature can discriminate red stimuli from green stimuli, there must be some mental quality that represents those physical properties. This property will have similarity and difference relations to other mental qualities that preserve, mirror, or are homomorphic to the structure that the physical properties have. These similarity and difference relations can be determined by presenting stimuli to the creature and determining whether the creature can discriminate between the two stimuli (Rosenthal 2024). Since this is a behavioral task, it could in principle be done unconsciously. Thus, on the quality space model, the unconscious qualitative states are purely functional states that stand in some similarity and difference relations and there is absolutely no problem with those kinds of states occurring unconsciously. They are qualitative in the sense of being non-conceptual/non-intentional and are individuated independently from consciousness.

The relative similarity and differences between these mental qualities are, on Lau's view, encoded in an architecture in the brain that lends itself to being labeled with an address. The visual cortex is topographically organized. Areas of the visual field that are closer together are represented by neurons in visual cortex that are closer to each other. There is a systematic mapping from the structure of these cortical areas to the visual field. Lau argues that the states that early sensory areas can be in can be labeled with an address. The higher-order monitoring system can then refer to the first-order states using these addresses. To use Lau's metaphor, it is somewhat like the way in which the words in the dictionary are laid out. If I tell you that I am thinking of a word on page 285 of the dictionary, and if that dictionary is standardized in a well-known way, then I might not know which word exactly it is, but I could narrow it down to a range (say beginning with a certain letter of the alphabet). This is the kind of content that the higher-order states have on Lau's view. They list the address of a first-order visual state and decide if it is noise or internally generated or veridical.

This view is different from the quotational models in that the first-order state is not quoted, it is not joined with the higher-order content to form a new conscious state. Rather on Lau's model the higher-order state acts as a 'bare pointer' that refers to the relevant state with its address. This indexing or pointing at the relevant first-order state renders it conscious, and one experiences the content of the first-order state.

As discussed in Chapter 4 (4.4.1), Lau has also postulated subjective inflation to account for the feeling of richness when we might not actually have it. Subjective inflation is behaviorally defined as a subjects' tendency to be more liberal in detection tasks involving peripheral vision or outside of focal attention even though these subjects are 'performance matched' in the sense of doing just as well at the relevant task (Knotts, Michel, Odegaard 2020).

However, this formal definition hides the fact that many of its defenders interpret it in a phenomenological way. That is to say that it is not interpreted in merely a behavioral way or in a way that could be accounted for by one's conscious judgments. It is a phenomenal datum for this view. We saw that the HOROR theory handles subjective inflation by postulating the relevant conceptual content in the HOROR. How does Lau's PRM account for it? The basic idea (developed in Knotts et al. 2020), is that in subjective inflation one will have the sense of more detail being present without representing that detail at the first-order level. As an analogy we are asked to think about amodal completion. Amodal completion is the name given to the phenomenon that when I see an object which is partially blocked by another object, I feel as though there is some sense in which I see the whole object, not just a part. This can result in some funny illusions.

One amusing one involves two pictures of a horse separated by an occluding black box. Importantly, the box has a length that is a few times longer than the horse image. One places the occluding box so that it partially blocks part of each horse picture. Specifically, one wants the front half of the back horse and the back half of the front horse to be occluded. The result is that one can see the front end of one horse coming out of the right-hand side of the box and the tail end of the other horse coming out of the left side of the box. That is not what one perceives, though. At least at first one has the very strong impression of seeing an unusually elongated horse. The visual system does not represent the part of the elongated horse that would have to be behind the box. One just has the sense of its presence. I have the sense of being aware of something that is not explicitly represented in the first-order states (there is no first-order representation of the middle part of the horse). So too, one might have the higher-order sense of having a lot of detail available to one even if one's actual phenomenology (encoded in one's first-order states) were sparse.[3]

But how does this happen? The first-order state had the same properties it does now before it was referred to (*ex hypothesi*). This is true in the case of the postulated qualitative red, as well as the postulated sense of presence in amodal completion. There is evidence that it can be done unconsciously (Emmanouil and Ro 2014). On PRM's account of subjective inflation, then, there must be a first-order unconscious feeling of presence or completion that the higher-order system points to. This immediately undercuts the notion of subjective inflation as an argument for the higher-order view (Lau and Brown 2019).

But we now have the familiar problem again. If the state was truly qualitatively red, or qualitatively felt like seeing the rest of the object, before being referred to, then what role can the first-order state play? What rules out that this mental quality was phenomenally conscious before being referred to by the higher-order system? It is only stipulation that can do so. There is nothing in the theory itself that will allow one to say that the unconscious qualitative states are not like anything for the subject.

One might respond that this is just the usual traditional higher-order approach. We have a divide-and-conqueror strategy in that we have one account of the mental qualities—in this case a functionalist account in terms of quality spaces. One then has another account of what makes us aware of those mental qualities—in this case a higher-order pointer indexing or pointing at the first-order state. Sure, the rationalization continues, the account is committed to unconscious qualities, but so are some other higher-order theories. One need not assume that this alone automatically commits one to some sort of dualism or fundamentalism about these qualities (and let's just ignore, says the proponent, for now that most who endorse this kind

---

[3] The foregoing account of subjective inflation is of course inspired by the relationalist account of higher-order theories. One could have a more robust account of inflation that posited rich contents to the higher-order states, or sparse concepts etc. as we saw in Chapter 4.

of view end up endorsing the latter view at some point as we have seen in previous sections. That is a peculiarity of them not the approach!). Nor, they continue, need one assume a first-order theory of phenomenal consciousness. Sure, folks who prefer the steep climb of the ascending road may do so, but why should the higher-order theorist worry?

There is a problem with the line of response. It overlooks a crucial difference between the way in which the non-relational versions of higher-order theory think about these unconscious mental qualities and the way in which the relational theory thinks about them. According to non-relational views like Rosenthal's HOT theory and Kriegel's self-representationalism, the first-order mental qualities are not phenomenally active. Their content is only phenomenologically manifest indirectly by being represented by the concepts in the relevant higher-order awareness. It is those concepts in the higher-order state that are phenomenally active. The first-order properties are in themselves phenomenally silent, as our discussion in Chapter 6 revealed. Whatever the differences between Rosenthal and Kriegel are, they agree that phenomenal character is represented character (putting aside some tricky terminological issues). There is no mystery how those kinds of first-order states could be unconscious. They are never really conscious in the sense of being phenomenologically manifest. This is exactly what Coleman complains about and causes him to search for an alternative view (Coleman 2018). But now these things that were originally hypothesized to occur in a completely non-conscious way are being postulated to occur consciously in some robust phenomenal sense.[4] How is this possible? Because they were pointed at? I think we are owed an argument that these borrowed postulates can do the required work.

As we have just discovered, Lau's version of spotlight theory has the same problem as other versions trying to explain the qualitative nature of first-order states. One could insist that it just is that way. Perhaps it

---

[4] Recall that even though Rosenthal and Weisberg say that the first-order mental quality is conscious, what they actually mean is that the higher-order state represents one as being in that state. What it is like for one is completely determined by that higher-order representation.

is just a fact about nature that when one tokens the address of a first-order representation of red, the 'redness' of the state 'lights up' and becomes a part of one's stream of consciousness. Perhaps there is just no explanation of this fact. That would be most distressing indeed! But nature may not care! I will come back to the empirical differences between this kind of view and HOROR in the final section. Before that, though, there is one final issue with PRM to discuss.

Lau wants to develop a view on which all of one's phenomenal character is determined by the first-order states and their contents. The inner awareness postulated on PRM is supposed to be a bare pointer with no content. However, there are moments where Lau seems to vacillate between a pure spotlight view and a joint-determination view.[5] We will discuss those kinds of views in more detail in the next section, but here recall that those views hold that one's overall phenomenal state is jointly determined by first-order and higher-order states. Both states are phenomenally active and jointly contribute to what is phenomenologically manifest.

There are two places where Lau seems to inadvertently slip into joint-determination. First, in his discussion of working memory he argues that when one is holding an image in working memory, and when there is a conscious experience during that period of time, that experience is different from an ordinary experience in that it lacks the 'here now' component (Lau 2022, 155). But in this case, is the missing 'here now' content supplied by the higher-order indexing machinery itself on Lau's account? Is the indication that a first-order representation is being held online in working memory an independent setting of the higher-order pointer? Or is this too something that we should find at the first-order level? If this is contributed by the pointer, then to that extent the view is a joint-determination view. As a result, it will have to rely on a non-traditional version of higher-order theory. If it is to be located at the first-order level, then we need an account of which first-order states/processes provide the 'here now' or working-memory aspect, and how does the higher-order pointer decide where to point in this case?

---

[5] When we wrote 'The Emperor's New Phenomenology' back in 2011, I think he was a joint-determinism enthusiast.

Perhaps this can be dealt with in a way that preserves PRM's spotlight credentials. There is another, related, worry in the vicinity. Lau seems to argue that it is the first-order qualitative states that are phenomenologically manifest, but closer inspection of his view leads one to wonder if this is really the case. This is because Lau argues that the higher-order system, in addition to merely pointing to the first order-state, also must implicitly know what the indexed states represent. The phenomenology is thus not really determined by the content of the first-order states, but rather by the higher-order knowledge that is implicit in the system.

As he himself says,

> I argue that higher-order mechanisms in the prefrontal cortex also implicitly "know" the mental quality space, at least approximately. That is because they have to know the spatial organization of sensory neurons, as well as what those neurons represent, in order to allow the relevant top-down processes to function. When the perceptual reality monitor "decides" that some neurons are representing the color red are correctly representing the world right now, by referring to those neurons correctly, the mechanism already has the information that the color is nothing like blue or silver. It may be somewhat more like brown, or orange, or pink, or maybe purple -but definitely nothing like the taste of vanilla ice cream -*at least for me*. (2022, 201; emphasis added)

But this makes it unclear whether Lau's view is truly a spotlight view. It now seems as though the first-order state itself is not what is being experienced. Is this 'implicit knowledge' had by the higher-order system anything like a conceptual representation of the first-order quality space?

To draw out the problem, suppose one has a sparse and degraded first-order representation of a cat. One may be groggy, or it may be dark. Whatever the case we end up with a degraded first-order representation. Now suppose that the PRM system then mistakenly tags that degraded representation as likely to be true, so one experiences it as real. Lau interprets this as experiencing the sparse representation as though it had all the details. Why isn't it the case that one has a sharp and clear experience of the vague first-order representation instead? It seems like one should become acutely aware that the details are missing. The response, as far as I can tell, is that the higher-order system refers to those first-order states and so the content is what they typically represent (what the prefrontal system "knows"). Thus, one experiences a cat there when one isn't perceiving a cat. This certainly gives the impression that it is the implicit content of the PRM system that is phenomenally active.

To make the point in another way, suppose that we imagine a case where one's higher-order perceptual reality monitoring system was transplanted into a different brain where the first-order states had different contents. When the higher-order system indexes some first-order state in this set-up, is what it is like determined by the actual content of the now new first-order state or the implicit knowledge of the original brain's first-order states? As I understand Lau's view it is by the implicit knowledge. So, even if this system is indexing an address that has green as its current content, but using an index from the original brain that was used to index a red first-order state, it should be like seeing red. This seems to suggest that Lau's perceptual-reality monitoring requires more than just an index. It requires something akin to knowledge, and that weakens the view because it seems like non-relationalism is being smuggled in when no one is looking.

If so, then Lau's view is unstable and seems poised to either collapse into a first-order view or inflate into a non-relational view.

7.3 Joint-Determination Views

Joint-determination views are closely related to the spotlight versions of the relational approach, but they differ in that they claim that both the first-order and higher-order components/states contribute something to the phenomenology of the subject. Joint-determination views have been less popular than the spotlight version, but there are at least two contemporary views that can be interpreted as joint-determination views.

7.3.1 Higher-Order Perception Theory

As we saw in the previous section, Lycan currently defends a nonstandard version of the spotlight view that I called 'Attentional Sifting' (they call it the Attention View). However, before that Lycan advocated what he called a Higher-Order Perception (HOP) theory (Lycan 1987; Lycan 1996). HOP is less popular than it once was, but it was a main player and should be fit into our taxonomy.

Lycan construes the inner sense he is interested in as a kind of scanner or monitor whose function is to represent the first-order states of the animal's mental life. The monitored state is thereby rendered conscious. HOP is a traditional higher-order view on my way of classifying things. Lycan clearly accepts the Transitivity Principle, but does he accept the claim that one's phenomenal character is made of both first-order and higher-order elements? It is not entirely clear, but it does appear to be the case. For example, in his 1996 book *Consciousness and Experience* he discusses the case of a 'false positive,' which is what we have been calling radical misrepresentation. While discussing this issue (19–21) he says, "If... there is no first-order pain sensation at all but merely a mendacious representation of one, there is no reason to think that all or any of the usual functional effects would indeed ensue. You would be introspecting [conscious of] something which had some of the qualitative aspects of a pain, but important elements would be missing; you might be in the position of the morphine patients, who manifest "reactive dissociation," saying that they still feel the pain as intensely as ever but no longer mind it" (20). A little further on he says that this experience of pain one has in the case of radical misrepresentation (his false positives) would "not be phenomenally very like veridical awareness of pain" (21).

You could interpret these passages in many ways, but perhaps the most natural way to interpret them is as endorsing a kind of joint-determination view.[6] The first-order state supplies the qualitative

---

[6] For example, it could be the case that the content is missing in the higher-order perception because it is missing in the FO state. It is not clear that Lycan means for this higher-order perception to be exactly like the case where it occurs regularly.

character, and the inner sense provides the awareness of that character. Both are phenomenologically manifest.

Higher-order perception views are interesting, but they have fallen out of favor because no one has discovered a system that looks like an inner sense. Lycan's own postulation was that it was based on attention and the cognitive neurosciences have revealed, according to him, that attention does not work like an internal monitor (see section 7.2.3). There are other views that are inspired by this though.

7.3.2 Higher-Order State Space Model

Recently Steve Fleming has proposed a Higher-Order State Space (HOSS) model (Fleming 2020). This model is pitched at the computational level and as it stands is agnostic on the neural implementation of the computational details. These are matters of empirical determination. On the HOSS model there is a generative first-order network that encodes the perceptual content and a higher-order generative system that encodes an abstract 'aware' or 'not aware' content that is directed at the first-order content in a general way. There can be different levels of the awareness pointer that are supposed to correspond phenomenologically to how vivid or strong the experience is. We might imagine that on HOSS the higher-order pointer is pointing to the visual areas and saying that the subject is aware (with some scalar magnitude) of what those contents represent. The general idea behind this kind of approach, which is closely related to SOMA (discussed in Chapter 4) and PRM (discussed in the previous section), is that the brain must perform some sort of signal detection on itself. According to HOSS there is a higher-order awareness state that encodes a 'phenomenal magnitude' that can take different values. At the same time this phenomenal magnitude indexes some first-order states. What you experience is thus jointly determined by the first-order contents, which are phenomenally active, as well as the higher-order state that simply says, 'seen with x magnitude' (adjusted as necessary for modality). This model is generative in the sense that if you ran it starting with the higher-order awareness state, the model would generate the first-order state.

This allows HOSS to account for some aspects of misrepresentation cases. Suppose that one is viewing a stimulus, say a red square, and is having phenomenally conscious experience. According to HOSS this is because one has the first-order states representing the stimulus and a higher-order awareness state that says that you are in those states. But suppose, for some reason, that in another case the red square first-order states caused the higher-order awareness to index a green square state. Since the model is generative, activating that higher-order awareness state will result in the activation of the green square first-order state. Fleming suggests that the neural activity widely interpreted as global ignition may instead reflect this generative aspect of his higher-order model. This, once again, highlights the fact that we are not yet quite sure how to interpret the neural activity we are recording. That is perhaps old news. The point here is that Fleming's view allows that there can be mismatch, but it is self-correcting.

However, this will take some amount of time to occur. This is because the generative aspect of the higher-order system will need to send a signal to the visual areas in order to generate the missing first-order state. What are we to make of what happens in the time interval before the first-order state is generated? During that time, we have a first-order state representing red and the higher-order awareness saying that we are vividly perceiving the green state (by listing its address). Is there a conscious experience at that time? If so, what it is like for the subject? Which state is the conscious state in this case? The green state (which hasn't been activated yet)? Or the red state, which is active but not being indexed?

Taking this one step further we can see that there might be a way to block the generation of the first-order state. In the limit we can imagine this being done by inventing our hypothetical brain clamp from Chapter 5. More realistically, perhaps there could be some way to use transcranial magnetic stimulation, or something, to stop the neural activity that implements the generative signal to the first-order areas. If so, then we have a case of radical misrepresentation on HOSS. A natural prediction of the theory is that in such cases subjects should experience being aware of something very vividly, but without any specific content—a pure form of awareness—that is the job of the relevant higher-order state after all. Or will it be instead like seeing green (before the first-order state is generated)? If so, then this version would also collapse into a version of non-relationalism at least to the extent that there is a contribution from the higher-order element of the state. It must make this contribution without the subject being aware of it, and so in a way that goes beyond the traditional Transitivity Principle.

As I understand HOSS currently it is the former. The experience would be incomplete. When the first-order states occur by themselves, they occur without being experienced—that is, with there being nothing that it is like for the subject to be in those states. When that state occurs and is indexed by the higher-order state, then one experiences its content. This account shares similarities with spotlight views we discussed in the previous section, with the main difference being that when the higher-order state occurs by itself without the occurrence of a first-order state, then the subject is predicted to experience a pure awareness state. Awareness, but without any thing that one is aware of.[7]

I think the HOSS model is very interesting and makes empirical predictions that are worth testing. The main issue I have with HOSS is the reliance on the first-order states to provide the specific phenomenology that occurs in one's stream of consciousness. This is the same problem that I have with spotlight views that we discussed in the previous sections. I should point out that I am very sympathetic to the core idea that drives both HOSS and Perceptual Reality Monitoring models, which is that the brain needs some way to interpret its own functioning. I am especially sympathetic to the idea that part of the explanation for how the brain does this is via the use of pointers or indexes at the computational and neuronal levels. HOSS proposes a specific model for how this system might work. I think whether there is a HOSS-like element in HOROR, or a PRM-like element, or a combination, is an empirical matter.[8]

---

[7] Although hard to pin down I am confident that Axel Cleermans' SOMA model (briefly mentioned in chapter 4) is a joint-determination view (Fleming et al. preprint).

[8] Graziano presents his Attention Schema theory as an illusionist account of why we think that we have phenomenal consciousness rather than as an actual account of phenomenal consciousness, but one could take the Attention Schema as a theory of phenomenal consciousness. On this view the brain has the global workspace and attention and a stripped-down model of the attentional process itself. Thus, on this Attention Schema view one has the first-order representation and then attaches to it the

7.4 Comparing HOROR and Relational Versions of Traditional Higher-Order Theories

All the relational theories are interesting. Despite my general misgivings about traditional relational higher-order theories, I remain committed to the empirical adjudication of this dispute. Perhaps nature prefers consciousness to be somewhat magical. In addition, the HOROR theory as I presented it did postulate the existence of pointer content in the relevant HORORs. It is thus very important to see how the empirical predictions vary from these relational versions of higher-order theory.

7.4.1 Differing Empirical Predictions?

The argument of the previous sections is my primary reason for exploring conceptual/intentional versions of inner awareness. I feel strongly we should avoid non-representational views unless we run out of options.

As before, the most obvious place to start is with mismatch cases. PRM and HOSS each posit different mechanisms to handle mismatch cases. As just discussed in the previous section, Fleming allows that there can be an erroneous index issued by the higher-order system, and so mismatch which then will be corrected by top-down processes. Lau's PRM view allows for misrepresentation in the following way. Suppose one is viewing a green stimulus, but for whatever reason the resulting first-order state is a lowly activated red state and a highly activated green state. The higher-order discriminator may nonetheless select the lower activated red state, and then one would come to experience the stimulus as red. Since it is the first-order perception of green that is highly activated in this case, one would behave as seeing green (in effect acting as though one were consciously seeing green, even though they were experiencing red). Thus, misrepresentation can occur on PRM when the pointer points to the incorrect contents.

'consciousness' operator and then has a conscious state. One might think of this as an explicitly illusionist version of the joint-determination view.

Given all this there are some clear empirical implications. Maybe we could achieve this via hypnosis (Fleming and Cleermans preprint). Suppose that a subject was perceiving a happy face but had a sad face phenomenologically manifest. Given what we know about HOSS, we can predict that this mismatch will cascade back through the system, and the erroneous higher-order content will produce the incorrect first-order stimulus. We should thus see the first-order activity change in line with this back propagation (around 150–250 milliseconds after stimulus presentation). Of course, the original question raised in the previous section still applies. If what it is like during this time is like seeing the sad face, then it looks like this isn't really a joint-determinization view. Instead, it looks like a non-relational view. On the HOROR side, we can say we predict that the content of the experience can be decoded from the HOROR. However, since HOROR allows that the pointer content may include something HOSS-like as the pointer part, then it may be the case that we get this generative component on HOROR as well. The main difference would then amount to how exactly the phenomenal character was accounted for.

HOROR theory predicts that we could knock out the pointer content and not alter what is phenomenologically manifest. HOSS and PRM both insist that without any pointer content we would not have any phenomenal consciousness, and so no experience.

Another prediction here is that according to HOSS the pointer encodes a scalar magnitude, while on PRM the pointer seems to be capable of three discrete states (veridical, internally generated, and noise). This suggests, as discussed above, that there is some content associated with the pointer on PRM. We should be able to see the difference here cash out in an empirical prediction.

Another place the theories diverge is on the account of subjective inflation. All sides agree that subjective inflation is phenomenologically manifest. It really is part of our phenomenology that we feel as though we experience more than we represent at the first-order level. On HOSS subjective inflation may be due to a higher-order (implicit) misrepresentation of the noise in the sensory system (Fleming personal communication). PRM gives a first-order account of subjective inflation as akin to amodal completion. HOROR gives a higher-order account of this phenomenology. HOROR does not deny that there could be a first-order state corresponding to a representation having details that are not explicitly being represented. The HOROR theory does insist that in order for that to be phenomenologically manifest there must be a HOROR with that as part of its content. If that were decodable from the prefrontal cortex, then that would support the prefrontally implemented HOROR theory over PRM.

Another obvious way in which the theories diverge empirically is over the intentional/conceptual content of the higher-order state. According to HOROR the contents of the HORORs should be as rich as what is phenomenologically manifest. On HOSS and PRM that is not the case.

One interesting prediction that you might make from this difference is the possibility of adaptation effects for the higher-order state itself, especially as it relates to the experienced sense of vividness an experience has. HOSS predicts that there is a unidimensional code for this. HOROR predicts there is a content of the HOROR corresponding to this. Neither side knows where to localize these events in the brain. So, one possibility is to use sequential effects (Fleming et al. preprint). The basic idea is that if HOSS is right and the relevant higher-order states have no content other than this unidimensional code for level of awareness, then it should be possible to show adaptation effects across perceptual events. The basic idea here would be to present stimuli that range from either, all just barely visible to all very vividly visible. The ratio of the presented stimuli could vary from all vivid to some small percentage of them being very visible with the others being just above threshold. Immediately following this will be a stimulus that the subject must (a) detect and (b) discriminate. This test stimuli will be in a different location on the screen and in a different orientation. If there were an aspect of the higher-order state that was invariant, in the sense that the same set of neurons coded for it, we might expect adaptation. In this case we would expect that the subject's awareness of the test stimuli would vary in some systematic way with the percentage of stimuli that were highly visible.

So, if I am presented with a bunch of Gabor patches, let's say all just at threshold and barely above my ability to detect, and then right after presented with a Gabor patch with a different orientation (to the left, say) and at a different location, that was also just above threshold, then we should expect adaptation of the invariant part of the higher-order awareness. In this case it would mean a matched d' with a difference in how visible the stimulus was rated between the two cases. That would be evidence that the set of neurons encoding the vividness of the one stimulus was also involved in coding it for the other stimulus. It is invariant. Ideally, we would want a case where the subject's d' was matched, and so they were just as good at detecting the presence of the stimulus, and yet the subject seemed to indicate they were less (or more) aware of it. That would seem to indicate that the adaptation effect was in awareness itself and not in the first-order processing of the stimuli.

In such cases HOSS predicts that you should be able to get adaptation effects across different stimuli because the same neural system will encode the vividness for all of the stimuli regardless of where they are presented. For the HOROR theory there are a couple of different ways things could go. If there were cross-stimuli adaptation, HOROR would take that as evidence that the relevant HORORs are compositional (see Chapter 4, section 4.2.3). This would mean that the same set of neurons would encode the same element of each (or at least many) HORORs. Assuming that the HORORs are not compositional and that there is a unique HOROR for each stimulus, then we would predict no adaptation. If there were effects within one stimulus class but not another, we would then start to think that the neural coding was sparse in that sense. This is a very interesting way of trying to get at the underlying neural coding of these higher-order states. Are they atomistic, in the sense of each one being unique in terms of neural coding? Or are the compositional, in the sense that the same (or similar) sets of neurons encode the same (or similar) parts of different HORORs? If there are adaptation effects, then that counts against an atomistic structure for HORORs. This is because, if each experience results in a unique HOROR, or an update in the content of an existing one, then this should be able to be refreshed every time without wearing it out.

HOROR theory relies on pointer content but is neutral on the exact nature of how this is implemented. There may be a HOSS-like or PRM-like element in the content of the relevant HORORs.

One way we might try to decide between the two models of pointer contents is to focus on the difference between veridical experience and imagination (Fleming et al. preprint). HOSS predicts that there is a single code that varies from noise all the way through veridical/real that can be attached to first-order states. PRM predicts that the higher-order state encodes categories. These categories are noise, internally generated, and veridical. This difference should be decodable from the brain. One proposed way to test this (Fleming et al. preprint) is to see whether you can train a decoder to work across these domains. For example, if we had subjects either performing a perception task or an imagery task, say viewing an apple or imaging an apple, while in a scanner, then we could train a decoder to recognize these conditions. We might train the decoder to aim for the content of the experience (apple versus car), or the vividness of the experiences (strong or weak), or the modality, either perception or imagery.

HOSS and PRM make specific predictions in these cases. According to HOSS one should be able to successfully cross-decode in all conditions. A decoder trained to predict vividness on perceptions trials should be able to predict vividness in imagery trials as well. If no evidence were found for this, we would need to re-think HOSS. PRM can allow that this is the case because these states are not entirely separate. Atomistic HOROR predicts that we would get a negative answer to this question. This is because it predicts a distinct neural population (or distinct code in same population) for each experience. However, HOSS predicts that a decoder trained to predict vividness within perception trials will also be able to predict whether a trail is either perception or imagery, due to the same univariate code being employed. PRM denies that this is case because there is no common neural code between the vividness within perception category and the vividness within imagery category. PRM hypothesizes them to be distinct states.

That concludes my presentation of empirical differences between these theories.

Many of these questions remain open. The empirical work alluded to above is in the early stages of being planned by a group supported by the Templeton Accelerating Research on Consciousness initiative. Independently of that many researchers are investigating questions relevant to these issues.

Exciting times indeed!

8
Conclusion

We have finally arrived at the end of our long road. I have not really argued for the HOROR theory. I have tried to clarify what the theory is committed to and what might count as an empirical test of the theory. Some of those tests are being carried out as I am writing this. Others await more sophisticated tools and a deeper understanding of how brain functions are related to psychological functions. I remain hesitantly hopeful that something along the lines of a HOROR theory might provide at least an important part of the puzzle that is understanding consciousness, but I also expect that my contribution, if there is one, will be to clarify how to decisively falsify these kinds of theories.

In addition, I think that the taxonomy offered in Chapter 5 does a better job at dividing up the current landscape than does the traditional division into higher-order versus self-representational views. As we have seen some views that count as higher-order are non-relational in my sense, and some views that count as self-representational views are also non-relational. The non-relational self-representational views were mixed non-relational views that sought to guarantee the existence of the first-order state that was represented. But there is now a growing sense that what they really wanted was not just some relation but a relational account in the sense we have discussed. Truly relational views hold that the first-order state itself contributes its content to the stream of phenomenology. It is this division between truly representational views (what I have called non-relational since the other term was already used) and relational views that is at the heart of much theorizing in consciousness.

APPENDIX

The 2D Argument against Non-Physicalism

I don't know if physicalism is true, or even coherent! But I do know that it has not been refuted by any empirical or non-empirical arguments. One way to see this is via what I have called the two-dimensional argument against non-physicalism (Brown 2010). At this point in time the two-dimensional (2D) argument against physicalism is well known (Chalmers 2009), as are the many responses to it. However, there has been a recent development that has yet to be widely discussed. Some philosophers have argued that we have equally compelling reasons to think that dualism is false based on the conceivability of mere physical duplicates that enjoy conscious experience in just the way we do (Martin 1998; Sturgeon 2000; Frankish 2007; Brown 2010; Piccinini 2017 Balog 2024).

Before starting let us first note that for the purposes of this argument we will be accepting the two-dimensional (2D) semantic framework as argued for in Chalmers (2009). My aims do not so much depend on whether you (or I) accept this framework since I merely want to show how the parody argument works, and it is best put in the same terms as the argument against physicalism. This makes the argument especially strong in that it grants all the assumptions to the opponent that it can.

Since we are accepting the 2D framework we are accepting the formulation of physicalism according to which it must be necessarily true if true at all. This amounts to the conditional $P \supset Q$ being a priori and necessary (where P is a "conjunction of all microphysical truths about the universe, specifying the fundamental features of every fundamental microphysical entity in the language of microphysics"; Chalmers 2009) and Q is a qualitative truth like that I (or someone) feels pain or sees red. It is because physicalism is committed to this that the conceivability of zombies poses a problem. If P & ~Q is truly (conceivable and so) possible then $\sim \Box (P \supset Q)$ is true, but that is just the claim that physicalism is false.

What is often unnoticed, and what the 2D argument against non-physicalism trades on, is that the dualist is committed to a modal claim as well. Following Chalmers let us use 'T' as a 'that's all' claim so that 'PT' is the conjunction of P from above with a nothing else clause. This will rule out ghosts and other non-physical entities (like non-physical qualia) at any world where PT is true. Given this the dualist is committed to NP.

NP: $\Box(Q \supset \sim PT)$

NP says that if there is consciousness at a world, then it is not the case that all there is at that world is our physics. There must be something more according to the dualist. Given this the 2D argument against NP proceeds by invoking the conceivability, and hence possibility, of Q & PT, which is supposed to show that NP is false (i.e., ~ □ [Q ⊃ ~PT] not that physicalism is true).

To do this we begin by conceiving of a mere microphysical duplicate of me (or you) that we stipulate has phenomenal conscious experience in just the way that I (or you) do. I have called these creatures 'shombies' (Brown 2010). Frankish uses the term 'anti-zombie' but I prefer 'shombie' since it is not clear that Frankish and I mean the same thing when we say that PT & Q is conceivable. He has argued (Frankish 2016) that we do not have a neutral conception of consciousness and so must be employing a functionalist notion when we conceive of PT & Q. I deny that and insist that we have a neutral pre-theoretic notion of consciousness, and it is that neutral epistemic notion that shombies have. In addition, Frankish's argument is for the conclusion that cosnciusness is physical, where mine is for the conclusion that non-physicalism is false.

Shombies are in every physical way indistinguishable from you and have conscious experience in just the very same way that you or I do. There is nothing obviously contradictory about consciousness being physical, and many people seem to find it plausible that consciousness could be physical. We have evidence from as far back as Democritus and as recently as Ned Block that some people have found nothing obviously contradictory in the idea that the conscious mind is physical. Surely if someone is trying to give an account of how consciousness could be physical that person finds it conceivable that consciousness is physical! We would seem to have evidence that many philosophers should find shombies to be conceivable.

From there the argument has the same kind of structure as the original zombie argument in that we conceive of shombies and infer their possibility and from that we conclude that non-materialism is false.

(1) (PT & Q) is conceivable
(2) If (PT & Q) is conceivable then (PT&Q) is 1-possible
(3) If (PT & Q) is 1-possible then (PT&Q) is 2-possible
(4) If (PT & Q) is 2-possible then dualism is false

Premise one says that shombies are conceivable. By conceivable I mean ideal negative conceivability. This, roughly, is the idea that an ideally rational agent wouldn't find a contradiction in the proposed scenario. I do think a case can be made for the positive conceivability of shombies (envisioning a scenario by which it is true that shombies have phenomenal consciousness, like maybe a world where the theory in a certain book you might be reading is true?), but we don't need that for the present purposes. Something is 1-possible when there is a possible world where the primary intension of a statement is true, and something is 2-possible when there is a possible world where the secondary intension of a statement is true. These notions are technical, and we don't need to dwell on them here. It is enough for us to note that intensions in the sense used here are functions that take possible worlds as either actual or counter-factual and then deliver truth values. So, 'water is H_2O' has a primary intension that that takes any given possible world as actual (so there is water on Twin Earth as far as the primary intension goes). The secondary intension takes the actual world as given and delivers truth values based on that (so no water at Twin Earth).

It is important to note that the argument as formulated so far does not have a problem with Chalmers' objections based on the conceivability of physicalism (Chalmers 2009, 180). One of these is to what he calls the metamodal strategy of those like Yablo who argue that $\Box (P \supset Q)$ and $\sim \Box (P \supset Q)$ are both conceivable. That would require that we somehow conceive of modal rationalism itself being false. The argument as presented so far does not require this. We already accepted the 2D framework and we are not objecting to modal rationalism. Here I only aim to emphasize that PT & Q is conceivable and do not in any way rely on the conceivability of $\Box (P \supset Q)$.

This also resolves the other problem that Chalmers has with the shombie argument. He formulates the argument as using the questionable S5 axiom $\Diamond \Box P \supset \Box P$ in the following way

1 $\Box (P \supset Q)$ is conceivable
2 $\Box (P \supset Q)$ is possible
3 Since in S5 $\Diamond \Box P \supset \Box P$ it follows $\Box (P \supset Q)$ is true
4 So Physicalism is true

Interpreted this way the argument requires that we conceive of a necessary truth being possibly true. This argument resembles the ontological argument for the existence of God and is equally implausible for the same reason. It is certainly true that if $\Box(P \supset Q)$ is true at some possible world then it is true at ours, but that is exactly what is at issue. But the 2D argument presented here does not have this form. One is required merely to conceive of PT & Q being true. Doing this requires merely that one conceive of a world where consciousness is physical. One is not thereby conceiving that this is true in all possible worlds.

Importantly we can do this even if we do not know how consciousness could be physical. To give that story would be to give an account of how it is positively conceivable that consciousness be physical. As I said I am hopeful for such a story, but one does not need it here. All we need here is the claim that there is nothing contradictory in our finding out that consciousness really is just physical or that there was nothing more than our physics in our world. Just as we can conceive of an unknowable truth without knowing what the truth is, so too can we conceive of consciousness being physical without knowing what makes it true.

What lesson you draw from the shombie argument will largely depend on whether one antecedently accepts, or leans toward, physicalism or modal rationalism generally. If one finds both zombies and shombies conceivable, as one supposes Ned Block might, then one will be skeptical of a priori methods for helping us to answer questions about the nature of consciousness. On the other hand, if one tends to find shombies incoherent or inconceivable then one is a dualist, and if one finds shombies conceivable but zombies obscure then one is a physicalist.

At the very least we can see that it is a mistake to give up on phenomenal consciousness if one is a physicalist. Acknowledging the reality of phenomenal consciousness does not imply that we accept something inherently non-physical. It does not imply anything spooky or non-physical. Phenomenal consciousness is conceivably physical, and that is enough for us to look for an empirically adequate account of what its nature might be.

Acknowledgments

For better or worse, this book was written entirely by humans. I owe thanks to many people, but for right now I want to especially thank David Chalmers for his guidance and support. In addition, I am very grateful to Jacob Berger, Ned Block, Stephen Fleming, Michael Graziano, Joseph Gottleib, Alex Kiefer, Hakwan Lau, Joe LeDoux, Mathias Michel, Adriana Renero, David Rosenthal, Miguel Ángel Sebastián, Dan Shargel, Tony Ro, and three anonymous reviewers, for extremely helpful feedback and/or discussion on earlier versions of this project. I would also like to thank Jennifer Brown, without whom I couldn't have done any of this.

Works Cited

Aaronson, Scott. (2014). "Why I Am Not an Integrated Information Theorist (or The Unconscious Expander)." *Shteltl-Optimiszed*. https://www.scottaaronson.com/blog/?p=1799.

Armstrong, David M. (1968). *Materialist Theory of Mind*. Routledge.

Baars, Bernard J. (1988). *A Cognitive Theory of Consciousness*. Cambridge University Press.

Baars, Bernard J., Stan Franklin, and Thomas Zoega Ramsoy (2013). "Global Workspace Dynamics: Cortical "'Binding and Propagation"Propagation' Enables Conscious Contents." *Frontiers in Psychology* 4: 200.

Baddeley, A. D., and G. Hitch (1974). "Working Memory." *Psychology of Learning and Motivation* 8: 47–89.

Balog, Kati (2025). "The Rise and Fall of the Mind Body Problem." In *Meaning, Modality and Mind: Essays Commemorating the 50th Anniversary of Naming and Necessity*, edited by C. Besson, A. Hattiangadi, and R. Padró. Oxford University Press.

Beck, Ori (2019). "Rethinking Naive Realism." *Philosophical Studies* 176 (3): 607–633.

Berger, Jacob (2014). "Consciousness Is Not a Property of States: A Reply to Wilberg." *Philosophical Psychology* 27 (6): 829–842.

Berger, Jacob (2017). "How Things Seem to Higher-Order Thought Theorists." *Dialogue* 56 (3): 503–526.

Berger, Jacob, and Richard Brown (2021). "Conceptualizing Consciousness." *Philosophical Psychology* 34 (5): 637–659. https://doi.org/10.1080/09515089.2021.1914326.

Berger, Jacob, and Richard Brown (2022). "Rosenthal's Representationalism." In *Qualitative Consciousness: Themes from the Philosophy of David Rosenthal*, edited by Josh Weisberg, 123–141. Cambridge.

Berger, J., and M. Mylopoulos (2019). "On Scepticism about Unconscious Perception." *Journal of Consciousness Studies* 26 (11–12): 8–32.

Block, Ned (1986). "Advertisement for a Semantics for Psychology." *Midwest Studies in Philosophy* 10 (1): 615–678.

Block, Ned (1995). "On a Confusion about a Function of Consciousness." *Brain and Behavioral Sciences* 18 (2): 227–247.

Block, Ned (2002). "The Harder Problem of Consciousness." *Journal of Philosophy* 99 (8): 391–425.

Block, Ned (2007). "Consciousness, Accessibility, and the Mesh between Psychology and Neuroscience." *Behavioral and Brain Sciences* 30 (5): 481–548.

Block, Ned (2011a). "The Higher Order Approach to Consciousness Is Defunct." *Analysis* 71 (3): 419–431.

Block, Ned (2011b). "Perceptual Consciousness Overflows Cognitive Access." *Trends Cogn Sci.* 15 (12, December 15): 567–575. https://doi.org/10.1016/j.tics.2011.11.001.

Block, Ned (2019). "Empirical Science Meets Higher-Order Views of Consciousness: Reply to Hakwan Lau and Richard Brown." In *Blockheads! Essays on Ned Block's Philosophy of Mind and Consciousness*, edited by A. Pautz and D. Stoljar, 199–213. MIT Press.

Block, Ned (2023). *The Border Between Seeing and Thinking*. New York: Oxford University Press.

Bourget, David, and David Chalmers (2021). *Philosophers on Philosophy: The 2020 PhilPapers Survey*. https://philarchive.org/archive/BOUPOP-3.

Braddon-Mitchell, David, and Frank Jackson (1996). *The Philosophy of Mind and Cognition: An Introduction*. Malden, MA: Blackwell.

Brown, Richard (2006) "What Is a Brain State?" *Philosophical Psychology* 19 (6): 729–774.

Brown, Richard (2007). "The Mark of the Mental." *Southwest Philosophy Review* 23 (1): 117–124.

Brown, Richard (2010). "Deprioritizing the A Priori Arguments against Physicalism." *Journal of Consciousness Studies* 17 (3–4): 47–69.

Brown, Richard (2012a). "The Myth of Phenomenological Overflow." *Consciousness and Cognition* 21 (2): 599–604.

Brown, Richard (2012b). Review of Rocco J. Gennaro: *The Consciousness Paradox: Consciousness, Concepts, and Higher-Order Thoughts*, Notre Dame Philosophical Reviews. https://ndpr.nd.edu/news/the-consciousness-paradox-consciousness-concepts-and-higher-order-thoughts/.

Brown, Richard (2012c). "The Brain and Its States." In *Being in Time: Dynamical Models of Phenomenal Experience*, edited by Shimon Edelman, Tomor Fekete, and Neta Zach, 211–238. Advances in Consciousness Studies 88. John Benjamins Press.

Brown, Richard, ed. (2013). *Consciousness Inside and Out: Phenomenology, Neuroscience, and the Nature of Experience*. Dordrecht: Springer Studies in Brain and Mind.

Brown, Richard (2014). "Consciousness Doesn't Overflow." *Cognition Frontiers in Psychology* 5 (1399). https://doi.org/10.3389/fpsyg.2014.01399.

Brown, Richard (2015). "The HOROR Theory of Phenomenal Consciousness." *Philosophical Studies* 172 (7): 1783–1794.

Brown, Richard (2019). "Consciousness, Higher-Order Theories of." *Routledge Encyclopedia of Philosophy, Taylor and Francis*. https://www.rep.routledge.com/articles/thematic/consciousness-higher-order-theories-of/v-1. https://doi.org/10.4324/9780415249126-V051-1.

Brown, Richard, Hakwan Lau, and Joseph E. LeDoux (2019). "Understanding the Higher-Order Approach to Consciousness." *Trends in Cognitive Sciences* 23 (9): 754–768.

Brown, Richard, and Joseph LeDoux (2020). "Higher-Order Memory Schema and Conscious Experience." *Cognitive Neuropsychology* 37 (3–4): 213–215.

Brown, Richard, and Pete Mandik (2012). "On Whether the Higher-Order Thought Theory of Consciousness Entails Cognitive Phenomenology, or What is it like to Think that one Thinks that P?" *Philosophical Topics* 40 (2): 1–12.

WORKS CITED

Byrne, Alex (2022). "Rosenthal on Mental Qualities." In *Qualitative Consciousness*, edited by Josh Weisberg, 109–122. Cambridge University Press.

Carruthers, Peter (2000). *Phenomenal Consciousness: A Naturalistic Theory*. New York: Cambridge University Press.

Carruthers, Peter (2005). "Consciousness: Essays From a Higher-Order Perspective." Oxford: Oxford University Press.

Carruthers, Peter (2019). "Human and Animal Minds: The Consciousness Questions Laid to Rest." New York: Oxford University Press.

Carruthers, Peter, and Rocco Gennaro (2020). "Higher-Order Theories of Consciousness." In *The Stanford Encyclopedia of Philosophy* (Fall edition), edited by Edward N. Zalta. https://plato.stanford.edu/archives/fall2020/entries/consciousness-higher/.

Caston, Victor (2002). "Aristotle on Consciousness." *Mind* 111 (444): 751–815.

Chabris, C., and D. Simons (2011). *The Invisible Gorilla*. HarperCollins.

Chalmers, David J. (1996). *The Conscious Mind: In Search of a Fundamental Theory*. Oxford University Press.

Chalmers, David J. (2006). "Perception and the Fall from Eden." In *Perceptual Experience*, edited by Tamar S. Gendler and John Hawthorne, 49–125. Oxford University Press.

Chalmers, David. (2009). "The Two-Dimensional Argument Against Materialism." In *The Oxford Handbook of Philosophy of Mind*, edited by Brian McLaughlin, Ansgar Beckermann, and Sven Walter, 141–206. Oxford University Press.

Chalmers, David (2013a). "Panpsychism and Panprotopsychism." *Amherst Lecture in Philosophy* 8: 1–35. http://www.amherstlecture.org/chalmers2013/.

Chalmers, David J. (2013b). "The Contents of Consciousness: Reply to Hellie, Peacocke and Siegel." *Analysis* 73 (2): 345–368.

Chalmers, David (2018). "The Meta-Problem of Consciousness." *Journal of Consciousness Studies* 25 (9–10): 6–61.

Chalmers, David J. (2021). *Inferentialism, Australian Style*. Proceedings and Addresses of the American Philosophical Association 92.

Chalmers, David J., and Kelvin J. McQueen (2022). "Consciousness and the Collapse of the Wave Function." In *Consciousness and Quantum Mechanics*, edited by Shan Gao, 11–63. Oxford University Press.

Cleeremans, A. (2022). "Theory as Adversarial Collaboration." *Nat Hum Behav* 6: 485–486. https://doi.org/10.1038/s41562-021-01285-4.

Cleeremans, Axel, Dalila Achoui, Arnaud Beauny, Lars Keuninckx, Jean-Remy Martin, Santiago Muñoz-Moldes, et al. (2020). "Learning to Be Conscious." *Trends in Cognitive Sciences* 24 (2): 112–123.

Coleman, Sam (2015). "Quotational Higher-Order Thought Theory." *Philos Stud* 172: 2705–2733. https://doi.org/10.1007/s11098-015-0441-1.

Coleman, Sam (2018). "The Merits of Higher-Order Thought Theories." *Trans/Form/Ação* 41 (s1): 31–48.

Coleman, Sam (2022) "Fred's Red: On the Objectivity and Physicality of Mental Qualities." *Synthese* 200: 301. https://doi.org/10.1007/s11229-022-03772-1.

Crane, T. 1998. "Intentionality as the mark of the mental." In *Contemporary Issues in the Philosophy of Mind*, edited by A. O'Hear, 229–251. Cambridge: Cambridge University Press.

Dennett, D. C. (1976). "Are Dreams Experiences?" *The Philosophical Review* 85 (2): 151–171.
Dretske, Fred (2007). "What Change Blindness Teaches about Consciousness." *Philosophical Perspectives* 21 (1): 215–220.
Emmanouil, T. A., and T. Ro (2014). "Amodal Completion of Unconsciously Presented Objects." *Psychon Bull Rev.* 21 (5, October): 1188–1194. https://doi.org/10.3758/s13423-014-0590-9.
Farrell, Jonathan (2018). "Higher-Order Theories of Consciousness and What-It-Is-Like-Ness." *Philosophical Studies* 175 (11): 2743–2761.
Fleming, S. (2020). "Awareness as Inference in a Higher-Order State Space." *Neuroscience of Consciousness* 2020 (1): 2020, niz020. https://doi.org/10.1093/nc/niz020.
Fodor, Jerry A. (1975). *The Language of Thought*. New York: Thomas Y. Crowell.
Frankish, Keith (2007). "The Anti-zombie Argument." *Philosophical Quarterly* 57 (229): 650–666.
Frankish, Keith (2016). "Illusionism as a Theory of Consciousness." *Journal of Consciousness Studies* 23 (11–12): 11–39.
Frankland, Steven M., and Joshua D. Greene (2020a). "Two Ways to Build a Thought: Distinct Forms of Compositional Semantic Representation across Brain Regions." *Cerebral Cortex* 30 (6, June): 3838–3855. https://doi.org/10.1093/cercor/bhaa001.
Frankland, S. M., and J. D. Greene (2020b). "Concepts and Compositionality: In Search of the Brain's Language of Thought." *Annu Rev Psychol* 71 (4, January): 273–303. https://doi.org/10.1146/annurev-psych-122216-011829.
Graziano, M. S. A., A. Guterstam, B. J. Bio, and A. I. Wilterson (2020). "Toward a Standard Model of Consciousness: Reconciling the Attention Schema, Global Workspace, Higher-Order Thought, and Illusionist Theories." *Cognitive Neuropsychology* 37: 155–172.
Gennaro, Rocco J. (2022). "Higher-Order Theories of Consciousness." *Internet Encyclopedia of Philosophy*. https://iep.utm.edu/higher-order-theories-of-consciousness/.
Gennaro, Rocco J. (2012). *The Consciousness Paradox: Consciousness, Concepts, and Higher-Order Thoughts*. MIT Press.
George A. Mashour, Pieter Roelfsema, Jean-Pierre Changeux, and Stanislas Dehaene (2020). "Conscious Processing and the Global Neuronal Workspace Hypothesis." *Neuron* 105(5): 776–798. https://doi.org/10.1016/j.neuron.2020.01.026.
Gennaro, Rocco J. (2020). "Cotard Syndrome, Self-Awareness, and I-Concepts." *Philosophy and the Mind Sciences* 1 (1): 1–20.
Gertler, Brie (2011). "Renewed Acquaintance." In *Introspection and Consciousness*, edited by Declan Smithies and Daniel Stoljar, 89–123. Oxford University Press.
Giacino, J. T., S. Ashwal, N. Childs, R. Cranford, B. Jennett, D. I. Katz, et al. (2002). "The Minimally Conscious State: Definition and Diagnostic Criteria." *Neurology* 58 (3, February 12): 349–353. https://doi.org10.1212/wnl.58.3.349.
Giustina, Anna (2022). "An Acquaintance Alternative to Self-Representationalism." *Philosophical Studies* 179: 3831–3863.
Gomez-Lavin, J. (2021). "Working Memory Is Not a Natural Kind and Cannot Explain Central Cognition." *Review of Philosophy and Psychology* 12: 199–225. https://doi.org/10.1007/s13164-020-00507-4.

Gottlieb, Joseph (2015). "Presentational Character and Higher Order Thoughts." *Journal of Consciousness Studies* 22 (7–8): 103–123.

Gottlieb, Joseph (2022). "The Higher-Order Map Theory of Consciousness." *Australasian Journal of Philosophy* 100 (1): 131–148.

Green, D. M., and J. A. Swets (1966). *Signal Detection Theory and Psychophysics*. John Wiley.

Harman, G. (990). "The Intrinsic Quality of Experience." *Philosophy of Mind and Action Theory: Philosophical Perspectives*. 4: 31–52.

Hellie, Benj (2007). "Higher-Order Intentionalism and Higher-Order Acquaintance." *Philosophical Studies* 134 (3): 289–324.

Hobson, J. Allan, Nicholas Tranquillo, and Anthony Shin, eds. (2021). *Conscious States: The AIM Model of Waking, Sleeping, and Dreaming*.

Kammerer, François (2022). "How Can You Be So Sure? Illusionism and the Obviousness of Phenomenal Consciousness." *Philosophical Studies* 179 (9): 2845–2867.

Kant, Immanuel (1724). *Critique of Pure Reason*. Macmillan Company.

Knotts, J. D., Matthias Michel, and Brian Odegaard (2020). "Defending Subjective Inflation: An Inference to the Best Explanation." *Neuroscience of Consciousness* 2020 (1). https://doi.org/10.1093/nc/niaa025.

Koenig, Lua, Haley G. Frey, Vasili Marshev, Emily R. Thomas, Ned Block, David Chalmers, et al. (2023). "Adjudicating between First-Order and Higher-Order Theories of Consciousness: The Role of Prefrontal Cortex." In *List of Abstracts for the Association for the Scientific Study of Consciousness talks June 2023*, 116. https://theassc.org/wp-content/uploads/2023/06/ASSC26-Abstract-List-Final.pdf.

Kolb, B., I. Whishaw, and G. C. Teskey (2023). *An Introduction to Brain and Behavior*. 7th ed. Macmillan Learning.

Kozuch, Benjamin (2021). "Underwhelming Force: Evaluating the Neuropsychological Evidence for Higher-Order Theories of Consciousness." *Mind and Language* 37 (5): 790–813.

Kriegel, Uriah (2003). "Consciousness as Intransitive Self-Consciousness: Two Views and an Argument." *Canadian Journal of Philosophy* 33 (1): 103–132.

Kriegel, Uriah (2009). *Subjective Consciousness: A Self-Representational Theory*. Oxford University Press.

Kriegel, Uriah, and Kenneth Williford, eds. (2006). *Self-Representational Approaches to Consciousness*. MIT Press.

Kripke, Saul A (1980). *Naming and Necessity: Lectures Given to the Princeton University Philosophy Colloquium*. Cambridge, MA: Harvard University Press.

Lamme V. A. F. (2018). "Challenges for Theories of Consciousness: Seeing or Knowing, the Missing Ingredient and How to Deal with Panpsychism." *Philos Trans R Soc Lond B Biol Sci*. 373, 1755 (September 19): 20170344. https://doi.org/10.1098/rstb.2017.0344.

Lau, H. (2022). *In Consciousness We Trust*. Oxford University Press.

Lau, Hakwan, and Richard Brown (2019). "The Emperor's New Phenomenology? The Empirical Case for Conscious Experience without First-Order Representations." In *Blockheads! Essays on Ned Block's Philosophy of Mind and Consciousness*, edited by Adam Pautz and Daniel Stoljar, 171–197. MIT Press.

WORKS CITED

Lau, H. C., and R. E. Passingham (2006). "Relative Blindsight in Normal Observers and the Neural Correlate of Visual Consciousness." *Proc Natl Acad Sci USA* 103 (49, December 5): 18763–18768. https://doi.org/10.1073/pnas.0607716103.

Lau, Hakwan, and David Rosenthal (2011). "Empirical Support for Higher-Order Theories of Conscious Awareness." *Trends in Cognitive Sciences* 15(8): 365–373.

LeDoux, Joseph (2019). *The Deep History of Ourselves: The Four-Billion-Year Story of How We Got Conscious Brains*. Viking Press.

LeDoux, Joseph (2024). *The Four Realms of Existence*. Harvard Press.

LeDoux, Joseph, and Richard Brown (2017). "A Higher-Order Theory of Emotional Consciousness." *Proceedings of the National Academy of Sciences of the United States of America* 114 (10): E2016–E2025.

Lee, Andrew Y. (2019). "The Microstructure of Experience." *Journal of the American Philosophical Association* 5(3): 286–305.

Lee, A. Y. (2023). "Degrees of Consciousness." *Noûs* 57 (3): 553–575. https://doi.org/10.1111/nous.12421.

Lee, J. (2023). "What Is Cognitive about 'Plant Cognition'?" *Biol Philos* 38 (18). https://doi.org/10.1007/s10539-023-09907-z.

Levine, Joseph (2001). *Purple Haze: The Puzzle of Consciousness*. Oxford University Press USA.

Levine, Joseph (2007). "Two Kinds of Access." *Behavioral and Brain Sciences* 30 (5–6): 514–515.

Levine, Joseph (2010). Review of Uriah Kriegel, *Subjective Consciousness: A Self-Representational Theory*. *Notre Dame Philosophical Reviews* 2010 (3).

Lewis, David (1979). "Attitudes de dicto and de se." *Philosophical Review* 88 (4): 513–543.

Liang, Caleb, and Timothy Lane (2009). "Higher-Order Thought and Pathological Self: The Case of Somatoparaphrenia." *Analysis* 69 (4): 661–668.

Locke, John (1689). *An Essay Concerning Human Understanding*. London: Oxford University Press.

Long, Robert (2021) "The Pretty Hard Problem of Consciousness." *Effective Altruism Forum*. https://forum.effectivealtruism.org/posts/Qiiiv9uJWLDptH2w6/the-pretty-hard-problem-of-consciousness#The_pretty_hard_problem_of_consciousness.

Ludlow, Peter, Yujin Nagasawa, and Daniel Stoljar, eds. (2004). *There's Something About Mary: Essays on Phenomenal Consciousness and Frank Jackson's Knowledge Argument*. MIT Press.

Lycan, Willian G. (1987). *Consciousness*. Bradford Books / MIT Press.

Lycan, Willian G. (1996). *Consciousness and Experience*. Cambridge, MA: MIT Press.

Lycan, William G. (2001). "A Simple Argument for a Higher-Order Representation Theory of Consciousness." *Analysis* 61 (1): 3–4.

Malcolm, N. (1956). "Dreaming and Skepticism." *The Philosophical Review* 65(1): 14–37.

Mandik, Pete (2009). "Beware of the Unicorn: Consciousness as Being Represented and Other Things that Don't Exist." *Journal of Consciousness Studies* 16 (1): 5–36.

Mandik, Pete (2016). "Meta-Illusionism and Qualia Quietism." *Journal of Consciousness Studies* 23, nos. 11–12: 140–148.

Neander, K. 2017, *A Mark of the Mental: in Defense of Informational Teleosemantics.* Cambridge, MA: MIT Press.

McClelland, Tom (2020). "Self-representational Theories of Consciousness." In *The Oxford Handbook of the Philosophy of Consciousness*, edited by Uriah Kriegel, 458–481. Oxford University Press.

Mehta, Neil (2022). "The Fragmentation of Phenomenal Character." *Philosophy and Phenomenological Research* 104 (1): 209–231.

Melloni, L., L. Mudrik, M. Pitts, K. Bendtz, O. Ferrante, U. Gorska, et al. (2023). "An Adversarial Collaboration Protocol for Testing Contrasting Predictions of Global Neuronal Workspace and Integrated Information Theory." *PLoS One* 18 (2, February 10): e0268577. https://doi.org/10.1371/journal.pone.0268577.

Michel, M. (2020). "Consciousness Science Underdetermined: A Brief History of Endless Debates." *Ergo* 6 (28).

Michel, Matthias (2022). "Conscious Perception and the Prefrontal Cortex A Review." *Journal of Consciousness Studies* 29, nos. 7–8: 115–157.

Michel, Matthias, and Jorge Morales (2020). "Minority Reports: Consciousness and the Prefrontal Cortex." *Mind and Language* 35(4): 493–513.

Millikan, R. G. (1984). *Language, Thought and Other Biological Objects.* Cambridge, MA: MIT Press.

Mole, Christopher (2020). "Consciousness and Attention." In *The Oxford Handbook of the Philosophy of Consciousness*, edited by Uriah Kriegel, 498–519. Oxford.

Myers, D. G., and C. N. DeWall (2020). *Psychology.* 13th ed. New York: Worth Publishers.

Neale, S. (1990). *Descriptions.* Cambridge, MA: MIT Press Books.

Nagel, Thomas (1974). "What Is It Like to Be a Bat?" *Philosophical Review* 83 (October): 435–450.

Neander, K. (1998). "The Division of Phenomenal Labor: A Problem for Representational Theories of Consciousness." *Nous* 32: 411–434. https://doi.org/10.1111/0029-4624.32.s12.18.

Odegaard, B., R. T. Knight, and H. Lau (2017). "Should a Few Null Findings Falsify Prefrontal Theories of Conscious Perception?" *J Neurosci.* 37 (40, October 4): 9593–9602. https://doi.org/10.1523/JNEUROSCI.3217-16.2017.

Okon, Elias, and Miguel Ángel Sebastián (2020). "A Consciousness-Based Quantum Objective Collapse Model." *Synthese* 197 (9): 3947–3967.

Owen, A. M., M. R. Coleman, M. Boly, M. H. Davis, S. Laureys, and J. D. Pickard (2006). "Detecting Awareness in the Vegetative State." *Science* 313 (5792, September 8): 1402. https://doi.org/10.1126/science.1130197.

Papineau, David (2002). *Thinking about Consciousness.* Oxford University Press.

Passingham, R. (2021). *Understanding the Prefrontal Cortex.* Oxford University Press.

Pautz, Adam (2020). "Representationalism about Consciousness." In *Oxford Handbook of the Philosophy of Consciousness*, edited by Uriah Kriegel, 405–437. Oxford University Press.

Pautz, Adam (Forthcoming). "Naive Realism v Representationalism: An Argument from Science." In *Contemporary Debates in the Philosophy of Mind*, edited by Jonathan Cohen and Brian McLaughlin, 405–437.

Pereplyotchik, David (2012). "Why Believe in Demonstrative Concepts?" *Consciousness and Cognition* 21 (2): 636–638.

Pereplyotchik, David (2013). "Some HOT Family Disputes: A Critical Review of The Consciousness Paradox by Rocco Gennaro." *Philosophical Psychology* 28 (3): 434–448.

Pereplyotchik, David (2017). "Pain and Consciousness." In *The Routledge Handbook of the Philosophy of Pain*, 210–220. Routledge.

Perry, John (1979). "The Problem of the Essential Indexical." *Noûs* 13 (1): 3–21.

Persaud N., M. Davidson, B. Maniscalco, D. Mobbs, R. E. Passingham, A. Cowey, et al. (2011). "Awareness-Related Activity in Prefrontal and Parietal Cortices in Blindsight Reflects More than Superior Visual Performance." *Neuroimage* 58 (2, September 15): 605–611. https://doi.org/10.1016/j.neuroimage.2011.06.081.

Pressman, M. R. (2011). "Sleep Driving: Sleepwalking Variant or Misuse of Z-drugs?" *Sleep Med Rev.* 15(5, October): 285–292. https://doi.org/10.1016/j.smrv.2010.12.004.

Pylyshyn, Z. W. (2001). "Visual Indexes, Preconceptual Objects, and Situated Vision." *Cognition* 80: 127–158.

Peters, Megan A. K., and Hakwan Lau (2015). "Human Observers Have Optimal Introspective Access to Perceptual Processes Even for Visually Masked Stimuli." *eLife* 4: e09651.

Peters, Megan A. K., Robert W. Kentridge, Ian Phillips, and Ned Block (2017). "Does Unconscious Perception Really Exist? Continuing the ASSC20 Debate." *Neuroscience of Consciousness* 2017 (1): nix015, https://doi.org/10.1093/nc/nix015.

Phillips, Ian (2021a). "Scepticism about Unconscious Perception Is the Default Hypothesis," *Journal of Consciousness Studies* 28, nos. 3–4: 2021.

Phillips, Ian (2021b). "Blindsight Is Qualitatively Degraded Conscious Vision." *Psychological Review* 128 (3): 558–584.

Piccinini, Gualtiero (2017). "Access Denied to Zombies." *Topoi* 36 (1): 81–93.

Picciuto, Vincent (2011). "Addressing Higher-Order Misrepresentation with Quotational Thought." *Journal of Consciousness Studies* 18, nos. 3–4: 109–136.

Piccolino, Marco, and Marco Bresadola (2013). *Shocking Frogs: Galvani, Volta, and the Electric Origins of Neuroscience*. Online ed. Oxford Academic. https://doi.org/10.1093/acprof:oso/9780199782161.001.0001.

Prinz, Jesse. (2007). "Mental Pointing: Phenomenal Knowledge Without Concepts." *Journal of Consciousness Studies* 14 (9–10): 184–211.

Prinz, Jesse (2012). *The Conscious Brain: How Attention Engenders Experience*. Oxford University Press.

Raccah, Omri, Ned Block, and Kieran C. R. Fox (2021). "Does the Prefrontal Cortex Play a Necessary Role in Consciousness? Insights from Intracranial Electrical Stimulation of the Human Brain." *The Journal of Neuroscience* 41: 2076–2087.

Raineri, C. (2021). "What's So Naïve about Naïve Realism?" *Philos Stud* 178: 3637–3657. https://doi.org/10.1007/s11098-021-01618-z.

Rahnev, D., B. Maniscalco, T. Graves, et al. (2011). "Attention Induces Conservative Subjective Biases in Visual Perception." *Nat Neurosci* 14: 1513–1515.

Renero, A. (2014). "Consciousness and Mental Qualities for Auditory Sensations." *Journal of Consciousness Studies* 21, nos. 9–10: 179–204.

Renero, Adriana (Forthcoming). *Kripke's Knowledge Argument against Materialism.* Philosophical Perspectives.

Renero, Adriana, and Richard Brown (2022). "A HORORible Theory of Introspective Consciousness." *Journal of Consciousness Studies Rolls.* https://www.frontiersin.org/articles/10.3389/fpsyg.2020.00655/full.

Rosenthal, David M. (1980). "Keeping Matter in Mind." *Midwest Studies in Philosophy* 5(1): 295–322.

Rosenthal, David M. (1986). "Two Concepts of Consciousness." *Philosophical Studies* 49 (May): 329–359.

Rosenthal, David M. (1997). "A Theory of Consciousness." In *The Nature of Consciousness: Philosophical Debates,* edited by Ned Block, Owen Flanagan and Guven Guzeldere. MIT Press.

Rosenthal, David M. (2005). *Consciousness and Mind.* Oxford University Press.

Rosenthal, D. (2010a). "How to Think about the Mental Qualities." *Philosophical Issues* 20: 368–393. https://doi.org/10.1111/j.1533-6077.2010.00190.x.

Rosenthal, David M. (2010b). "Consciousness, the Self and Bodily Location." *Analysis* 70 (2): 270–276.

Rosenthal, David (2011a). "Exaggerated Reports: Reply to Block." *Analysis* 71 (3): 431–437.

Rosenthal, David (2011b). "Awareness and Identification of Self." In *Consciousness and the Self New Essays,* edited by JeeLoo Liu and John Perry, 22–50. New Essays.

Rosenthal, David (2020). "Competing Models of Consciousness." *Cogn Neuropsychol* 37, nos. 3–4 (May–June): 176–179.

Rosenthal, David. (2022). "Mental Appearance and Mental Reality." In *Qualitative Consciousness,* edited by Josh Weisberg, 243–271. Cambridge University Press.

Rosenthal, David (2024) "Methodological Considerations for the Study of Mental Qualities." In *Conscious and Unconscious Mentality: Examining Their Nature, Similarities and Differences,* edited by Juraj Hvorecký, Tomáš Marvan, and Michal Polák, 91–129. London and New York: Routledge.

Rosenthal, David, and Josh Weisberg (2008). "Higher-Order Theories of Consciousness." *Scholarpedia* 3 (5): 4407.

Sauret, Wesley, and William G. Lycan (2014). "Attention and Internal Monitoring: A Farewell to HOP." *Analysis* 74 (3): 363–370.

Searle, John R. (2002). *Consciousness and Language.* New York: Cambridge University Press.

Sebastián, Miguel Ángel (2013). "Not a HOT Dream." In *Consciousness Inside and Out: Phenomenology, Neuroscience, and the Nature of Experience,* edited by Richard Brown, 415–432. Springer Studies in Brain and Mind.

Sebastián, Miguel Ángel (2022a). *Being Self-Involved Without Thinking About It: Confusions, Virtues and Challenges of Higher-order Theories (in) Qualitative Consciousness: Themes from the Philosophy of David Rosenthal.* Cambridge, MA: Cambridge University Press.

Sebastián, M. Á. (2022b). "First-Person Perspective in Experience: *Perspectival De Se Representation* as an Explanation of the Delimitation Problem." *Erkenn* 2022. https://doi.org/10.1007/s10670-022-00564-4.

Segundo-Ortin, M., and P. Calvo (2022). "Consciousness and Cognition in Plants." *Wiley Interdiscip Rev Cogn Sci.* 13 (2, March):e1578. https://doi.org/10.1002/wcs.1578.

Seth, A. (2021). *Being You: A New Science of Consciousness*. Dutton Press.

Seth, A. K., and T. Bayne (2022). "Theories of Consciousness." *Nat Rev Neurosci.* 23 (7, July): 439–452. https://doi.org/10.1038/s41583-022-00587-4. Epub 2022 May 3. PMID: 35505255.

Schurger, Aaron, and Michael Graziano (2022). "Consciousness Explained or Described?" *Neuroscience of Consciousness* 2022 (1): niac001. https://doi.org/10.1093/nc/niac001.

Schwitzgebel, Eric (2014). "The Crazyist Metaphysics of Mind." *Australasian Journal of Philosophy* 92 (4): 665–682.

Sergent, C., M. Corazzol, G. Labouret, et al. (2021). "Bifurcation in Brain Dynamics Reveals a Signature of Conscious Processing Independent of Report." *Nat Commun* 12: 1149. https://doi.org/10.1038/s41467-021-21393-z.

Shea, Nicholas (2018). *Representation in Cognitive Science*. Oxford University Press.

Shargel, Daniel (2016). "The Insignificance of Empty Higher-order Thoughts." *Journal of Cognition and Neuroethics* 4 (1): 113–127.

Silins, Nicholas (Forthcoming). *The Conscious Theory of Higher-Orderness*. Oxford Studies in Philosophy of Mind.

Smith, Joel. (2020). "Self-Consciousness." In *The Stanford Encyclopedia of Philosophy*, edited by Edward N. Zalta. https://plato.stanford.edu/archives/sum2020/entries/self-consciousness/.

Sosa, Ernest (2003). "Privileged Access." In *Consciousness: New Philosophical Perspectives*, edited by Quentin Smith and Aleksandar Jokic, 238–251. Oxford University Press.

Sperling, G. (1960). "The Information Available in Brief Visual Presentations." *Psychological Monographs* 74: 1–29.

Strawson, Galen (1994). *Mental Reality*. Cambridge, MA: MIT Press.

Sturgeon, Scott (2000). *Matters of Mind: Consciousness, Reason and Nature* (1st ed.). Routledge. https://doi.org/10.4324/9780203424551.

Thompson, Evan (2014). "Waking, Dreaming, Being: Self and Consciousness in Neuroscience, Meditation, and Philosophy." Cambridge University Press.

Tian, Karen, Brian Maniscalco, Michael Epstein, Olenka Graham Castaneda, Angela Shen, Giancarlo Arzu, et al. (2023). "An Adversarial Collaboration to Test Predictions of First-Order and Higher-Order Theories of Consciousness Using Subjective Inflation." In *List of Abstracts for the Association for the Scientific Study of Consciousness talks June 2023*. https://theassc.org/wp-content/uploads/2023/06/ASSC26-Abstract-List-Final.pdf.

Tononi, G., M. Boly, M. Massimini, et al. (2016). "Integrated Information Theory: From Consciousness to Its Physical Substrate." *Nat Rev Neurosci* 17: 450–461. https://doi.org/10.1038/nrn.2016.44.

Tye, Michael (2009). *Consciousness Revisited: Materialism Without Phenomenal Concepts*. MIT Press.

Tye, Michael (2021). *Vagueness and the Evolution of Consciousness: Through the Looking Glass*. Oxford University Press.

Valenstein, E. S. (2005). *The War of the Soups and the Sparks: The Discovery of Neurotransmitters and the Dispute over How Nerves Communicate.* Columbia University Press.

Van Gulick, R. (2022). "Consciousness and Self-awareness—an Alternative Perspective." *Rev. Phil. Psych.* 13: 329–340. https://doi.org/10.1007/s13 164-022-00622-4.

Weisberg, Josh (2008). "Same Old, Same Old: The Same-Order Representational Theory of Consciousness and the Division of Phenomenal Labor." *Synthese* 160 (2): 161–181.

Weisberg, J. (2011). "Abusing the Notion of What-It's-Like-ness: A Response to Block." *Analysis* 71 (3): 438–443.

Weiskrantz, Lawrence (1997). *Consciousness Lost and Found: A Neuropsychological Exploration.* New York: Oxford University Press.

Windt, Jennifer M. (2019). "Dreams and Dreaming." *The Stanford Encyclopedia of Philosophy*, edited by Edward N. Zalta. https://plato.stanford.edu/archives/sum2021/entries/dreams-dreaming/.

Windt, J. M., T. Nielsen, and E. Thompson (2016). "Does Consciousness Disappear in Dreamless Sleep?" *Trends Cogn Sci.* 20 (12, December): 871–882. https://doi.org/10.1016/j.tics.2016.09.006.

Wu, Wayne (2014). "Being in the Workspace, from a Neural Point of View: Comments on Peter Carruthers, 'On Central Cognition.'" *Philosophical Studies* 170 (1): 163–174.

Yaron, I., L. Melloni, M. Pitts, and L. Mudrik (2022). "The ConTraSt Database for Analysing and Comparing Empirical Studies of Consciousness Theories." *Nat Hum Behav.* 6 (4, April): 593–604. https://doi.org/10.1038/s41562-021-01284-5.

Young, B. D., A. Keller, and D. Rosenthal (2014). "Quality-Space Theory in Olfaction." *Frontiers in Psychology* 5: article 1. https://doi.org/10.3389/fpsyg.2014.00001.

Zahavi, Dan (2005). *Subjectivity and Selfhood: Investigating the First-Person Perspective.* Cambridge, MA: Bradford Book/MIT Press.

Zahavi, Dan, and Uriah Kriegel (2015). "For-Me-Ness: What It Is and What It Is Not." In *Philosophy of Mind and Phenomenology*, edited by D. Dahlstrom, A. Elpidorou, and W. Hopp, 36–53. Routledge.

Index

For the benefit of digital users, indexed terms that span two pages (e.g., 52–53) may, on occasion, appear on only one of those pages.

access consciousness, 43–44, 58–59, 72–73
attention, 4–5, 24, 40, 109–11, 133, 203–5
awareness, 37–39, 41–42, 93–96, 98–99
   The Ascending Road, 60–61, 116, 195–96, 199, 203, 210–11
   deflationary accounts of inner awareness, 10–11, 60
   inner awareness, 1–2, 6, 10, 58–59, 65–68, 119–21

blindsight, 40, 43–44, 81–82, 136, 137–38
Block, Ned, 16–17, 19–20, 52, 59–60, 132–33, 139, 175–76

Chalmers, David, 17, 23, 53–54, 94, 109–11, 196–97
change blindness, 16–17, 101–5, 128, 131–33
central challenge of consciousness science, 9–10, 54, 116–17, 162
Coleman, Sam, 201–2
content of HORORs
   indexical/pointer, 12–13, 19–20, 76–77, 79–82, 85–86, 93, 98–72, 220
   intentional, 62, 78–79, 87, 127–28, 172–73, 203–5
   phenomenally silent vs. phenomenally active, 12–13, 65, 77–78, 80–81, 149, 154–55, 211
   phenomenologically manifest, 8–9, 12–13, 28, 62–63, 71, 85–87, 94–95, 215–16
   rich vs. sparse, 15, 101–5, 128–29, 209–10, 213–14, 222

creature consciousness, 32, 33–36

dreamless sleep, 34–35

empirical predictions
   mismatch cases, 15, 97–101, 131, 140, 179–80, 184, 190, 217, 219
   empty higher-order states, 18, 81–82

first-order theory, 5–7, 58, 73
Fleming, Steve, 10–11, 124, 216–18

Gennaro, Rocco, 21–22, 120, 145, 161–62, 165, 179, 182, 183–86, 192–93
Global Workspace Theory, 4, 124, 206–7

hard problem, 45–46
   harder problem, 52
   hard enough problem, 53, 54, 56
   meta problem, 53–54, 96–97, 188
   pretty hard problem, 52–53, 54
   real problem, 53–54, 55, 97
Hellie, Benj, 23, 109–10, 195–97, 203
higher-order state space model, 10–11, 24, 124, 216–18
higher-order theory
   traditional, 144–47
   neural implementation of, 6, 127–29, 192–93
   non-traditional, 12, 19–20, 143, 157–58, 160–66, 212
higher-order thought theory, 1–2, 12, 18–20, 21–22, 97, 108–9, 168–79, 185–86

HOROR theory
  the HORORibly Simple Argument, 73–76, 83, 188
  rich HOROR v. sparse HOROR, 15–17, 103–109, 123, 128–129

illusionism, 9, 48–52
integrated information theory (IIT) 4–5, 6, 53
introspective Consciousness, 15, 41–43, 108–14

Kriegel, Uriah, 21–22, 170, 177–81, 191–92, 211

Lau, Hakwan, 10–11, 17, 53, 81–82, 119, 137–38, 207
local recurrency, 4, 55, 141–42
locked-in syndrome, 37–38
Lycan, William, 24, 74, 203–4, 215–16

mental, 62–65
mental quotation, 24, 200–3, 208–9

non-conceptual states, 29–30, 83, 120n.4, 125–26, 206, 207–8
non-physicalism, 9, 47–48, 197, 200, 225
non-relational higher-order theories
  mixed vs. pure, 18–19, 153–54, 158, 167–80, 183, 184–85

perceptible red, 14, 28n.2, 83–84, 92–93, 113–87, 188–89
perceptual reality monitoring, 10–11, 207–14, 218
perspectival de se content, 89–91
phenomenal consciousness
  phenomenologically manifest content, 8–9, 12–13, 85–87, 88, 90, 91n.5, 102–3, 109, 110–11, 211, 215–16
  subjective vs phenomenal character of, 13, 27–29, 69, 86, 182, 188, 199
phenomenal properties, 23–24, 27–33, 48–49, 62–63, 195–97
plant consciousness, 35–36

prefrontal cortex, 15–16, 119–26, 127, 137–38, 191–92, 213, 220–21

qualitative character, 28, 62–63, 69–70nn.6–7, 93n.6, 163–64, 198

relational higher-order theories
  spotlight, 19–20, 23–24, 154–58, 197–214
  joint-determination, 20, 24, 150, 154–58, 184–85, 195, 202n.2, 212, 214–18, 218n.7
representationalism, 29–30, 59–60, 65–68, 74, 170, 171, 191–92
Roomba (robotic vacuum) 35
Rosenthal, David, 10–11, 21, 58, 85–86, 108, 115–16, 145–46, 167–69, 171–72, 186–87

Sebastian, Miguel, 84, 89, 123
self-consciousness, 41–43, 44, 87n.2, 120, 192
self-representationalism, 59–60, 180–83, 192, 211
shombies, 47, 50, 51, 226, 228
Silins, Nico, 10, 59, 60–61
somatoparaphrenia, 22, 178
somnambulism, 37
state consciousness, 11–12, 39–41
  as phenomenal consciousness, 39
  separability from phenomenal consciousness, 40
subjective Inflation, 137–42, 209–10, 220–21

Transitivity Principle, 11–12, 18, 58, 72, 115–16, 117–18, 149, 150, 151, 154–59, 160–62
transparency, 28n.2, 42–43, 73, 95, 109–12, 116–44

unresponsive wakefulness, 36

visual form agnosia, 22–23, 185

Wide-Intentionality View, 21–22, 74, 183–86
working memory, 19–20, 66–64, 81, 100–1, 107, 134, 135–36, 212